Editor: Anne Hardy

Associate Editor: Stan Garrod

Senior Editors: Andrew Allentuck, Nicholas Macklem

Regional Editors: Penny Anderson, Rhonda Anderson, Steve Angelo, Jean Cook, Janet Goodall, Peter Gove, Linda Greenaway, Grant Heckman, Christopher Knapper, Katherine LeButt, Carol Matthews, Paul Miller, Joan Polfuss, Ann Ripley, Ian Robertson, Ann Sherman Shirley Spafford

Contributing Editors: Elaine Butcher, John Butcher, Roger Eaton, Sheila Gordon-Payne, Judith Hardy, Elizabeth Macklem, Mary Martin, Brent McFadyen, Michael McKenna, Catherine McNair, Ian Mitchell, Katherine Hall Page, Don Saunderson, Alfred von Mirbach

Production: Michael Macklem

Anne Hardy

Where to Eat in Canada

FORTY-SIXTH YEAR
16-17

We acknowledge the support of the Government of Canada through the Canada Book Fund for our publishing activities.

ISBN 978 0 7780 1437 9

Front cover by Paul Gauguin

Printed in Canada by Coach House Printing

PUBLISHED IN CANADA BY OBERON PRESS

HOW TO USE THIS GUIDE

The restaurants recommended in this guide have been arranged alphabetically by location, from Abbotsford in British Columbia to Yellowknife in the Northwest Territories. Each entry begins with the name of the city, town or village in which the restaurant is located, followed by the name and address of the restaurant and its telephone number. Next comes the entry itself, printed in roman type, followed by two or three lines, in italic type, indicating the hours during which the restaurant is open for business. The entry ends with a quantity of other useful information: does the restaurant have a full liquor licence or is it licensed for beer and wine only? What credit cards does it take? If the restaurant is in an urban centre, does it have free off-street parking? Do you need to book a table? Is there wheelchair access to the front door and the washrooms?

If you already know what restaurant you want to go to, look up the restaurant in the guide, selecting first the name of the centre and then the name of the restaurant. You will find a heading like this:

LAKE LOUISE, Alberta   **MAP 96**
THE POST HOTEL   ☆☆☆
200 Pipestone Road   **$325 ($625)**
(800) 661-1586

At left, you will find the name, address and telephone number of the restaurant, all arranged under Lake Louise. The first line on the right means that Lake Louise is represented by Map Number 96. Look for Number 96 on the map of Alberta. Once you've found it, consult your road-map for the most convenient route to Lake Louise. Often a quick check of the entry in the guide will help you to find your way.

The second line indicates how many stars the restaurant has earned. The maximum is three, and there are only twenty restaurants in the guide that have earned this rating. Another 87 have earned two stars and 140 have earned one. We consider a further 83 restaurants to be good buys, which doesn't necessarily mean that they are unusually cheap, though it usually does. They are indicated by a pointing finger.

The third line indicates the price. The first (and often the only) figure indicates the average cost of dinner for two with a modest wine, applicable taxes and a tip of 15%. Dinner for two is taken to mean two appetizers, two main courses, one sweet, two coffees and three glasses of an open wine. Where a restaurant has earned two stars, the cost of half a bottle of wine is included. Where a restaurant has earned three stars, the cost of a full bottle is part of the estimated price. The wines chosen are not the cheapest the establishment has to offer, nor are they the most expensive. Where, as in the case of the Post Hotel, a second figure in parentheses follows the first, this second figure indicates the average cost of dinner, bed and breakfast. The presence of this figure means that we recommend not only dinner but also, if convenient, an overnight stay.

If you don't know where you want to go, turn to the maps. Find yourself on the map that shows the province you are in. Select the nearest number and then look it up in the Index. Under the number you'll find all the centres represented by that number. Let's suppose that the nearest number is 204, which stands for the city of Toronto. Look up Toronto in the Index to Southern Ontario and you'll find that there are three other centres with the same number, each enclosed in parentheses. This means that these centres are all in the immediate vicinity of Toronto, too close to be given a number of their own. They are Creemore, Markham and Port Credit. Now look up Toronto in the main body of the guide, where you'll find all 38 restaurants that we recommend in the city itself. If you then look up the other three centres, you will find three more restaurants in the area that we also recommend.

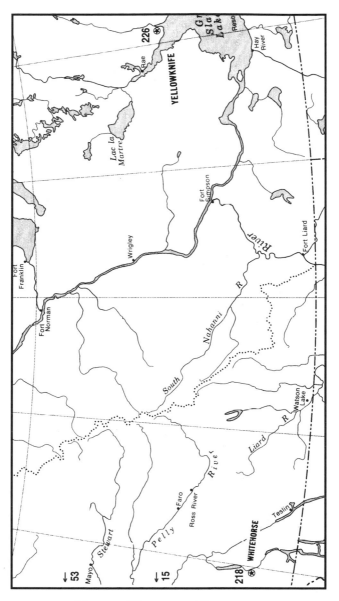

YUKON & NORTHWEST TERRITORIES

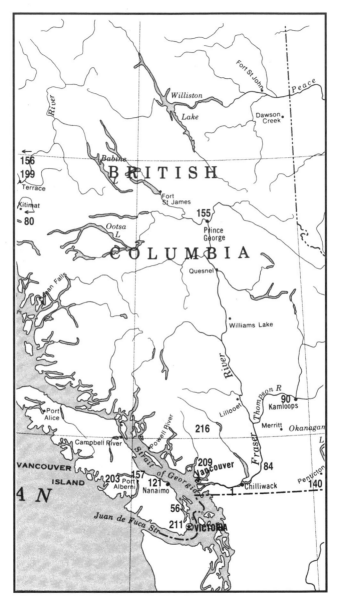

← 156
199
Terrace

Kitimat
80

Williston
Lake

Fort St John

Peace

Dawson
Creek

River

Babine

B R I T I S H

Fort
St James

155

Ootsa
L

Prince
George

C O L U M B I A

Quesnel

Williams Lake

River

Fraser

Thompson R

90
Kamloops

Lillooet

Merritt

Okanagan
L

216

84

209
Vancouver

Chilliwack

140
Penticton

Powell River

Port
Alice

Campbell River

Strait of Georgia

VANCOUVER

ISLAND

203
Port
Alberni

157

121
Nanaimo

4 N

56

Juan de Fuca Str

211

VICTORIA

BRITISH COLUMBIA

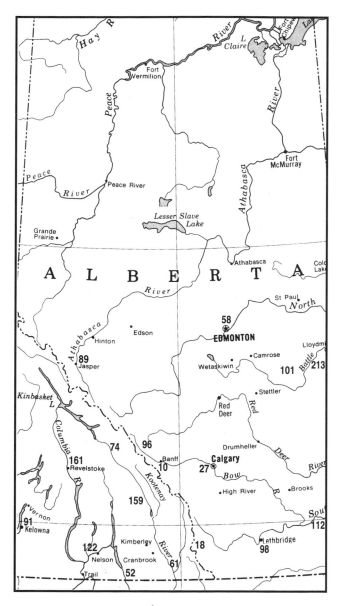

ALBERTA

Wollaston

Lake

Brochet

Cree
L

Reinde

Lake

Lake

Ly
La

La
Loche

R

Churchill

Île-à-
la-Crosse

Lac
la Ronge

La Ronge

Cold
Lake

Flin Flo

Meadow
Lake

Saskatchewan

Nipawin

Saskatchewan

154

nster

Prince Albert

R

Melfort

Hudson
Bay

North
Battleford

S A S K A T C H E W A N

River

182
Saskatoon

Kindersley

Yorkton

Saskatchewan

Qu'Appelle

Melville

R

Swift Current

Moose Jaw

160 ✪ **REGINA**

94

185

Assiniboia

Weyburn

Estevan

SASKATCHEWAN

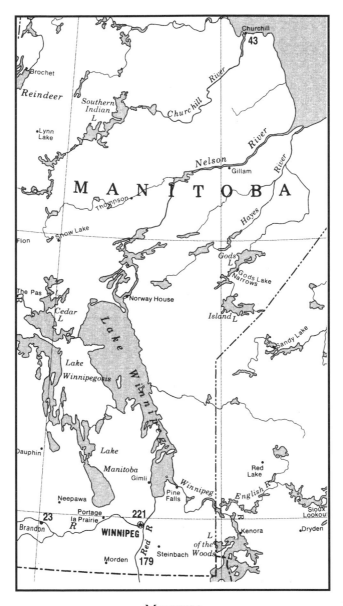

MANITOBA

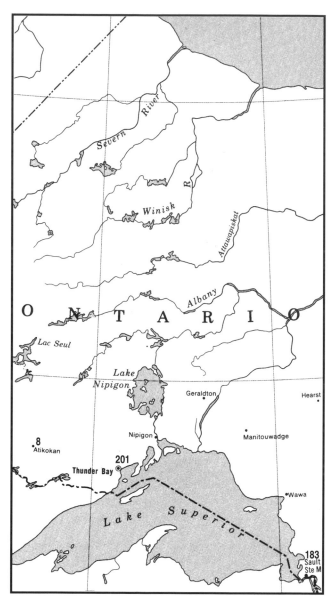

Northwestern Ontario

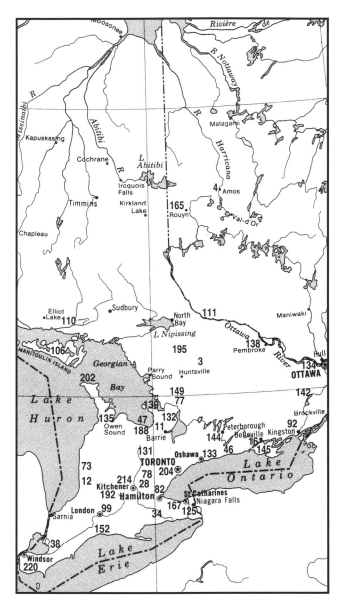

SOUTHERN ONTARIO

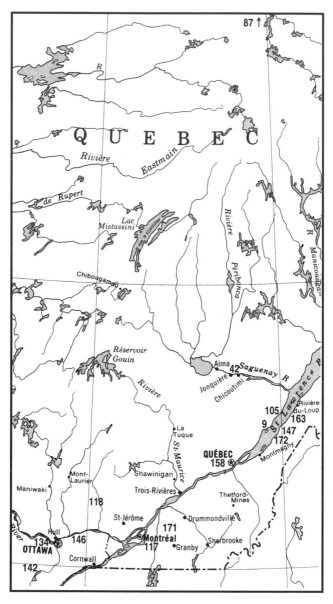

CENTRAL QUEBEC

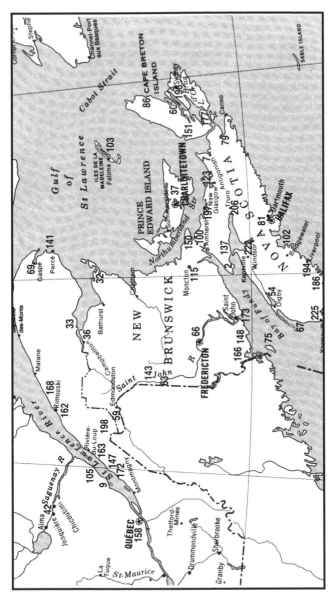

EASTERN QUEBEC & THE MARITIMES

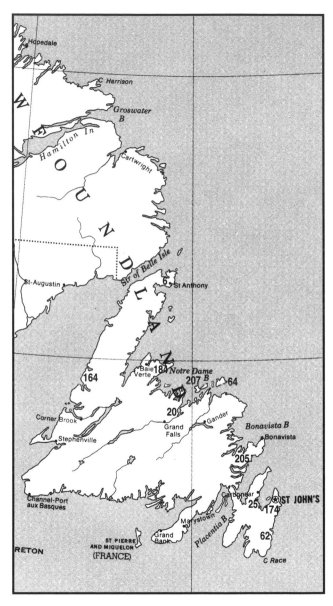

Hopedale

C Harrison

Groswater B

Hamilton In

L A B R A D O R

Cartwright

St-Augustin

Str of Belle Isle

St Anthony

164

Baie Verte 184 Notre Dame

207 B

64

20

Corner Brook

Grand Falls

Gander

Stephenville

Bonavista B

Bonavista

205

Channel-Port aux Basques

Carbonear

25 174 ST JOHN'S

Marystown

Grand Bank

Placentia B

62

ST PIERRE AND MIQUELON (FRANCE)

RETON

C Race

NEWFOUNDLAND & LABRADOR

INDEX TO MAPS

ABBOTSFORD, B.C.

MAP 1

CLAYBURN VILLAGE STORE
34810 Clayburn Road
Clayburn
(604) 853-4020

$50

The Clayburn Village Store is closed for the months of January, May and September. That's when Bryan and Trish Haber take off, perhaps to a food festival in California, perhaps to Betty's Tea-Shop in York, where they buy a special rare Assam tea for the Village Store back home. (Theirs is the only cream tea with clotted cream to bc had anywhere this side of Victoria.) Trish makes all their own chutneys, pickles, cheese scones, sticky walnut buns and sticky-toffee puddings. Every year they bring home new soup recipes, and their recipe for carrot-and-coconut soup has been published in *Bon Appetit*. We also like their caramelized onion soup with garlic and parmesan cheese, though many of the customers seem to prefer the Thai coconut-and-squash soup. Bryan Haber is also keen on British ales, which he buys from Samuel Smith's Yorkshire Brewery in Tadcaster. There's Imperial Stout, Nut Brown and Teddy Porter, and he now has an organic ale and an organic cider as well. There's always an assortment of British candies on the candy counter, all sold from big glass jars, just the way they used to be in the nineteen-thirties. But they didn't have a frozen-yogurt machine then. He has one now that lets him choose whatever flavour the customer feels like.
Open Tuesday to Saturday 10 am to 5 pm. Closed on Sunday and Monday. Licensed. Master Card, Visa. &

ADVOCATE HARBOUR, N.S.

MAP 2

WILD CARAWAY
3721 Highway 209
(902) 392-2889

☆☆☆
$95 ($175)

The drive from Halifax to Advocate Harbour takes about four hours. The menu at Wild Caraway changes every two weeks and concentrates on local seafood and greens from Andrew Aitken and Sarah Griebel's garden. Andrew and Sarah like to forage for fiddleheads, wild mushrooms, sea greens, cattails and lamb's quarters. Dinners start with parsnip tortellini, perhaps, or local scallops. The menu is always innovative and features such things as halibut with lemon beurre blanc, local flounder and cold-smoked char. Sometimes the sweet is something as simple (and delightful) as wild strawberries. They have home-brew ginger beer and rhubarb lemonade on their wine-list. Prices are remarkably low and the service is at once warm and knowledgeable. Wild Caraway is a gem.

Open Monday and Thursday to Sunday 11 am to 8 pm from the middle of May until late October. Closed on Tuesday and Wednesday. Licensed. Master Card, Visa. ♿

ALGONQUIN PARK, Ontario   MAP 3
AROWHON PINES   ☆
Highway 60   **$200 ($625)**
(866) 633-5661

All the recipes at Arowhon Pines were developed over the years, then put onto a computer in such detail that no hired chef could put a foot wrong. And so it has worked out. Meals are planned a week in advance, which means that nobody ever gets the same meal twice. As you enter the great hexagonal dining-room, you're confronted by a large buffet table, where there are several soups (beautiful pumpkin in the fall), a number of pâtés and terrines, braised short-ribs, scotch eggs, smoked mousse of lake trout, honey-garlic chicken wings and a wild-rice salad. You can eat as much of any of these as you like. When you sit down at your table—don't try to book a window table, because it's first come first seated—there's a choice of four entrées, one of which will be fish, another a vegetarian dish. The sweets are all famous, so try to save room for one. There's a huge assortment of pies, tarts and cakes, at least one of which will be hot. Maple mousse is a specialty of the house. The coffee is excellent, but you have to bring your own bottle—there's no corkage fee. Lunch is also served buffet-style on weekends only. The price in parentheses above covers three meals a day for a couple, plus all the recreational facilities on offer.

Open daily 12.30 pm to 2 pm, 6.30 pm to 8 pm from 3 June until 10 October. Bring your own bottle. Master Card, Visa. Book ahead. &

ALGONQUIN PARK   MAP 3
BARTLETT LODGE   ☆
Highway 60   **$185 ($495)**
(866) 614-5355

No-one forgets their first visit to Bartlett Lodge. The Lodge is on Cache Lake about fifteen miles east of the West Gate. You drive to the far end of the car park, where you'll find a free telephone to the Lodge. A boat comes to pick you up in about two minutes. (In fine weather they come in a custom-built Giesler; if it's raining, they come in a covered pontoon boat.) On the far side you're offered a complete dinner for 67.50 a head. It's made by Dave Fortune, an Ottawa-based chef who will be on the job for another year or two, maybe more. The meal begins with a selection of charcuterie, followed by a seasonal soup, then perhaps a mushroom risotto, then one of four or five entrées (wild salmon, say, or beef tenderloin) and finally something like key-lime pie or a vegan almond tart with avocado. Coffee is on the house. If you spend the night there won't be any television, but breakfast is a feast and you'll have your own canoe.

Open daily 6 pm to 8 pm from early May until mid-October. Bring your own bottle. Master Card, Visa. You must book ahead.

AMHERST, N.S.
See LORNEVILLE.

This is a guide to Canadian restaurants from coast to coast—the first ever published and the only one of its kind on the market today. Nobody can buy his way into this guide and nobody can buy his way out.

AMOS, Quebec

MAP 4
☆☆
$135

LE MOULIN
100 1 avenue o
(819) 732-8271

Jean-Victor Flingou is an excellent cook who enjoys his work. But after more than twenty years on the job, he's turned the evening meal over to his son, Maxim, who now has a new menu. Amos was a very small city when Jean-Victor started out, and he used to cook what he felt like cooking. But there's more competition these days and food costs are constantly increasing. He and his son still bring in all their seafood from Montreal, and that means Atlantic salmon, scallops, shrimps and occasionally red tuna. He used to ignore pork, but it's on the menu now (with two mustards), along with rack of Alberta lamb. In the evening the plat du moment may be quail, duck, sweetbreads or bison. They also use a lot of chicken, because the kitchen needs chicken bones for its stock. At noon the menu du jour costs just 20.00; if you have more than that, ask for the feuilleté of strawberries. It's available all day and it's delightful.

Open Monday to Friday 11 am to 2 pm, 5 pm to 9 pm, Saturday 5 pm to 9 pm. Closed on Sunday. Licensed. Amex, Master Card, Visa. Book ahead. ⅃

ANCASTER, Ontario

(MAP 82)
☆
$135

THE MILL
548 Old Dundas Road
(905) 648-1828

The Mill in Ancaster is one of the most conservative restaurants in its group. But the chef, Jeff Crump, helped to found the Ontario chapter of the slow-cooking movement, and has long been an advocate of local organic produce. He has some interesting appetizers, among them a scallop bouillabaisse with mussels and clams, pear-and-parsnip soup and a risotto with sour apples, gouda and aged sherry. The most interesting of his main dishes is the confit duck leg, with moist flesh and crisp skin—a great dish. There's also a dry-aged rib-eye of beef, lamb with parsnips, sturgeon with apple and cabbage and roasted pheasant with candied sweet potato and roasted pears. Sweets depend largely on the time of year. Our favourite is the clementine pie with meringue. The champagne Sunday brunch is as good as any in this part of the country.

Open Tuesday to Friday 11.30 am to 10 pm, Saturday 5 pm to 10 pm, Sunday 9.30 am to 2.30 pm (brunch), 5 pm to 8 pm. Closed on Monday. Licensed. Master Card, Visa.

L'ANSE–AUX–MEADOWS, MAP 6
Newfoundland
THE NORSEMAN ☆☆
(877) 623–2018 **$150**

Adrian Nordhof loves the life here, which is good news for admirers of the Norseman. The Norseman is a café and art gallery right next door to the Viking Settlement. It's more than twenty years since we discovered Adrian's wife, Gina Hodge and her mother, who were still open at the very end of the season. They have a fine menu and a warm and happy dining-room. Adrian still does most of the cooking and has taken a couple of courses as a sommelier as well. He has a different wine-list every year, based on his travels in Europe. "We won't give our guests anything," Gina will tell you, "that we wouldn't give ourselves." They buy everything they can locally; their cod was swimming an hour before it turned up on your plate. The same is true of the lobster. The mussels come from down the road and so does the snow crab. The fish plant in St. Anthony sells the best shrimp Gina has ever eaten, and every day they make a chowder of cod and salmon with onions, saffron and port wine. If you don't like fish, ask them for roast chicken, duck confit or Welsh lamb, which they import because it's better than the local product. Next year they're taking over the bed-and-breakfast next door, which used to be run by Gina's mother. They also own two state-of-the-art cottages on the seashore, which they bought from the author,

Annie Proulx.
Open daily noon to 9 pm from 25 May until 20 September. Licensed. Diners, Master Card, Visa. Book ahead if you can. &

L'ANSE-AUX-MEADOWS
See also ST.-LUNAIRE-GRIQUET.

ANTIGONISH, N.S.   MAP 7
GABRIEAU'S BISTRO   ☆☆
350 Main Street   **$170**
(902) 863-1925

Gabrieau's has a wonderful wine-list, offering such things
as Rothschild's petit mouton, several barolos (all properly
aged) and, at the other end of the list, two or three from
Luckett, among them the celebrated Phone Book. There
are all the usual crabcakes and raw oysters, as well as perfectly fresh Atlantic salmon, Berkshire pork and lovely
local lamb. Most remarkable of all is the sushi menu with
its tuna sashimi and its shrimp tempura. You can order à
la carte or ask for a sushi platter, which is loaded with Nigiri sushi of all sorts. There's also a tapas menu, normally
only offered at the bar but available by request in the dining-room, with a wide selection of Asian choices like
miso scallops and Thai green shrimp curry. This is an
amazing restaurant.
*Open Monday to Thursday 11 am to 9 pm, Friday 11 am to
9.30 pm, Saturday 4 pm to 9.30 pm. Closed on Sunday. Licensed. All cards.* &

ATIKOKAN, Ontario   MAP 8
TOWN & COUNTRY
(807) 597-2533   **$95**

John and Stephanie Torbiak started the Town & Country
in 1983. John runs the hotel, Stephanie runs the restaurant. She knows her market and never takes any old
favourites off the menu. In fact, she recently added two
Thai curries, a chicken and a shrimp. She makes a good
quiche too. If you don't want a big meal, just ask for a

soup and a salad. The soups are always homemade and everything on the menu—the steaks and the pasta—is cooked to order. Stephanie gets tired by the end of the season, but everyone likes her cooking and that makes it all worthwhile.

Open Monday to Saturday 9 am to 9 pm. Closed on Sunday. Licensed. Amex, Master Card, Visa.

BAIE ST.-PAUL, Quebec   MAP 9

Baie St.-Paul is such an important centre on the north shore that we're taking a chance on one or two suggestions. A La Chouette at 2 rue Leblanc (telephone (418) 435-3217) is the best place to stay. It's bright and colourful, with seven bedrooms and stunning breakfasts. Ginette Guérette puts a lot of thought and energy into the planning and preparation of the meal, offering four varieties of toast, all made from local flour. For lunch and dinner, everyone's favourite is the Mouton Noir at 43 rue Ste.-Anne (telephone (418) 240-3030). It has a spacious deck overlooking a sleepy river and the restaurant is decidedly picturesque. We ourselves haven't had much luck with the kitchen, but other travellers have been more fortunate. It's open every day in season for both lunch and dinner. It has a licence and takes most cards

BALA, Ontario   **(MAP 77)**
BALA HOUSE
3047 Highway 169   **$45**
(519) 216-7954

We don't know how they can afford to keep this place going. Nobody here has had any experience of running a restaurant, but they do know how to smoke meat. One traveller writes to tell us that he drives for miles for one of their pulled-pork sandwiches. They don't coat the meat with barbecue sauce, so you get to taste the pork, which is smoked for ten hours on the smoker out back. The bacon cheeseburgers have as many admirers as the pulled pork. They come with their own sauce and twice-fried potatoes. There are only two small tables in the place, though there are more outside in summer. If the chef isn't busy in the kitchen you can listen to him playing his guitar.

Open Monday, Tuesday and Thursday to Sunday 11 am to 8 pm. Closed on Wednesday. No liquor, no cards. No reservations.

BANFF, Alberta *MAP 10*

Banff has a number of surprisingly good inexpensive restaurants. Bumpers at 537 Banff Avenue (telephone (403) 762-2622) even encourages children. It's at the far end of town and doesn't look much from the outside. But inside it's a different story. They have swift, cheerful service and an all-you-can-eat salad bar. They specialize in well hung Alberta beef, and they sell a lot of triple-A prime rib. The Balkan at 120 Banff Avenue (telephone (403) 762-3454) was opened in 1982 by a Greek couple who had a lot of old family recipes. The cooking has always been completely authentic and the prices are as low as ever. The thing to have here is the so-called arni-psito, which is a version of lamb Greek-style, and it's a stunning dish. A few years ago, they decided to try something new, so they brought in a belly-dancer, and every Tuesday and Thursday invited customers to throw their plates on the floor. Some people love this sort of thing and the place is always crowded. The St. James Gate at 207 Wolf Street (telephone (403) 762-9355) is an Irish-style pub where they have 24 beers on tap and 30 single malts. Everybody admires the choice of beers and nearly everybody likes their barley soup, their meatloaf and their spicy shepherd's pie. The cooking is good, the helpings big and the prices fair. The Balkan and the St. James are open all day every day, Bumpers every evening from 5 pm to 10 pm. They all have a licence and take most cards.

BANFF   MAP 10
EDEN   ☆☆☆
Rimrock Resort Hotel   **$275**
30 Mountain Avenue
(888) 746-7625

Eden is built into the side of a mountain, and it's very beautiful. Even those who complain about the high prices admit that the view from the dining-room is stunning.

The presentation and the service are beyond compare. The wine pairings are inspired. The wine-list is extraordinary. It has 70,000 bottles from all over the world. The vegetarian tasting menu (seven courses for 103.00) has a number of their best dishes—try the Jerusalem artichoke soup and you'll see what we mean. The à la carte is up-to-the-minute. One dinner we will never forget began with a complimentary cup of ravioli in a truffle broth. The salad of squashes and pumpkin is exquisite. The Thunder Creek pork with peach-and-mustard glaze is marvellous. The yuzu with green tea, black sesame and mango is absolutely perfect. The fact is, we have nothing at all to criticize.

Open Tuesday to Sunday 6 pm to 9 pm from 1 June until mid-October, Wednesday to Sunday from mid-October until 31 May. Closed on Monday in summer, Monday and Tuesday in winter. Licensed. Amex, Master Card, Visa. Book ahead if you can. &

BANFF   **MAP 10**
NOURISH   ☜❏
211 Bear Street   **$75**
(403) 760-3933

More and more people are looking for a vegetarian restaurant these days, and this is a good one. The portions are generous and most people will want to share their meal. (Half a Caesar salad is a meal in itself.) All the soups are full of flavour and so are the nachos. There are two dozen of them. The big hit with everybody, however, is the wild-mushroom ravioli; meat-eaters often go to Nourish just for this dish. They have an impressive list of wines and plenty of seats at the bar.

Open daily (including Christmas) 11.30 am to 4 pm, 5 pm to 9.30 pm. Licensed. No cards.

Every restaurant in this guide has been personally tested. Our reporters are not allowed to identify themselves to the management or to accept free meals. We accept no advertisements. We accept no payment for listings. We depend entirely on you.

BARRIE, Ontario   **MAP 11**
THE CRAZY FOX
135 Bayfield Street   **$150**
(705) 737-5000

Coos Uylenbroek and his wife, Lawna, came to Barrie in
1986. They settled in a charming Victorian house on
Bradford Street. When, a few years later, he moved up-
market, his new dining-room could not have been more
different. He got a dramatic two-storey restaurant with
a bar downstairs and tables on a balcony upstairs. The
kitchen itself is behind a striking wall of glass. After all
these years there are bound to be nights when the cooking is not at its best, but the kitchen is still as creative as
ever, turning out things like breast of chicken crusted
with pecans and stuffed with goat-cheese on a bed of
caramelized pears. The ingredients are always of the best,
the steaks tender and the vegetables correctly cooked.
Summer and winter you'll find some fresh berries at the
end of the meal and a blood-orange sorbet made without
sugar. The wine-list is quite expensive, but you can get a
flight of three different two-ounce glasses of wine much
more cheaply.
*Open Tuesday to Friday 11.30 am to 11 pm, Saturday 5 pm to
11 pm. Closed on Sunday and Monday. Licensed. Amex, Master Card, Visa. Free parking.*

BAYFIELD, Ontario   **MAP 12**
THE BLACK DOG   ☆
5 Main Street N   **$160**
(519) 565-2326

For years the Little Inn and the Red Pump were thought
to be the two best restaurants in Bayfield. You won't go
wrong with either of them, but in our opinion the Black
Dog now takes first place. Like the other two, it's in an
historic building that was built in 1850 and is now the
oldest commercial building on the street. It's always been
known for its twenty draft beers and its many single-malt
whiskies. But it's the kitchen we're interested in at the

moment. They make their curried shrimp with lemon grass and coconut broth, their snails with mushrooms and herbs de provence, their milkfed liver with buttermilk mash, their flat-iron steak with chimichurri.

Open daily 11 am to 5 pm (lunch), 5 pm to 9 pm (dinner) from 1 May until Labour Day, Wednesday to Sunday 11 am to 5 pm, 5 pm to 9 pm from Labour Day until 30 April. Closed on Monday and Tuesday in winter. Licensed. Amex, Master Card, Visa. Book ahead if you can. &

BAY FORTUNE, P.E.I.   (MAP 37)
THE INN AT BAY FORTUNE   ☆☆
758 Highway 310   **$275**
(902) 687-3745

As everyone knows by now, David Wilmer sold the Inn at Bay Fortune last year to his long-time friend and colleague, Michael Smith. David is now spending most of his time down the road at the Inn at Spry Point (telephone (902) 583-2400), which will in future be run as a bed-and-breakfast with wine and appetizers. Michael Smith's celebrity has already brought full houses to Bay Fortune, where the dining-room is now called Fire Works. Fire Works has a huge open hearth, a rotisserie, a grill, a smoke-house and an oven. In the dining-room they've developed a so-called feast format, featuring local produce from the Inn's marvellous organic garden cooked over an open fire. Dinner is served informally at several butcher-block tables. There's a gin-and-tonic station, an oyster station, a sausage station and a station offering smoked salmon with a lemon-caper aioli where you can meet your neighbours cocktail-party style. Dinner takes three or four hours, and most people have been impressed by both the cooking and the presentation. The garden salad has about fifty different greens, herbs and flowers. The steaks are cooked *à point* and the salt-crusted halibut and the charcuterie board have both been widely praised. In 2016 they will have finished remodelling the seventeen bedrooms, all in high style, and they may offer lunch as well. The old house, built by Elmer Harris in 1913, is still beautiful, the bay at the foot of the garden still lovely. *Open daily 6 pm to 9 pm from 20 May until 30 September. Licensed. All cards. Book ahead.*

BEAMSVILLE, Ontario (MAP 167)
AUGUST ☆
5204 King Street **$105**
(905) 563-0200

How a town of 12,000 people can support a restaurant as good as August we cannot imagine. Beth Ashton is very serious about regional cuisine. Her first partner, Marc McKerracher, had a big garden. Clayton Gillie, who replaced McKerracher, has no garden, but is passionate about foraging for organic produce. Lunch, which used to be a small, simple affair, is now as varied and plentiful as anyone could hope for. We can recommend the soups and the house-made pasta, which changes several times a week. They smoke their own fish and cure their own beef; they bake their own bread and make their own sweets. Every weekday they offer a club sandwich on toasted tomato bread. On Sundays they offer andouille sausages and potato hash with two eggs and cheddar cheese. In the evenings they add spiced chicken with brown sugar and mustard for 20.25, which is pretty hard to beat (locavore with local cheeses, house-made pickles and salmon gravlax costs about half that). An Ontario lamb rack is more and so is the dry-rub flat-iron steak. Wines are all raised on or near the Beamsville Bench and several are sold by the glass as well as the bottle. If you bring your own bottle, corkage is free on Wednesday. *Open Tuesday to Saturday 11.30 am to 3 pm, 5 pm to 9 pm, Sunday 9 am to 3 pm (brunch). Closed on Monday. Licensed. Master Card, Visa.* ♿

This is a guide to Canadian restaurants from coast to coast—the first ever published and the only one of its kind on the market today. We accept no advertisements. Nobody can buy his way into this guide and nobody can buy his way out.

BEAVER CREEK, Yukon   MAP 15
BUCKSHOT BETTY'S   ☞
Highway 1   **$65**
(867) 862-7111

Betty is one of those people of whom one says, "They
don't make them like that any more." Her real name is
Carmen Hinson and nothing has changed here since we
first wrote about her—except that she has added two
more cabins (to make seven) and stopped renting rooms
in her own house. One of the cabins has a fine view and
all of them are very quiet. Carmen still works far too
hard. She has some help in the summer, but all winter she
works by herself, taking an occasional hour or two off to
chop wood. There are about 45 seats inside and 45 on the
wrap-around deck outside. Carmen does all her own baking—bread, cookies, brownies and hamburger buns, and
whatever else she feels like making. That might be pecan
pie, carrot cake or apple strudel. Her homemade soups
are full of flavour and her sandwiches are like no others.
Beaver Creek is an ideal place to stop after the magnificent but scary drive from Whitehorse.
Open daily 6.30 am to 10.30 pm (or later) from mid–April until
mid–October, daily 7 am to 9 pm from mid–October until mid–
April. Licensed. Master Card, Visa. ♿

BELLEVILLE, Ontario   MAP 16
L'AUBERGE DE FRANCE   ☞
304 Front Street   **$70**
(613) 966-2433

Jean-Marc Salvagno made his name in Avignon years ago
before moving to Toronto and, more recently, to
Belleville, where he opened his own bistro and bakery.
If you come for lunch, you choose your soup, your
quiche, your salad and your sandwich at the counter and
it's brought to you in the small seating area at the rear.
There are usually about half a dozen sandwiches on offer,
all made with house-made bread. The sweets are made
on the premises, and our favourite is the raspberry tart.

Once a month they offer what they call a chef's table, which has an innovative menu that costs only 40.00 a head.
Open Monday to Friday 10 am to 6 pm, Saturday 9 am to 6 pm. Closed on Sunday. Licensed. All cards. ♿

BELLEVILLE
See also BRIGHTON.

LE BIC, Quebec (MAP 162)
CHEZ SAINT-PIERRE ☆☆
129 rue du Mont St.-Louis $215
(418) 736-5051

Colombe Saint-Pierre has three children, but that hasn't kept her away from the kitchen that's become her passion. Le Bic is only ten miles west of Rimouski, but Chez Saint-Pierre isn't that easy to find. It's on a back street facing a car park and you'll probably have to ask your way. In these simple surroundings, Colombe is cooking as well as anyone in Quebec. Most of her ingredients come from neighbouring farms. She gets her pork from St.-Gabriel. She forages for mushrooms, for mountain spinach and salsify des prés. Sorrel grows wild on the shoulders of local roads. Colombe likes to begin her meals with something like ravioli of chanterelles or scallops marinated in Chinata paprika and finished with lemon and sundried tomatoes—a compelling and dramatic dish. She'll continue, perhaps, with fillet of bison or gravlax of Arctic char. She'll end with a chocolate financier, a biscuit bavarois or a plate of local cheeses. The choice of French and Italian wines matches the menu in quality and finesse. Chez Saint-Pierre is a restaurant you must discover for yourself. Be sure to book ahead.
Open Wednesday to Sunday 5 pm to 9.30 pm from 1 until 31 May, Tuesday to Sunday 11.30 am to 2 pm, 5 pm to 9.30 pm from 1 June until 31 August, Wednesday to Sunday 5 pm to 9.30 pm from 1 September until 30 April. Closed on Monday and Tuesday in the spring, fall and winter, on Monday in summer. Licensed. Master Card, Visa.

BLAIRMORE, Alberta   **MAP 18**
HIGHWOOD
11373 20 Avenue   **$55**
(403) 562-7878

The setting here may be pretty unprepossessing and the
service spotty, but the cooking is well worth everything.
The menu is long but familiar. There's butter chicken,
but before you laugh it off take note that many people
think the butter chicken at Blairmore makes two of the
same dish in Calgary. There's a buffet lunch that costs all
of 13.00 with rice and naan. We've had complaints of
bone in both the chicken and the lamb, but this is all halal
meat and the samosas and pakoras are as good as the butter chicken. The chai tea is never too sweet. We suggest
you stop here the next time you're near the Crow's Nest
Pass. Blairmore is about twelve miles from the border between Alberta and British Columbia.
Open Monday to Saturday 11 am to 2 pm, 4.30 pm to 8 pm.
Closed on Sunday. Licensed. Master Card, Visa.

BLOOMFIELD, Ontario   **(MAP 145)**
THE HUBB AT ANGELINE'S   ☆
433 Main Street   **$130 ($235)**
(613) 393-3301

Angéline's was one of the first upscale restaurants in
Prince Edward County, long before it became a trendy
destination for Toronto people. The place is still owned
by the Fida family, but the renamed Hubb bistro has been
run for several years by the chef, Elliot Reynolds, and his
wife, Laura Borutski. We like to start with sweetbreads
and kohlrabi with yellow plums and crisp shallots, followed by pan-roasted halibut served with confit tomatoes
and garlic scapes. Our favourite sweets are the raspberry
pavlova and the mascarpone jelly-roll. The menu is seasonal and every fall they put on a three-course *prix-fixe*—
pulled-pork croquettes, duck meatballs or seared trout
and lemon pudding. There's a good list of local wines,
plus a number of ciders and draft beers. For hotel resi-

dents there's an excellent breakfast buffet.
Open Thursday to Saturday 5 pm to 9 pm. Closed Sunday to Wednesday. Licensed. All cards. &

BOTWOOD, Newfoundland   **MAP 20**
DOCKSIDE   ☆
243 Water Street   **$135**
(709) 257-3179

We seem to have known about Dockside since the beginning of time, but it's actually only 22 years since Jim Stuckless converted an old hardware store into a notable tourist destination. Botwood is set in stunning countryside and was an important base during the Second World War. Nowadays the kitchen here has a big reputation. Jim taught himself to cook when he took the place over, and he's still in the kitchen (halftime) today, though he's sold Dockside to Sandra Gill. The menu is still short and filled with the sort of food he himself has always liked to eat. That means fresh local greens in summer and root vegetables in winter. The beef is all triple-A from Alberta and people tell us they've never had a better New York steak. The skin-on breast of chicken is stuffed with savoury and served with orange and grand marnier; the cod is pan-fried and comes in by the boatload. We only hope Jim continues to make his apple torte and his partridge-berry kuchen. Dockside is only twenty minutes by car from the Trans Canada by Highway 350.
Open daily noon to 2 pm, 5 pm to 8 pm. Licensed. All cards. &

BRACEBRIDGE, Ontario   **(MAP 77)**
ONE FIFTY-FIVE
155 Manitoba Street   **$140**
(705) 645-1935

This is a pleasant restaurant, quiet and well served. But the cooking is not what it used to be. The beef carpaccio comes with far too many greens and far too little carpaccio of beef. The gravlax of salmon, which is the best of the appetizers, runs out too often. Other than that, there's only panko-crusted goat-cheese and a Caesar salad. There's a good shrimp risotto to follow and the yellow perch, dressed with lemon and parsley, is always carefully prepared. The sweets are made in house, but the flourless-chocolate cake is rather disappointing. Too many of the wines come from Chile and Argentina, too few from Niagara. Prices, however, are very modest.

Open Tuesday to Sunday 11.30 am to 2.30 pm, 5 pm to 9.30 pm from 1 April until 15 February. Closed on Monday. Licensed. Amex, Master Card, Visa. Book ahead if you can. &

BRACEBRIDGE   (MAP 77)
RIVERWALK
1 Manitoba Street   **$150**
(705) 646-0711

Bracebridge now has at least two useful restaurants: One Fifty-Five and Riverwalk. Both are open year-round and both occupy heritage houses. One Fifty-Five is up the hill on Manitoba Street; Riverwalk overlooks the falls down at the foot of the street. Its menu is seasonal, starting with charcuterie (a variety of cured meats and pickles) and going on to breast of chicken with lovely crackling skin, Muskoka lamb (now a rarity) and a couple of steaks. David Friesen makes a point of using ingredients grown in the Muskoka region whenever he can. His wines, however, come from California, Australia, Italy and Chile as well as the Niagara Region.

Open Tuesday to Sunday 11.30 am to 2.30 pm, 5.30 pm to 8.30 pm (shorter hours in winter). Closed on Monday. Amex, Master Card, Visa. Book ahead if you can.

BRACKLEY BEACH, P.E.I.   (MAP 37)
THE DUNES   ☆
(902) 672-2586   **$145**

Emily Wells, who cooked here for many years, has left to open her own restaurant in New Glasgow, P.E.I. (see below). A number of visitors, however, have been excited by the work of her successor, Norman Day. Already he's won an award for his seafood chowder. But he has many other good ideas as well: slow-braised lamb shanks, fresh Atlantic salmon with yellow curry and a splendid chocolate torte. His wine-list is short, but there's always plenty of good drinking on it—Edna Valley chardonnay for one. The coffee is excellent.

Open daily 11.30 am to 4 pm, 5.30 pm to 10 pm from 15 June until 15 October. Licensed. Amex, Master Card, Visa. Book ahead. &

BRANDON, Manitoba   MAP 23
BLUE HILLS BAKERY   ☜❒
1229 Richmond Avenue   **$45**
(204) 571-6762

This little bakery café comes from another age. It has seven or eight tables, no decorations, and a soup and sandwich that cost exactly 10.17. Kelly and Becky, who run the place, go from strength to strength. They've made no compromises and people like their food. Vegans and vegetarians come here and so do people who want a turkey dinner. Both owners are Hutterites and both are passionate about fresh organic produce. They buy all their grains and vegetables from nearby organic farms. They make all their own granola and their own bread and serve them for breakfast until eleven o'clock on weekdays and one o'clock on Saturdays. Every noon they offer old-fashioned soups and chicken chowder, as well as sandwiches, salads and a quiche or perhaps shepherd's pie. Their pies are frozen, but their coffee comes in fresh from Salt Spring Island.

Open Monday to Saturday 7 am to 5 pm. Closed on Sunday. No liquor. Master Card, Visa. &

BRIER ISLAND, N.S.
See FREEPORT.

The map number assigned to each city, town or village gives the location of the centre on one or more of the maps at the start of the book.

BRIGHTON, Ontario (MAP 16)
THE GABLES ☆
14 Division Street N **$160**
(613) 475-5565

Dieter Ernst hasn't changed his menu in the last two years. Why should he? Everyone thinks that every dish he serves is the best they've ever eaten. It's true, Dieter Ernst is a master chef. If you try his pastry you'll see what we mean. As for his meat and fish, they're all cooked perfectly *à point*. Notice that his whipping cream is the real thing, his snails are like no other and his wienerschnitzel is tender and full of flavour. His roasted duck with red cabbage and cherries, his Black Angus steak, his cod, salmon, scallops and rainbow trout all have their admirers. Dieter makes his own sweets and if the apple strudel is still on the menu you should ask for it. There are some surprising wines from Prince Edward County, as well as several single malts and a number of grappas. The dining-room is elegantly furnished and Kirsten Ernst is a charming and attentive hostess.
Open Wednesday to Friday 11.30 am to 2 pm, 5.30 pm to 9 pm, Saturday 5.30 pm to 9 pm. Closed Sunday to Tuesday. Licensed. Master Card, Visa. Book ahead if you can. &

BRIGUS, Newfoundland MAP 25
THE COUNTRY CORNER
14 Water Street **$45**
(709) 528-1099

Brigus is on Conception Bay, built around a sheltered harbour and surrounded by hills. It was established in 1612 and looks much as it did before Confederation, one of the few towns in the province that does. The Country Corner has twelve seats, a covered patio and a gift shop. The menu is small, but the ingredients are fresh and usually local. The specialty of the house is cod chowder, always served with a tea-biscuit. A second menu lists nothing but gluten-free dishes. At noon they specialize in turkey and beef sandwiches. The pick of the sweets is

the wonderful blueberry crisp, made with just-picked blueberries and served with ice cream.
Open daily 8 am to 8 pm from Victoria Day until Thanksgiving. No liquor. Master Card, Visa.

BURLINGTON, Ontario   (MAP 82)
BLACKTREE   ☆☆☆
Roseland Plaza   **$165**
3029 New Street
(905) 681-2882

Matteo Paonessa has worked with some of the best chefs in Canada, including Marc Thuet, Susur Lee and Michael Stadtländer. He likes to begin his meals with an *amuse bouche* of veal cheeks with bilberry jam or candied Norwegian steelhead trout with gooseberries. Next comes a small loaf of bread, sprinkled with sea-salt and still warm from the oven. Appetizers include pan-seared foie gras, octopus with lemon grass, confit of red deer and an apple soup. Main courses always include some gnocchi, some fish and some game. Once we had a partridge in a pear tree (shredded partridge with pear jam and enoki mushrooms). On another occasion we had salt-crusted black cod with pickled carrots, rutabaga and maitake mushrooms. After that we were offered an orange-and-fig upside-down cake. Blacktree is without doubt the best restaurant in this part of the country.
Open Wednesday to Saturday 6 pm to 10 pm. Closed Sunday to Tuesday. Licensed. Master Card, Visa. Book ahead if you can. ♿

BURLINGTON   (MAP 82)
PANE FRESCO   ☞
414 Locust Street   **$45**
(905) 333-3388

Pane Fresco is a bakery and café located close to the lakeshore in downtown Burlington. They sell a lot of artisanal bread, which is handmade and contains no artificial preservatives. Apart from the bread, the menu used to be very limited. In the last couple of years, however, it's been much enlarged. They now always serve two soups, one of which is usually roasted red pepper with crumbled goat-cheese. Some of the specials, like chicken parmigiano, with fresh basil, tomato and bocconcini cheese, are available only on certain days of the week. Others (like quiche) are offered every weekday. There used to be just two salads every day; now they are up to six. One of the best dishes is a slow-braised brisket with brie, onions, baby greens and horseradish. For dessert there are countless brownies, croissants, cannolis and handmade biscottis. Occasionally there's a bread pudding as well.

Open Monday 8 am to 4 pm, Tuesday to Thursday 8 am to 6 pm, Friday and Saturday 8 am to 7 pm, Sunday 8 am to 4 pm. No liquor, no cards. &

BURLINGTON (MAP 82)
SPENCER'S ☆
1340 Lakeshore Road **$125**
(905) 633-7494

Spencer's on the Waterfront is a little less formal than its sister restaurant, the old Mill in Ancaster. You can start with soup, raw oysters, beef tartar, mussels, house-smoked albacore tuna, pork belly or foie gras—an exceptional list of choices. The best of the main courses is either the Arctic char with beluga lentils and chorizo or the lobster bake with clams, mussels, corn and new potatoes. There are also several steaks and slow-braised short-ribs. The best of the sweets is now the roasted peaches and plums with yogurt, peach compote and plum sorbet. The Sunday brunch is worth every cent of the 47.00 it costs.

Open Monday to Saturday 11.30 am to 4.30 pm (lunch), 4.30 pm to 9.30 pm (dinner), Sunday 9.30 am to 3.30 pm (brunch), 5.15 pm to 9 pm. Licensed. Master Card, Visa. Free parking. &

Nobody but nobody can buy his way into this guide.

41

CALGARY, Alberta

MAP 27

THE BLACK PIG
825 1 Avenue NE   **$120**
(403) 460-0350

The Black Pig is a Spanish restaurant and the specialty of
the house, as the name implies, is Iberico ham. Apart
from that, the main dishes are few and far between, but
Larry Scammell has a number of interesting appetizers,
among them lamb meatballs, crisp pork belly and an excellent beef tartar. The wine-list is all Spanish, and the
best drinking (as usual) is from Rioja. The Cune reserva
costs 12.00 a glass and 60.00 a bottle, and it's worth every
dollar.
Open Tuesday and Wednesday 5 pm to 10 pm, Thursday to
Sunday 10 am to 3 pm, 5 pm to 10 pm. Closed on Monday. Li-
censed. Master Card, Visa. ♿

CALGARY   MAP 27

BLINK   ☆☆
111 8 Avenue SW   **$190**
(403) 263-5330

Blink has wonderful service. The waiters not only bring
your meal promptly and with a smile; they also know the
score of the current baseball game and will hug you if
your team wins. The kitchen likes to start with a parfait
of foie gras or a gorgeous squash soufflé. Wild Pacific halibut may follow, crusted with bone marrow. Rib-eye of
beef is always on the menu and so is Arctic char. The meal
will end with a lovely chocolate pâté with ginger ice
cream. There's an unusual Long Meadow chardonnay to
drink and also a half-bottle of Blue Mountain for only
30.00. The Long Meadow is quite a bit more.
Open Monday to Friday 11 am to 2 pm, 5 pm to 10 pm, Satur-
day 5 pm to 11 pm. Closed on Sunday. Licensed. All cards. Book
ahead if you can. ♿

Our website is at www.oberonpress.ca. Readers wishing
to use e-mail should address us at oberon@sympatico.ca.

CALGARY   **MAP 27**
BOXWOOD
340 13 Avenue SW   **$115**
(403) 265-4006

Boxwood was opened a few years ago by the River Café. It occupies a small grassy park between Twelfth and Thirteenth Avenues. They have a short menu and take no reservations. At noon there are just two or three dishes—one fish and a couple of chicken. Dinner is much the same, though they add some rotisseries, among them Driview lamb. They make their own still and sparkling water (but not their lemonade) and list a number of wines, among them Wise Guy sauvignon blanc and Rook merlot, both from the Columbia Valley. There's an open kitchen and friendly service. Prices are low for Calgary. *Open daily 11 am to 10 pm. Licensed. Amex, Master Card, Visa. No reservations.*

CALGARY   **MAP 27**
CENTRAL GRAND
Central Landmark   **$60**
1623 Centre Street NW
(403) 277-2000

Central Grand is on the second floor of the Central Landmark building at the southwest corner of Centre Street and the Trans Canada Highway. You park and enter from the south and take an elevator to the restaurant level. Central Grand is large and well appointed and has a long menu featuring things like Singapore fried noodles, Malaysian chow fun, shredded-pork vermicelli and salted fish, but it's better to come in before two o'clock for their dim sum, which makes a wonderful display of squid, shrimps, duck feet, chicken feet, pulled pork and stuffed eggplant. The place is full of celebrities feasting on chicken feet at bargain prices. At least they don't order chow mein. *Open daily 10 am to 3 pm, 5 pm to 10 pm. Licensed. Amex, Master Card, Visa.*

CALGARY   **MAP 27**
MODEL MILK   ☆
308 17 Avenue SW   **$150**
(403) 265-7343

Model Milk occupies the old Model Milk Dairy building
and it has a lively, original menu. The menu begins with
small plates of milkfed-veal sweetbreads, fried quail, elk
tartar and albacore tuna. Milkfed veal is rare everywhere
except Montreal and at Model Milk the sweetbreads,
served with charred romaine, are lovely. So is the elk tartar and the raw tuna. Large plates come next and there's
rump of lamb from Driview Farms, rainbow trout, line-
caught halibut and Wagyu beef (cheap at 36.00). The best
of these—not counting the Wagyu beef—is the halibut,
which is served in a light broth with cucumber and kelp.
They make their own ice cream and it shows. Their
cheese comes from the Drunken Cow and their apple
crisp is made with hand-picked apples. They make their
own sparkling water too and carry a fine pinot noir from
the Willamette Valley in Oregon. The service is well informed and the prices are reasonable.
Open Monday to Saturday 5 pm to 1 am, Sunday 5 pm to 10
pm. Licensed. Amex, Master Card, Visa. Book ahead if you
can. ♿

CALGARY   **MAP 27**
THE NASH
925 11 Street SE   **$195**
(403) 984-3365

The Nash is Michael Noble's latest venture The name
comes from the old National Hotel, where the restaurant
occupies the ground floor. The renovation is stylish. The
menu is ambitious, offering Ahi tuna as an appetizer,
along with rotisserie chicken and seafood chowder. The
main courses are less remarkable, and even the best of
them, the chicken ravioli, is not particularly inviting. The
lemon cream with blackberries is, however, a splendid
dish. The wines are expensive—the Tantalus riesling is

44

one of the cheapest at 66.00 a bottle. Just ask for a glass of Tawse, which costs only 12.00, and keep your money. *Open Tuesday to Sunday 11.30 am to 2.30 pm, 5 pm to 9.30 pm. Closed on Monday. Licensed. Amex, Master Card, Visa. Free parking.* &

CALGARY   MAP 27
NOTABLE   ☆
4611 Bowness Road NW   **$150**
(403) 288-4372

Michael Noble's restaurant is inconveniently located in the northwest of the city. It's a strange place, serving pizza and burgers as well as such conventional things as ravioli and bison. But the man in the kitchen knows what he's doing. The organic spring salmon is a marvellous dish. So is the Alberta beef tartar with house-made mustard. The beef tartar one has seen before, but the house-made mustard is a special treat. Albacore tuna is skilfully served in a niçoise salad, which is a refreshing change. The trout is served as a whole fish, simply grilled. Not that Notable is inexpensive. Blue Mountain chardonnay costs 76.00 a bottle, Four Graces pinot noir from the Willamette Valley costs 124.00 and the cabernet sauvignon from Cakebread costs all of 152.00. Michael Noble has an inconvenient location, an original menu and good cooking.
Open Tuesday to Friday 11.30 am to 11 pm, Saturday 11 am to 11 pm, Sunday 11 am to 9 pm. Closed on Monday. Licensed. Amex, Master Card, Visa. Book ahead if you can. &

CALGARY   MAP 27
OX & ANGELA   ☆
528 17 Avenue SW   **$135**
(403) 457-1432

This is a Spanish restaurant, which means wonderful Iberico ham, made from black pigs, or the much cheaper serrano ham, which is made from white pigs. These can both be had as a main course or as an appetizer—Persian dates, say, stuffed with serrano ham. They also have tapas servings of salt cod, albacore tuna, simply grilled, steamed clams, pan-seared scallops, beef short-ribs and patatas bravas. Take the Iberico ham every time. To drink, ask for one of the riojas—Hacienda Lopez de Haro comes by the glass for 11.00. They also have several Portuguese sherries for the same price. You can always drink Canadian if you like—Blue Mountain, Tawse, Mission Hill or Joie—but that would be a pity. In case you're wondering, the Ox is in charge of the kitchen; Angela manages the front of the house.

Open Monday to Friday 11.30 am to 11 pm, Saturday and Sunday 11.30 am to 2 pm (brunch), 5 pm to 11 pm. Licensed. Amex, Master Card, Visa. &

CALGARY   **MAP 27**
PIGEON-HOLE   ☆
306 17 Avenue SW   **$140**
(403) 452-4694

Pigeon-Hole is right next door to Model Milk, where the chef first made his name. His menu here is broadly similar, offering Driview lamb tartar, leg of duck, milk-fed veal, line-caught salmon, calamari tostada, octopus and salted cod. Avoid the calamari and ask instead for the charred cabbage or the chicken-liver mousse. If you're tired of raw tuna, try the grass-fed beef, which is great. The Tantalus from the Okanagan is the best of the white wines and is priced at 14.00 a glass or 68.00 a bottle. The service is amazing.

Open Monday to Saturday 5 pm to 1 am, Sunday 5 pm to 10 pm. Licensed. Amex, Master Card, Visa. Book ahead if you can. &

CALGARY   **MAP 27**
RIVER CAFE   ☆
Prince's Island Park   **$175**
(403) 261-7670

At the River Café they do a lot of their own farming and

employ the kitchen staff to seed and cultivate their crops. In spite of these virtues, we've had some disappointments at the restaurant lately. The fish-and-game board is not what it used to be and they no longer make their fine fish pie. And the quiches can be overcooked. The dinner menu works better than lunch, offering such good things as tuna tataki, squash terrine and striploin of bison. And there's still plenty of good drinking, much of it from Joie Farm, Tantalus, Tawse and Norman Hardie—the last two commonplace in the East but rarely seen in the West. *Open Monday to Friday 11.30 am to 2.30 pm, 5.30 pm to 10 pm, Saturday and Sunday 10 am to 3 pm (brunch), 5.30 pm to 10 pm. Licensed. Amex, Master Card, Visa. Book ahead if you can.* &

CALGARY   **MAP 27**
TEATRO   ☆☆
200 8 Avenue SE   **$190**
(403) 290-1012

Teatro occupies an old bank building on 8 Avenue SE. It's very well appointed, very well served and very expensive. They got a new chef last year and made a completely new start. These days you begin with fried squid (a tender, delightful dish). Follow that with terrine of foie gras with coffee, carpaccio of beef or in-house charcuterie. The grilled Arctic char with wild mushrooms is a remarkable creation; the pickerel and breast of duck are less exciting, but the beef and the lamb all come from Alberta. The wine-list is skilfully chosen. All the wines by the glass are just what they should be (Blue Mountain and Poplar Grove among them). At the other end of the list there are no fewer than seven sassicaias, eight ornellaias and a number of sweet wines from Château d'Yquem. Teatro is open late, which makes it the place to go after a play at the performing arts centre or a concert by the Calgary Philharmonic. Both are quite nearby.
Open Monday to Thursday 11.30 am to 2.30 pm, 5 pm to 11 pm, Friday 11.30 am to 2.30 pm, 5 pm to 11.30 pm, Saturday 5 pm to 11.30 pm, Sunday 5 pm to 10 pm. Licensed. All cards.

Book ahead. ♿

CALGARY   **MAP 27**
VERO BISTRO MODERNE   ☆
209 10 Street NW   **$195**
(403) 283-8988

Vero makes a specialty of gnocchi, offering sweet potato
as an appetizer and organic potato as a main course. If
Driview lamb is on the daily menu, ask for that; if not,
ask for either the potato gnocchi or the caramelized scallops—the baby squid is often sold out and the bouillabaisse is indifferent. The wine-list is impressive, and you
have a choice between two barolos, one at 83.00, the
other at 160.00. Sangiovese is available by the glass at
13.50, by the bottle at 58.00.
*Open Tuesday to Friday 11 am to 2 pm, 5 pm to 10 pm, Satur-
day and Sunday 10 am to 2 pm (brunch), 5 pm to 10 pm. Closed
on Monday. Licensed. Master Card, Visa. Book ahead if you
can.* ♿

CALGARY
See also CANMORE.

CAMBRIDGE, Ontario   **MAP 28**
LANGDON HALL   ☆☆
1 Langdon Drive   **$290 ($525)**
(800) 268-1898

Langdon Hall was built on a lavish scale more than a hundred years ago. The bedrooms are luxurious, the dining-
room splendid. They belong to the order of Relais &
Châteaux and their new chef's menu is very grand, starting with dressed crab (a fine dish) and seared foie gras.
The main dishes are all rather self-important. There's
roasted loin of beef and pickled lamb's tongue; there's
milk-poached veal and guinea-hen with chanterelles and
madeira; there's halibut with Jerusalem artichokes and
baby turnip. To end the meal there's an (irresistible)
bavarois of violets. They have almost a thousand labels

in the cellar, most of them very expensive. Altogether there are eight or more vosne-romanées and 23 pommards, all of them premier-cru. There's a long list of wines from Niagara, but a plain glass of riesling from Tawse costs at least 20.00. Money, they say, is for spending.

Open daily noon to 2.30 pm, 5.30 pm to 9.30 pm. Licensed. All cards. Book ahead.

CAMPOBELLO ISLAND, N.B. (MAP 75)
FAMILY FISHERIES
1977 County Road 774 **$55**
Wilson's Beach
(506) 752-2470

This is one of the very few good restaurants on Campobello Island. If you find every table full, just go to the carry-out window, where everything is the same as inside. The menu is surprisingly long, but the best thing on it is the whole lobster. The lobster stew is almost as good, and there are those who think the lobster sandwich is better than either. The haddock is good too—it's absolutely fresh and perfectly cooked. As for the pan-fried scallops, you won't get better anywhere on this shore. They come with cornmeal and real mashed potatoes. Start with an appetizer of smoked salmon and end with blueberry or raspberry pie. (They pick the raspberries in their own garden and serve them with real whipped cream.) Everything is cooked to order and the service is slow, but sitting back and slowing down, as somebody once said, is one of the things you come to the Maritimes for.

Open daily 11.30 am to 8.30 pm. No liquor. Master Card, Visa.

Every restaurant in this guide has been personally tested. Our reporters are not allowed to identify themselves to the management or to accept free meals. We accept no advertisements. We accept no payment for listings. We depend entirely on you. Recommend the book to your friends.

CAMPOBELLO ISLAND (MAP 75)

JOCIE'S PORCH
724 Highway 774   **$30**
Welshpool
(506) 752-9816

Jocie's has a front porch 70 feet long furnished with Adirondack chairs and a couple of swings. They have a lovely view of Friars Bay, which is filled with bald eagles and finback whales. The menu is short, but everything comes fresh from the kitchen. The coffee is marvellous and so are the teas. They also have some well conceived soups, fine chillis, interesting sandwiches and lovely sweets. On Friday nights there are jam sessions where local people come with their guitars and everyone joins in.

Open Monday to Saturday noon to 5 pm. Closed on Sunday. No liquor. Master Card, Visa.

CANMORE, Alberta (MAP 27)

THE CRAZY WEED   ☆
1600 Railway Avenue   **$150**
(403) 609-2530

We've had some complaints about the Crazy Weed since they moved away from Main Street. We suspect that this is because the prices have gone up—or maybe some people just like to complain. We've never had a poor meal here, though we do miss the old café. Jan Hrabec's daughter has joined her mother in the kitchen and she's interested in many different cuisines: Vietnamese meatballs dipped in chilli and lime, ceviche of albacore tuna, slow-roasted spare-ribs, spicy Indian noodles and kung pao chicken wings. Most of the important dishes are now called big plates, but you don't need to spend the earth if you don't want to. In fact, the pan-roasted chicken with its prune tagine costs only 22.00. They have more than two hundred wines and several Canadian chardonnays in their cellar.

Open Monday to Friday 11.30 am to 3 pm, 5.30 pm to 9.30

pm, Saturday and Sunday 5.30 pm to 9.30 pm. Licensed. Master Card, Visa. Book ahead if you can. ᘒ

CANMORE (MAP 27)
THE TROUGH ☆
725 9 Street **$200**
(403) 678-2820

Cheryl and Richard Fuller (a mother and son) run the kitchen at the Trough. They have only ten tables, and inevitably the prices are high. Most people come here for the bruschetta or the jerk-spiced baby back ribs with pineapple, watermelon and mint. If you prefer fish, you'll find that the catch of the day is delicately seasoned and lightly cooked. The menu is short and the sweets are a high point—we still remember their date pudding. They have a generous list of Canadian and foreign wines, among them some good merlots from California. They may need more chardonnays, but they have some excellent grappas.
Open Tuesday to Sunday 5.30 pm to 9 pm. Closed on Monday. Licensed. Master Card, Visa.

CAP A L'AIGLE, Quebec (MAP 105)
AUBERGE DES PEUPLIERS ☆
381 rue St.-Raphael **$175 ($375)**
(418) 665-4423

It's nearly two hundred years since the Tremblay family came to Charlevoix, and forty years since they turned their homestead into a small hotel that many of us grew to love. Ferdinand Tremblay himself began to modernize the house. He installed a new bar and enlarged the dining-room. The new bedrooms are small, but they're comfortable enough to bring people back year after year. Dominique Truchon, a local boy, was in charge of the kitchen for many years. Since he left to establish his own restaurant (Chez Truchon in La Malbaie, see below) there have been some weak moments in the cooking. But we usually choose to dine and spend the night here. Last year

the chef was Gilles Bernard, whose bouillabaisse was a splendid thing. So was his mango-and-scallop ceviche with green onions. The menu has always been strong on local produce, which really means Charlevoix County lamb, duck and duck foie gras. There's a four-course table d'hôte for 52.00, or 62.00 with cheese. Sweets have never been a feature, but the salmon and trout are both perfect. The wine-list is French and has its strengths and weaknesses, but there are several good wines by the glass.
Open daily 8 am to 10.30 am, 6 pm to 10 pm. Licensed. All cards. Book ahead. ♿

CARAQUET, N.B.   MAP 32
HOTEL PAULIN
143 boulevard St.-Pierre o   **$160 ($315)**
(866) 727-9981

We stopped writing about the Hôtel Paulin, because it didn't seem serious about taking non-residents. We're recommending it again this year, because it's the best place to stay in town and a good place to eat. Three generations of the Paulin family have made this one of the oldest family-run hotels in the country. Built in 1891, it's a good example of turn-of-the-century Acadian architecture. It's been completely redecorated inside, with three luxurious suites on the third floor, each of which has a lovely view of the Baie des Chaleurs. After running the place alone for 30 years, Gérard Paulin married Karen Mersereau and found himself with a first-class chef. She loves to cook and for about 50.00 guests get course after course of fascinating dishes. She changes her menu every day, always emphasizing regional produce. That of course means local seafood from the bay, local lamb and local cheeses, as well as hand-picked fiddleheads, chanterelles and strawberries. Everything is beautifully prepared. The service, however, is slow.
Open daily (if anyone is staying at the hotel) 7 pm to 8.30 pm. Licensed. Master Card, Visa. You must book ahead. ♿

Nobody but nobody can buy his way into this guide.

CARAQUET   MAP 32
MITCHAN SUSHI   ☆☆
114 boulevard St.–Pierre o   **$95**
(506) 726-1103

You wouldn't expect to find a good Japanese restaurant in the heart of Acadian country, but there are those who think that Mitchan Sushi is the best restaurant of its kind in New Brunswick. Certainly, they have an enormous selection of sushi, sashimi, tempura, teriyaki and shrimp and pork dumplings. The sweets are quite ambitious. They make their own ice cream (green-tea, red-bean and black-sesame). The dining-room is attractive and the plating will remind you of a bouquet of flowers. The prices are all surprisingly low.

Open daily noon to 3 pm, 6 pm to 11 pm from early May until late November, by appointment only Wednesday 5 pm to 9 pm, Thursday and Friday 11.30 am to 1.30 pm, 5 pm to 9 pm, Saturday and Sunday 5 pm to 9 pm from late November until early May. Licensed. Master Card, Visa. Closed on Monday and Tuesday in winter.

CARLETON–SUR–MER, Quebec   MAP 33
LE MARIN D'EAU DOUCE
215 route du Quai   **$140**
(418) 364-7602

We've been coming to this old house by the sea for years. The place was built in 1820 overlooking the beach. There's a jetty at the back and a bright, cheerful dining-room. Mustapha Benhamidou is at his best with seafood, but he's also interested in adapting refined French cuisine to such local dishes as veal chops and merguez de canard, as well as cod and salmon. Sweets are not a big thing with him, but wine is, and most of his wines come, not from Niagara or Prince Edward County, but from France or Italy. It's usually a good idea to order from the menu du jour, which always has some fish on it.

Open Monday to Saturday 5 pm to 9 pm. Closed on Sunday. Licensed. All cards.

CAYUGA, Ontario   **MAP 34**
THE TWISTED LEMON   ☆
3 Norton Street W   **$145**
(905) 772-6636

The Twisted Lemon opened in the summer of 2009, and already people are driving long distances for a meal here. Chef Dan Megna and his wife, Laurie Lilliman, have brought many years of experience to their dream. For instance, Megna learned a lot about the best produce from Mark McEwan, and at the Twisted Lemon nearly everything they use grows right here in Haldimand County. Dinner starts with a complimentary bowl of lemon twists and goes on to pan-seared scallops with house-made blueberry barbecue sauce. The kitchen is at its best with scallops and you should be sure to ask for them. For only about 20.00 you can then have gnocchi with sweet potatoes and for 23.00 there's great pappardelle made to an old family recipe. They also do pan-seared salmon with apple-brandy, breast of chicken and rack of lamb with prosciutto. If you feel like an adventure, order the teriyaki beef heart or the loin of kangaroo. The wine-list offers an ambitious selection of wines from the Old World and the New.
Open Tuesday 5 pm to 9 pm, Wednesday to Friday 11.30 am to 2 pm, 5 pm to 9 pm, Saturday 4.30 pm to 9 pm. Closed on Sunday and Monday. Licensed. Master Card, Visa. Book ahead.

CEDAR, B.C.   **(MAP 121)**
CROW & GATE PUB
2313 Yellow Point Road   **$70**
(250) 722-3731

In 1972 Jack Nash, an Englishman, built the Crow & Gate on ten acres of scenic property in Cedar, near Nanaimo. The Crow & Gate was the first neighbourhood pub in the province. The place is pure Yorkshire, with its low wooden ceilings, oil paintings and wood-burning fireplaces. There's no deep fryer here, no fish and chips. What they have is country-style meat pies, the best of

54

which, of course, is the steak-and-kidney pie. There are other good things too, like the oyster stew, the crab-cake, the stilton quiche, the English trifle and the sticky-toffee pudding. You order and pay up front and the food is brought to your table, so there's no waiting ever.
Open daily 11 am to 11 pm. Licensed. Master Card, Visa. &

CEDAR (MAP 121)
MAHLE HOUSE ☆☆
2104 Hemer Road **$150**
(250) 722-3621

Located a few miles south of Nanaimo, the Mahle House occupies an old heritage house standing on a one-acre property. Stephen and Tara Wilson buy their ingredients locally and cook everything with care. Most people like to start with the truffled wild mushroom arancini with brie or the legendary porcupine prawns wrapped in kataifi with wasabi mayonnaise. When it comes to the main course, you have to choose among the rack of lamb with garlic, the grilled leg of lamb with rosemary and grainy mustard, the duck two ways and the hanger steak with fries. For vegetarians they offer a curried lentil-and-goat-cheese phyllo roll stuffed with cauliflower and chick peas in coconut milk. Naida Hobbs continues to prepare her celebrated peanut-butter pies, which make a perfect sweet. The three-course *prix-fixe* costs just 39.00 (on Thursdays and Fridays only). There's also a surprise menu for 44.00.
Open Wednesday to Sunday 5 pm to 9 pm. Closed on Monday and Tuesday. Licensed. Amex, Master Card, Visa. Book ahead if you can. &

CHARLO, N.B. MAP 36
LE MOULIN A CAFE ☆☆
210 Chaleur Street **$50**
(506) 684-9898

This tiny place (eight tables in summer, five in winter) has a huge reputation. The chef, Christian Paquet, worked abroad for almost a quarter of a century before returning to the town where he started. He knows what the customers here want: soup (he makes five every day), pizza (he makes several), Acadian dishes and fresh local fish, which is really exceptional. There's always a daily special as well—scallop linguine, tilapia or curried seafood. Andrea Boudreau, his partner, makes all the bread-rolls and the pies, which are fabulous The strawberry is still our favourite, but don't overlook the coconut, the butterscotch or the pumpkin. They keep many teas and coffees on the list, and everything is very cheap. *Open Tuesday to Sunday 10 am to 8 pm. Closed on Monday. Bring your own bottle. Master Card, Visa. Book ahead if you can.*

CHARLOTTETOWN, P.E.I.   MAP 37

We always urge visitors to the Island to go to the Farmer's Market, which is held every Saturday morning. Most of the produce is organic, and you can snack on smoked salmon or some of the best sausages you've ever tasted. Not far away, on a short stretch of Great George Street, there are several attractive restaurants. Leonhard's Café and Bakery at 142 Great George Street (telephone (902) 367-3621), has some of the best coffee in town. The young German owner also makes fine homemade bread and pastries, glorious Florentines, homemade stews and big, substantial sandwiches. This is a perfect place for lunch, but they aren't open for dinner and are closed on Sunday. Beanz at 138 Great George Street (telephone (902) 892-8797) is an espresso bar, but they also have soups, sandwiches and salads, and their squares, cookies and cheesecakes are all wonderful. They're open all day every day and take Master Card and Visa, but there's no liquor. Along the street from Beanz, at 144 Great George Street (telephone (902) 368-8886), is Shaddy's, a nice, comfortable Lebanese restaurant that has the only upright broiler in Charlottetown. The best thing they do is the shawarma with tabouleh. As for the falafel in a pita, one visitor thought it the best in the world. We ourselves admire the lamb kebabs and the kofta. The pastries all come from Montreal, where the chef spent ten years before coming here. Shaddy's is open all day Monday to Friday and all afternoon Saturday and

Sunday, has a licence and takes Master Card and Visa. The Daniel Brenan Brickhouse at 125 Sydney Street (telephone (902) 566-4620) is now just called the Brickhouse. It has an open kitchen and a counter, where you can sit and talk to the chef. Sadly, the cooking is inconsistent. Some of the dishes (but not all) can be ordered gluten-free, and we've heard good things about the charcuterie and the blue mussels. They're now open Monday to Thursday 11 am to 10 pm, Friday and Saturday 11 am to 11 pm, Sunday 11 am to 10 pm, have a licence and take Amex, Master Card and Visa. The Pilot House at 70 Grafton Street (telephone (902) 894-4800) specializes in seafood, draft beer and scotch whisky. The menu lets you choose between pub food and such important things as chicken, pork, scallops and salmon. The scallops are served with a mushroom risotto, the salmon in a maple glaze. They also have a fine lobster sandwich and excellent fish and chips. They're open all day every day but Sunday, have a licence and take all cards. Emily Wells opened Local 343 at 98 Water Street (telephone (902) 569-9343) in the summer of 2015. It's right next to the Delta Hotel, which makes it convenient for everyone. There are about 15 tables, but one has to climb stairs to get there. You can count on good local produce, and you can be sure that there's no deep-frying in the kitchen. Keep an eye out for the crab-cakes and the chowder. There's a takeout on the ground floor that serves salads, quiches and meat pies. Local 343 is open every day, has a licence and takes most cards.

CHARLOTTETOWN   MAP 37
BUONO MANGIA
193 Kent Street   **$100**
(902) 370-6676

This unassuming little place is about the best Italian restaurant on the Island. Hooie and her partner, Ian, serve everything with homemade fettuccine or cannelloni, sometimes tagliatelle. As for their fettuccine Alfredo, it's about the lightest we can remember. Every evening there are seven or eight main dishes, plus a nightly special. Those who should know say that Buono Mangia has the freshest food in town. Everything is local (even the cheese) and the ice cream is beautiful. The food is hot and cheap and there's a short wine-list that offers five reds and five whites. But there are only 30 seats, so be sure to book ahead.

Open Tuesday to Friday 11.30 am to 2.30 pm, 4.30 pm to 9 pm, Saturday 4.30 pm to 10 pm. Closed on Sunday and Monday. Licensed. Master Card, Visa. Book ahead.

CHARLOTTETOWN   MAP 37
HIMALAYAN INDIAN CUISINE
Midtown Plaza   **$100**
375 University Avenue
(902) 892-7450

Charlottetown has long needed an authentic Indian restaurant and this, at last, is it. It's owned by a Nepalese family and it opened in 2014. They serve a variety of Indian and Nepalese dishes, among them a few tandoori specialties. The big sellers are the kormas, the saags and the biryanis. Naan or rice comes with each of these and you can choose to have your food mild, medium or hot. The only sweet is mango sorbet and the best thing to drink is the mango lassi.

Open daily 11.30 am to 9.30 pm. Licensed. Master Card, Visa.

CHARLOTTETOWN   MAP 37
TERRE ROUGE
72 Queen Street   **$100**
(902) 892-4032

Terre Rouge was once a grocery store, but now it looks more like a French bistro or an old-style New York bar. The kitchen is interested only in produce that grows nearby—local oysters, pork, beef and lamb, fish and shellfish. The cooking is simple and straightforward. Arctic char, for instance, may be served with smoked potatoes, rotisserie chicken with lightly-whipped mash. Usually they offer at least three different varieties of beet. The waiters are young and eager and the service is always quick, though the cooking is not. At Terre Rouge they aim to provide good food, not fast food, and good food

takes time to prepare.
Open daily 8 am to 10 pm. Licensed. Amex, Master Card, Visa. &

CHARLOTTETOWN
See also BAY FORTUNE, BRACKLEY BEACH, GEORGETOWN, MONTAGUE, MURRAY HARBOUR, NEW GLASGOW, ST. PETERS BAY, SOURIS, SUMMERSIDE, VICTORIA-BY-THE-SEA.

CHATHAM, Ontario   MAP 38
CHURRASCARIA
525 Grand Avenue E   **$125**
(519) 355-1279

We can't quite believe that a restaurant in Chatham can last from one year to the next, but the fact is that this year Churrascaria is still in business and is as good as ever, if not better. Brian Machado's menu offers a number of Portuguese specialties such as bacalhau (pan-seared fillet of cod), santola (crab-legs) and Portuguese free-range chicken, as well as every variety of char-grilled steak, among them organic fig-crusted New York steak finished with pork *jus* and cooked *à point* for just 22.95. Churrascaria serves three meals a day for next to nothing. Breakfast starts at 4.99 for two eggs with bacon or, for 2.00 more, Portuguese pastries filled with custard or (for 12.95) Norwegian salmon with provolone cheese and roasted red peppers. For lunch or dinner, you can expect fresh Atlantic salmon or Lake Erie pickerel and a glass or two of Portuguese wine. Dinner, however, closes early. Don't come late.
Open Tuesday to Thursday 8 am to 2 pm, 5 pm to 8 pm, Friday and Saturday 8 am to 9 pm, Sunday 8 am to 2 pm. Closed on Monday. Licensed. Amex, Master Card, Visa. &

The price rating shown opposite the headline of each entry indicates the average cost of dinner for two with a modest wine, tax and tip. The cost of dinner, bed and breakfast (if available) is shown in parentheses.

59

CHELSEA, Quebec (MAP 134)
LES FOUGÈRES
783 route 105 **$140**
(819) 827-8942

Les Fougères was completely renovated in late 2015. It now has a full-length bar with an open kitchen and new tables and chairs. The furniture was made locally and it's very beautiful. Strangely, the cooking seems now to have improved. Their curried shrimp with mango chutney, their confit of duck with goat-cheese and poached pears and their braised short-ribs are all lovely dishes. They have one unusual sweet—buffalo-milk jelly—and their sticky-toffee pudding is much lighter than most. The wine-list is short but useful. Les Fougères is an easy drive from Ottawa and the dining-room is warm and comfortable. Charles Part has been in charge of the kitchen here for longer than we can remember, and he and his wife, Jennifer Warren, deserve a lot of credit for their dogged persistence.
Open Wednesday to Friday noon to 10 pm, Saturday and Sunday 10 am to 4 pm (brunch), 4 pm to 10 pm (dinner). Closed on Monday and Tuesday. Licensed. Amex, Master Card, Visa. Book ahead.

CHEMAINUS, B.C. (MAP 56)
ODIKA ☆
2976 Mill Street **$125**
(250) 324-3303

Odika is much the best restaurant in Chemainus. They offer excellent food and great service in homey, comfortable surroundings. It's close to the ferry from Salt Spring, which makes it a convenient place to stop. Lunch and dinner both start with coconut-breaded prawns or Cajun crab-cakes crusted with panko, followed in the evening by African lamb shanks Ngondo. They're slow-cooked and served in a squash-seed sauce with plantain mash and braised kale. After that, go for either the cheesecake with a coulis of raspberry and rhubarb or the plum-and-berry

crumble with black-pepper ice cream.
*Open Sunday to Thursday 11 am to 9 pm, Friday and Saturday
11 am to 10 pm. Licensed. All cards.* &

CHESTER, N.S.   (MAP 81)
NICKI'S   ☆
28 Pleasant Street   **$100**
(902) 275-4342

Nicki Butler once owned the Captain's House, which in
its day was the leading restaurant in town. But Nicki's is
now the best place to eat within miles. Nicki herself is
still in the kitchen and does a lot of the cooking. Most of
the produce she uses is local. Fish often comes in off the
boats in nearby Lunenburg. Most of the meat also comes
from Nova Scotia. The wine-list is small, carefully chosen
and very cheap. You can drink well for less than 45.00 a
bottle. There's no printed menu; you simply look at the
blackboard and make your choice. Every Sunday there's
a celebrated carvery that offers lamb, beef, chicken and
pork. The sweets are all house-made; keep an eye out for
the rhubarb crumble.
*Open Wednesday to Sunday 5 pm to 9 pm from 1 May until 15
October. Closed on Monday and Tuesday. Licensed. All cards.
Book ahead if you can.* &

CHICOUTIMI, Quebec   MAP 42
LA VOIE MALTEE   ☞
777 boulevard Talbot   **$80**
(418) 549-4141

We remember some great meals in Chicoutimi, most of
them at Chez Amato. Amato, however, has gone and the
Voie Maltée has not. It's filled with students and it's
crowded and noisy. They have ten micro-brews, including a blond Pilsner made on the premises from local ingredients. They have several dishes based on beer and the
best of them is probably the beef stroganoff with ale. The
cooks are fond of cheese and if you ask for the macaroni
and cheese with crab or a cheeseburger made with foie

gras you'll see why. There are at least two first-class appetizers (spiced shrimp and salmon Caesar) and one excellent sweet (tiramisu with beer). The food is all good and very cheap. A second Voie Maltée has now opened at 2509 rue St.-Dominique in Jonquière (telephone (418) 542-4373) and a third at 1040 boulevard Pierre Bertrand (telephone (418) 683-5558) in Quebec.

Open Monday to Friday 11.30 am to 3 am, Saturday and Sunday noon to 3 am. Licensed. All cards. No reservations.

CHURCHILL, Manitoba   MAP 43
GYPSY'S
253 Kelsey Boulevard   **$120**
(204) 675-2322

Climate change is making life difficult in these parts. Polar bears no longer have thick ice to hunt on and they wander farther and farther away in search of any kind of food, leaving Churchill without its main tourist attraction. So the town is advertising beluga-whale tours and dog-sled trips instead. Tony De Silva came here from Montreal thirty years ago and his restaurant has always been known for the consistency of its cooking. The menu at Gypsy's never changes—Arctic char, Manitoba pickerel and a number of Portuguese dishes like chicken marinated in white wine, bifana sandwiches and imported cheeses. Tony is an expert on French pastry and he has several different kinds of bread, including Portuguese papo secos, as well. He's also something of an expert on Portuguese wines. No wonder that Gypsy's, which seats a hundred people, is often full, polar bears or no polar bears.

Open Monday to Saturday 6 pm to 10 pm from 1 March until 30 November. Closed on Sunday. Licensed. All cards.

This is a guide to Canadian restaurants from coast to coast—the first ever published and the only one of its kind on the market today. We accept no advertisements. Nobody can buy his way into this guide and nobody can buy his way out.

CLARK'S HARBOUR, N.S.   (MAP 186)
WEST HEAD TAKEOUT
81 Boundry Street   **$45**
(902) 745-1322

About 800 people live in Clark's Harbour, which is the only settlement on Cape Sable Island. Everybody enjoys getting there and everybody admires the white-sand beaches, which are important for bird-watchers. There are many rare species to be seen, including 20% of the world's piping plovers, an endangered species. The West Head Takeout is a tiny building at the end of the town wharf, with a fish-processing plant on either side. This year they have a licence (or so they say) and tour buses are stopping at the door. The place looks like nothing from the outside and there's little to indicate what goes on inside. Still, the Takeout is busy from morning till night. It used to be called the Seaview, but if the name has changed the fish hasn't. It's easy to recommend the lobster roll, which is as good as any we've tasted. They also have a scallop burger for 4.25 and very fresh fish and chips for 8.95. Anyone who finds himself within 25 miles of this place and doesn't come in for a meal is making a mistake.

Open daily 10.30 am to 8 pm from late March until late September. Licensed. No cards. &

COBBLE HILL, B.C.   (MAP 56)
AMUSE ON THE VINEYARD
840 Cherry Point Road   **$125**
(250) 743-3667

The Amuse Bistro has moved once again, this time from the Unsworth Vineyards to Cherry Point, where Bradford Boisvert is still in the kitchen. He's simplified the menu, but he still offers a fine apple bisque and a tomato soup with spinach and olives. For a fresh experience, try the locally foraged chanterelles in a brandy-cream sauce on toast. In the evening, he does a fine job with the rack of organic lamb. He's known for flamboyant sweets, but what we like is the apple cobbler with homemade ice cream and honey.

Open Wednesday to Sunday 5 pm to 9 pm. Closed on Monday and Tuesday. Licensed. Master Card, Visa. Book ahead in summer. &

COBBLE HILL (MAP 56)
BISTRO AT MERRIDALE CIDER ☆
1230 Merridale Road **$80**
(250) 743-4293

You'll find the bistro in the middle of a working cider farm, where they're offering produce grown by farmers and cheese-makers in the nearby Cowichan Valley, paired with local Merridale cider. You can eat outside on the patio overlooking the apple orchards or inside, where they have a traditional fieldstone fireplace. There are some fine salads to start with, dressed in a reduction of cider. Next come short-ribs on wild-mushroom polenta with gorgonzola. In the evening they add North Island sablefish, braised in orange, mirin and soy and served on a green papaya salad. The apple pie is made with apples grown right here on the Merridale farm.

Open Monday to Thursday noon to 3 pm, Friday and Saturday noon to 3 pm, 5 pm to 9 pm, Sunday 10.30 am to 3 pm (brunch). Licensed. Master Card, Visa. &

COBOURG, Ontario **MAP 46**
WOODLAWN INN ☆
420 Division Street **$125 ($295)**
(905) 372-2235

It's more than 25 years since the Della Casa family bought this fine old inn and installed Stephen Della Casa as *sommelier,* with a list of 300 wines and two dozen single malts. The kitchen buys whatever it can from nearby suppliers, though its most popular dish is the Dover sole, which is deboned at the table and is probably the best (flash-frozen or not) this side of Dover. There's also Atlantic salmon, and beef cooked with rosemary and red wine and served with polenta and creamy spinach. Sunday brunch still costs only 17.95, for which there's a station where omelettes are made to order one at a time and beef and turkey carved on demand. The Woodlawn Inn is a good place for a special occasion or for a weekend break. It now has comfortable beds and excellent service. *Open Monday to Saturday 11.30 am to 2 pm, 5.30 pm to 8.30 pm, Sunday 11.30 am to 2 pm (brunch), 5.30 pm to 8 pm. Licensed. All cards.* &

COLLINGWOOD, Ontario   MAP 47
DUNCAN'S
60 Hurontario Street   **$110**
(705) 444-5749

There's nothing all that special about Duncan's, except that if you're a stranger in town they'll make sure you feel at home. The menu is huge and literally never changes. People come here for the chicken club sandwich, the quesadillas, the baked brie in phyllo and the wild-mushroom ravioli. Prices are higher in the evening, when you can have a fine ten-ounce striploin with blue cheese or a fillet of Atlantic salmon in puff pastry. (The chicken stuffed with goat-cheese is big enough to keep two people full for a week.) The kitchen isn't much interested in sweets, but there's a big wine-list. They're very busy at noon, when it's a good idea to book ahead.
Open Monday to Thursday 9 am to 8 pm, Friday and Saturday 9 am to 10 pm, Sunday 9 am to 4 pm. Licensed. Master Card, Visa. &

COLLINGWOOD   MAP 47
GUSTAV'S CHOPHOUSE
Georgian Bay Hotel   **$125**
10 Vacation Inn Drive
(705) 445-9422

Two new steak houses have opened this year in Collingwood and Gustav's is the more promising of the two. The Georgian Bay Hotel has been entirely renovated and the owners have picked the best chef and the best pâtissière they could find. Both are at Gustav's now, and the pâtissière is certainly amazing. But they're still scanning local farms to find out where the best produce is to be had. The restaurant is too new for us to say in any detail just what the chefs are doing. Further reports needed.

Open daily Monday to Wednesday 11 am to 11 pm, Thursday and Friday 11 am to midnight, Saturday and Sunday 8 am to 10 am (brunch), 11 am to midnight. Licensed. All cards. &

COLLINGWOOD   MAP 47
SANTINI
61 Hurontario Street   **$125**
(705) 443-8383

We used to say that the young couple who run this place seemed to be having a lot of fun. But now we're more conscious of the hard work they have to do. They began with a deli, which is at 166 Hurontario Street (telephone (705) 994-4200). It has twelve tables but no liquor and is open all day from Monday to Saturday. Recently they opened a beautiful full-service restaurant up the street in the old part of town. In our opinion the menu is just too long, but others disagree. Everyone admires the carpaccio, the salads and the sweets. The European sea-bass is very special.

Open Monday and Tuesday and Thursday to Sunday 11.30 am to 10 pm. Closed on Wednesday. Licensed. Master Card, Visa. &

COLLINGWOOD
See also THORNBURY.

COOMBS, B.C.   (MAP 157)
THE CUCKOO
2310 Alberni Highway   **$135**
(250) 248-6280

The Cuckoo is housed in a building that's at least 60 years old, but most of their visitors prefer to eat outside on the terrace. Wood-fired thin-crust pizzas are the best thing they do. Our favourite has always been the smoked salmon with capers and goat-cheese, but they say that the margherita is made the way it's been made for a hundred years. Then there's one made with six different cheeses, but we haven't tried it yet. They now offer homemade chilli oil and roasted garlic with every pizza they sell. People also like the gnocchi and the ocean-wise seafood—crab, mussels, clams, scallops and prawns. If you have children in tow, ask for the family-style three-course meal, which serves four. The most interesting of the sweets is a glass of port with asiago and gorgonzola cheese. There's a short wine-list and Vancouver Island beer on tap.

Open daily 11 am to 9 pm from early March until late December. Licensed. Master Card, Visa. &

COWICHAN BAY, B.C. (MAP 56)
THE MASTHEAD ☆
1705 Cowichan Bay Road **$130**
(250) 748-3714

This is a charming seaside hotel and it continues to be one of our favourites. Their menu changes little from year to year and still features locally sourced seafood, combined with the best of Cowichan Valley meat, fowl and vegetables. Their three-course fixed-price menu continues to be one of the best deals to be had anywhere, offering lobster bisque, poached red snapper or braised spare-ribs with Guinness, followed by an apple fritter topped with chocolate ganache and whipped cream—all for less than 35.00. Starters include weathervane scallops, seafood chowder and a Caesar salad. Even women admire the so-called man steak. We prefer the fresh crab or spot prawns, if they're available. They're steamed and served with drawn butter. The potatoes are cooked in duck drippings and for sweet there are always banana fritters with home-made ice cream.

Open daily 5 pm to 10 pm. Licensed. All cards. Book ahead if you can. &

CREEMORE, Ontario (MAP 204)
CREEMORE KITCHEN ☆
134 Mill Street **$130**
(705) 466-2900

Creemore is a pretty village. About a tenth of the residents work for Creemore Springs Brewery, perhaps the most notable of Ontario's craft breweries. The Creemore Kitchen is just across the street. Caesar Guinto (formerly executive chef at the Royal Ontario Museum) and his partner, Sam Holwell, have installed a cathedral ceiling and hemlock lining in two existing cottages and created a modern, though folksy, restaurant on the site. Here they serve some gorgeous things. Guinto was trained in France, but flirts with Filipino styles in his pork springrolls with sweet onion and potato jam. You might also get an eight-ounce sirloin steak or bangers and mash with house-made HP sauce, a quiche or some pasta. The fish of the day is always good, especially the pan-seared pickerel. There are apple fritters for sweet, as well as lavender meringue and Eton Mess. The wine-list is small, but there's always Creemore pilsner and lager on tap.
Open Monday, Thursday and Friday 11 am to 2.30 pm, 5.30 pm to 9.30 pm, Saturday and Sunday 11 am to 2.30 pm (brunch), 5.30 pm to 9.30 pm. Closed on Tuesday and Wednesday. Licensed. Master Card, Visa. Book ahead. ♿

CRESTON, B.C. MAP 52
REAL FOOD CAFE ☆☆
223 10 Avenue N **$135**
(250) 428-8882

Look for Creston at the foot of Kootenay Lake, just north of the border on Highway 7. At the Real Food Café everybody is fiercely loyal to the Creston Valley. The Kootenay Alpine Cheese Company, which is right in town, produces all their cheese. Tabletree produces their black-cherry juice, Kootenay Natural raises their chickens and their Angus beef. They're also loyal to the British connection. For instance, you can get fish and chips with mushy peas (served in a newspaper if you like), as well as sticky-toffee cake (made with white chocolate). You can also get what they call Britain's favourite dish, which is tikka masala. Vegetarian and gluten-free items appear right on the regular menu. There's a short list of local wines and a couple of Old Country beers as well. *Open Monday to Friday 11 am to 2 pm, 4.30 pm to 8 pm. Closed on Saturday and Sunday. Licensed. Master Card, Visa. Book ahead if you can.* &

DAWSON CITY, Yukon MAP 53
THE DRUNKEN GOAT ☆
950 2 Avenue **$125**
(867) 993-5868

We used to underestimate the Drunken Goat. The fact is that it's a lot more than a friendly place offering big helpings of Greek food. One reader swears that it's the best place to eat within 500 miles. The helpings are certainly large—that's true. But the Greek recipes are utterly authentic, and the grilled lamb is a masterpiece. The prices are high, even for the north, but nobody seems to complain. The Billy Goat bar has comfortable seating and a great open fireplace. In summer you can sit outside on the deck and enjoy a drink under the midnight sun. *Open daily 4.30 pm to 11 pm (shorter hours in winter). Licensed. Master Card, Visa.*

DIGBY, N.S. MAP 54
BOARDWALK CAFE
40 Water Street **$85**
(902) 245-5497

Esther Dunn was back in the kitchen full-time last summer. She makes everything herself: the quiches and the lasagne, of course, but also the bread and salad-dressings. Her pies are all brilliant—try the apple-lattice and see for yourself. In the evening you can expect fresh haddock, scallops (from Digby Bay), lobster and salmon. The Boardwalk doesn't have any bottled wines, just one or two house wines served by the glass. Inside, the restaurant is pretty plain, but the big windows look out on the harbour and the scallop fleet. The servers are all friendly and everyone has a good time here, especially if they have one of Esther's pies.

Open Monday to Friday 11 am to 2 pm from the beginning of March until late June, Monday to Saturday 11 am to 2 pm, 5 pm to 8 pm from late June until the end of September, Monday to Friday 11 am to 2 pm from 1 October until 20 December. Closed on Saturday and Sunday in the spring and fall, on Sunday in the summer. Licensed. All cards. &

DUNCAN, B.C.   MAP 56
HUDSON'S ON FIRST   ☆☆
163 First Street   **$125**
(250) 597-0066

Hudson's on First is situated just a block from downtown Duncan in an impeccably-restored century-old building. It has two Edwardian dining-rooms and a bar. Their cooking has been widely praised. Lunch is certainly an impressive meal, featuring a salad made with Dragonfly Farm greens, Daniel Hudson's own apples, spiced hazelnuts and goat-cheese. The rabbit terrine, the confit of duck and the dungeness crab with an organic-potato terrine are their most interesting appetizers. In the evening there's Arctic char, pan-seared scallops with lemon and roast breast of duck with braised red cabbage. For sweet they have a glazed lemon tart with lime and cilantro, a quince soufflé and a variety of house-churned sorbets and ice creams.

Open Tuesday to Friday 11 am to 2 pm, 5 pm to 8.30 pm, Saturday and Sunday 11 am to 2 pm (brunch), 5 pm to 8.30 pm. Closed on Monday. Licensed. Amex, Master Card, Visa. Book ahead.

Where an entry is printed in italics this indicates that the restaurant has been listed only because it serves the best food in its area or because it hasn't yet been adequately tested.

DUNCAN

MAP 56

RIVERWALK
200 Cowichan Way   **$90**
(877) 746-8119

Riverwalk features a fusion of First Nations traditions
with contemporary West Coast cuisine. The chef's platter is a quick way to get to know some of their best dishes
(crab-cakes, clam fritters and squid with red-pepper
horseradish). If you have plenty of time, ask for the slow-
roasted bison in a peppercorn barbecue sauce or the fish
and chips, made with either fresh halibut or salmon. The
Salish seafood platter offers wild Pacific salmon, cod and
prawns garnished with sea asparagus. Locally-farmed
venison also usually features prominently on the menu.
Open Monday to Saturday 10.30 am to 3 pm from 1 June until
30 September. Closed on Sunday. Licensed. Master Card, Visa.
Book ahead if you can. &

DUNCAN

MAP 56

VINOTECA
5039 Marshall Road   **$125**
(250) 748-2338

Bistro 161 has closed for good, but Fatima da Silva continues to work her magic in the kitchen at Vinoteca.
Vinoteca is located in a century-old family farmhouse on
the Zanata Vineyard. Its menu is based on simple Italian
country cooking, using food grown for the most part on
the Zanata farm. The Cowichan Valley is an important
producer of portobello mushrooms and the kitchen
makes extensive use of them here. We always start with
portobello-mushroom soup, but the duck terrine with
honey and orange is equally good and so is the seafood
salad with mussels, squid and shrimps marinated in
lemon, saffron and garlic. Pasta plays another leading role
on the menu, but if you don't want pasta, go for the veal
scaloppine with lemon and white polenta or the pan-
seared chicken with rosemary. The wines at Vinoteca are
not as good as the food, but the pinot grigio is probably

the best choice.

Open Wednesday and Thursday noon to 3 pm, Friday 11.30 am to 3 pm, Saturday and Sunday 11.30 am to 3.30 pm. Closed on Monday and Tuesday. Licensed. Master Card, Visa.

DUNCAN
See also CHEMAINUS, COBBLE HILL, COWICHAN BAY, MAPLE BAY, MILL BAY, SALTAIR.

DUNDAS, Ontario   **(MAP 82)**
QUATREFOIL   ☆
16 Sydenham Street   **$125**
(905) 628-7800

Quatrefoil occupies a century-old house in downtown Dundas. Fraser Macfarlane's cooking is a mixture of classical and modern French. He makes a nice version of calamari and a lovely gnocchi with maitake mushrooms and parmesan cheese. His striped bass comes with amazing pappardelle in a chestnut purée, his rainbow trout with a fine spinach risotto. The kitchen is adept with seafood, though Cumbrae's tenderloin is also flawless (and half the price at noon). When it comes to the sweets, the caramelized apple tart is better than the vanilla crème brûlée.
Open Tuesday to Saturday noon to 2.30 pm, 5 pm to 9.30 pm. Closed on Sunday and Monday. Licensed. Amex, Master Card, Visa.

EDMONTON, Alberta   **MAP 58**
CORSO 32   ☆☆
10345 Jasper Avenue   **$195**
(780) 421-4622

Corso 32 has changed a lot in the last year or so. It's all soft white inside, the service composed and calm. The menu is now quite small and offers only three main dishes, at least one of which, the Chinook salmon, is, however, beautifully cooked. You can start your meal with either speck or fried short ribs. The speck is delightful, the short ribs are too. The chocolate tart, long a fea-

ture of the menu, is still great. The wine-list is large and moderately priced: a bottle of chianti classico costs just 50.00, a bottle of dolcetto d'Alba 5.00 more.
Open daily 5 pm to 11 pm. Licensed. Amex, Master Card, Visa. Book ahead. ♿

EDMONTON   **MAP 58**
THE MARC
9940 106 Street   **$150**
(780) 429-2828

The Marc occupies the ground floor of a modern office block near the high-level bridge. Inside, it's all white with wide steel-and-glass windows. At noon they serve mushrooms on toast (their most successful dish), grilled flank steak, smoked salmon or trout, pulled duck, soup and fish. It all looks pretty ordinary until you notice that the mushrooms are wild and that the salmon and trout are house-smoked. It's not hard to tell the difference. Then in the evening they add grilled octopus, Cornish game hen, Arctic char, scallops with shimeji mushrooms and snails with bone marrow. There are only a couple of Okanagan wines, but one of them is the great Joie chardonnay from Naramata, the other a lovely syrah from Stag's Leap. The service is friendly, the prices modest.
Open Monday to Friday 11.30 am to 2.30 pm, 5.30 pm to 10 pm, Saturday 5.30 pm to 10 pm. Closed on Sunday. Licensed. Amex, Master Card, Visa. Book ahead. ♿

EDMONTON   **MAP 58**
NINETEEN   ★★
5940 Mullen Way NW   **$215/$110**
(780) 395-1119

Look for Nineteen beyond Whitemud Drive on the way to Nisku Airport. It may be (and is) an inconvenient location, but it's a sumptuous place with elegant service, a stunning wine-list and an enterprising menu. The kitchen has no hesitation about serving bone marrow, raw tuna, pork belly and foie gras. Loin of Alberta lamb comes with dijon mustard, chicken linguine with truffles. There are beef short-ribs, lamb shanks, chinook salmon and beef tenderloin. The cooking is poised and prices are modest. Recently they've started serving lunch from Thursday to Sunday. There's usually some Ahi tuna with a kale-and-quinoa salad, prawns with grilled romaine and yellowfin tuna crusted with pepper, as well as a daily pasta, a daily fish and a beef burger with basil mayonnaise. The wine-list is carefully chosen. There's a chardonnay from Cakebread, a pinot gris from Burrowing Owl, a sauvignon blanc from Dog Point and a cabernet sauvignon from Peter Lehmann.

Open Monday to Wednesday 3 pm to 11 pm, Thursday 11 am to 2 pm, 5 pm to 11 pm, Friday and Saturday 11 am to 2 pm, 5 pm to midnight, Sunday noon to 2 pm, 5 pm to 10 pm. Licensed. All cards. Book ahead. &

EDMONTON   **MAP 58**
NORTH 53°   ☆
10240 124 Street   **$125**
(587) 524-5353

This is a strange and wonderful restaurant. If you go to 10240 124 Street you'll find the door locked. North 53° is some distance along the street, at the corner of 103 Avenue. Inside, the place is chic and well served, but there's nothing on the menu that isn't grown or raised in Canada. Think twice. That means no chocolate, no coffee. Unless you order the five-course tasting menu, there are only a few dishes on the à la carte, all of them amazing. There's terrine of rabbit, heritage chicken, snow crab and salmon. The salmon comes with mustard greens, beautiful spinach, snap peas and gai lan. The snow crab is wonderful, with its duck egg, black butter and corn. There's Alberta mead to drink, Black Hills syrah from the Okanagan and a few imported wines—no coffee or chocolate but wines from California, Spain and Australia. The Black Hills is the pick of them all and it's available by the glass as well as the bottle. If you want a sweet after ten o'clock, when the kitchen is closed, they'll make you up butternut-squash ice cream with tuile, which is about the best thing on the menu. North 53° is full of new ideas—come and see for yourself.

Open Tuesday to Sunday 5 pm to 11 pm. Closed on Monday. Licensed. Amex, Master Card, Visa. Book ahead. &

EDMONTON   **MAP 58**
NUMCHOK WILAI
10623 124 Street   **$80**
(780) 488-7897

Numchok Wilai is still, we think, the best Thai restaurant in Edmonton. It may not be cheaper than the others, but the food is better; the service is cheerful and the atmosphere tranquil. They have a licence and offer Singha beer, which is the thing to drink. In the last year they increased the price of lunch to 12.95. For that you get a bowl of lemon-grass soup, a couple of spring rolls, coconut rice and your choice of red and green curries of beef and chicken, pad Thai and a variety of vegetarian dishes. In the evening they add several shrimp and mussel curries for only a few dollars more. The recipes are all authentic and everything has a taste. Some people prefer the hot-basil beef and chicken to the curries, but everybody likes the vegetables, especially the eggplant, and they do a nice, spicy mango salad with shrimps. If you find the coconut rice too sweet, try the sweet-and-sour pork with brown rice. Numchok Wilai is a streetfront restaurant with a comfortable arrangement of tables and chairs.

Open Monday to Friday 11.30 am to 2 pm, 5 pm to 9 pm, Saturday 5 pm to 9 pm. Closed on Sunday. Licensed. Master Card, Visa.

EDMONTON   **MAP 58**
RANGE ROAD   ☆
10643 123 Street   **$140**
(780) 447-4577

Range Road has been under construction, it seems, forever. They carry on, however, and the year before last were nominated one of the top ten new restaurants in the country. The place is all about farm-fresh produce. Their duck comes from Whistle Farm, their bison from Pilatus Farm, their pork belly from Nature's Green Acres. The pork belly is very good indeed; the bison is tender but lacks flavour. The best of all are the smoked mussels from Salt Spring Island, a lovely, memorable dish. So is the double-chocolate tart. They have a chardonnay and a pinot noir from Joie Farm in Naramata, as well as a good sauvignon blanc from Black Hills in Oliver. Range Road occupies premises once used by Blue Pear, but, unlike Blue Pear, it's a busy, crowded, noisy place.

Open Monday to Saturday 5 pm to 11 pm. Closed on Sunday. Licensed. Amex, Master Card, Visa. Book ahead.

EDMONTON   **MAP 58**
RED OX INN   ☆
9420 91 Street   **$175**
(780) 465-5727

If you're a stranger to Edmonton, the Red Ox Inn is hard to find. Head east on Whyte Avenue and turn north on 83 Street to a roundabout. The third exit from the roundabout is Connors Road. Turn right off Connors Road and find your way the few blocks to 91 Street. The Red Ox Inn has been completely redecorated and the menu, always innovative, now seems more exciting than ever. Currently they offer things like albacore tuna with radish, apple and an emulsion of jalapeno. Halibut with chanterelles and lemon grass comes next, or beef tenderloin with polenta or loin of lamb with falafel and Brussels sprouts. The great virtue of the restaurant is, however, still the wine-list, where you'll find Columbia Crest merlot, Fontanafredda barbera, Faively chardonnay and Burrowing Owl pinot gris, all at very reasonable prices. The Grgich Hills cabernet is more expensive at 65.00 for the half-bottle, but it's worth its weight in gold. A glass of Alvear Pedro Ximenez Anada sherry still costs only 9.00.

Open Tuesday to Sunday 5 pm to 9 pm. Closed on Monday. Licensed. Amex, Master Card, Visa. ⅃

EDMONTON MAP 58
SOLSTICE
10723 124 Street **$190**
(780) 488-4567

Solstice is a newcomer to Edmonton. It's dark and well served, with a short menu and a big wine-list. There are only a couple of appetizers (scallop risotto and tuna tartar) and several main dishes, among them lamb shanks, braised venison and beef tenderloin. Black cod is often offered as a daily special with squid ink—if you're allergic to squid ink (as many people are), be sure to ask them to leave it out. The cooking is very delicate. Native wines—there are imports as well—include Gehringer, Black Hills and, best of all, Burrowing Owl.
Open Monday to Saturday 5 pm to 11 pm. Closed on Sunday. Licensed. Amex, Master Card, Visa. &

EDMONTON MAP 58
ZINC
Art Gallery of Alberta **$140**
2 Sir Winston Churchill Square
(780) 392-2501

Zinc is all glass and steel, and the sun pours in its great west windows, making it a lovely place to be in fine weather. The kitchen is at its best with its lobster pot-pie, its cauliflower croquettes, its half-rack of lamb and its oregano chicken, at its worst with its beer-battered haddock, which screams for more salt. The flourless-chocolate torte is a fine way to end the meal and it costs only 8.00. The wine-list is full of good buys like Cakebread chardonnay and Black Hills syrah.
Open Tuesday to Saturday 11 am to 2.30 pm, 5 pm to 9 pm (later on weekends), Sunday 11 am to 2.30 pm. Closed on Monday. Licensed. Amex, Master Card, Visa. &

Every restaurant in this guide has been personally tested. Our reporters are not allowed to identify themselves or to accept free meals.

EDMUNDSTON, N.B.   MAP 59
LOTUS BLEU   ☆
52 chemin Canada   **$55**
(506) 739-8259

This bright and colourful little café is the best place to eat
in town, which of course isn't saying much. But it's saying something. They offer a different hot dish every day
of the week. We ourselves have had a first-class Indian-
style vegetable stew and a lovely dal. Sometimes there's
a quiche and there are always several good salads. The
vegetables are all organically grown and the bread comes
from Première Moisson in Montreal. The sweets are
made in-house and they have leaf teas of every sort. The
Lotus Bleu has been in business for seven years now and
every year has been a struggle. It deserves better.
Open Monday to Wednesday 7.30 am to 6 pm, Thursday and
Friday 7.30 am to 7 pm, Saturday 9.30 am to 5 pm. Closed on
Sunday. No liquor. Master Card, Visa. ♿

ENGLISHTOWN, N.S.   MAP 60
THE CLUCKING HEN   👉
45073 Cabot Trail   **$50**
(902) 929-2501

If you just got off the Englishtown ferry, chances are
you'll drive right past this little place. But if you started
the Trail at Baddeck you'll know that there aren't many
places like it on the road ahead of you. The cooking at
the Clucking Hen is simple, but the baking is special.
Everything is freshly made. You place your order at the
counter and it'll be delivered to your table. Everybody
seems to like their pan-fried haddock, their fish chowder
and their crab sandwich with tomato, red wine and mayonnaise, all on house-made bread. Oatcakes are a specialty
of the house, and there are always cinnamon rolls, butter
tarts and gingerbread with caramel.
Open daily 7 am to 8 pm from 1 July until 31 August (shorter
hours in the spring and fall). Licensed for beer and wine only.
Master Card, Visa. ♿

FERNIE, B.C.   **MAP 61**
THE CURRY BOWL
31 7 Avenue   **$80**
(250) 423-2695

We dropped this place from the guide a few years ago because it appeared to be deteriorating. But recent visits
have earned it a lot of superlatives, especially for the
won-ton soup made with miso broth and the lamb
korma, which one visitor calls "the best in recent memory." The kitchen specializes in Thai curries, though they
still have the Vietnamese summer roll and sesame salad
on the menu. They also have more than 50 beers on offer,
many of them made and sold by cottage breweries. Fernie
has the best powder snow in the Currie Bowl, after which
(with a different spelling) the restaurant is named.
*Open daily 5 pm to 10 pm. Licensed. Master Card, Visa. No
reservations.*

FERRYLAND, Newfoundland   **MAP 62**
LIGHTHOUSE PICNICS
Highway 10   **$60**
(709) 363-7456

Lighthouse Picnics have been offered for fourteen seasons
now and they're so popular that it's wise to call ahead before you come. Jill Curran and her staff of thirteen make
everything themselves and they can't keep up with the
demand. If you don't have a booking, just remember that
Ferryland is an hour's drive from St. John's and a thirty-
minute walk from the parking-lot. The lighthouse was
built in 1869 and operated by the same family for more
than a century. It had deteriorated badly over time but
the staff began restoration in their second year and
finished the job in 2004. Ferryland has had a colourful
history since it was founded by Lord Baltimore, but it has
never been more treasured than it is today. Visitors are
given a blanket and a flag to mark the place where they're
sitting. Then while they wait they get to watch the waves
breaking on the rocks below and the whales surfacing and

blowing. The picnics consist of a salad, a sandwich and a sweet, with a Mason jar of freshly-squeezed lemonade, all for 27.00. If it rains, you can sit inside. We like the sandwich filled with brie and chutney-glazed ham the best, but there's plenty of seafood close to hand—cold-water shrimp, salmon, crab—and curried chicken with mango. If you ask, they'll even make you a gluten-free picnic.

Open Wednesday to Sunday 11.30 am to 4.30 pm from 28 May until 2 October. Closed on Monday and Tuesday. No liquor. Amex, Master Card, Visa. Book ahead.

FIELD, B.C. (MAP 96)
TRUFFLE PIGS ☆
Kicking Horse Lodge **$150**
100 Centre Street
(250) 343-6303

There are only 169 permanent residents in Field, but everyone who comes here remembers the place. It's what people from the East think of when they think of Western Canada—a small town with a general store and mountains on all sides. Truffle Pigs opened in 1997 in the general store itself. Some time later they bought the Kicking Horse Lodge with the help of local people. Here they have ten tables and a modern kitchen. They have most of the best Okanagan wines on their wine-list. They have the best triple-A beef on their menu. They offer a variety of fruit pies, all made with local fruit. Breakfast means eggs benedict with Hutterite smoked sausages; lunch means bul-go-gi of pork-belly nachos. At night the longtime favourite is beef bourguignon, but they also offer elk short-ribs braised in beer and green-salt confit of duck. In summer there's a charcuterie platter of wild-boar terrine and smoked bison bünderfleisch.

Open daily 7 am to 10 am, 11 am to 3 pm, 5 pm to 9 pm from late May until the end of September (shorter hours in winter). Licensed. Amex, Master Card, Visa. No reservations. ♿

Nobody but nobody can buy his way into this guide.

FLORENCEVILLE, N.B.   MAP 63
FRESH   ☆☆
9189 Main Street   **$185**
(506) 392-6000

Fresh has had a great year, which is very good news. One has to worry about a place as special as this. Sara Caines opened it some ten years ago, in the first of three antique railcars parked on the track next to the Shogomoc railway station in the former village of Bristol. Her plan was to sell nothing but fresh food cooked from scratch, changing her menu every six weeks. She had only enough space for two, and it's not every chef who can keep up with Sara Caines. But James Freeman has stayed the course and with his four burners and small oven now offers a surprise menu that most visitors ask for. You tell him what ingredients you like and he cooks you something special. He also has a regular menu that starts with scallops spiked with whisky and a mushroom-and-eggplant bake and goes on to shrimp risotto and garden-fresh asparagus, lamb Wellington from New Zealand and beef tenderloin butchered in house. Sara works as waitress, bartender and maîtrise d'hôtel and she has amazing energy. She has only 26 seats, so you should book ahead. The wine-list is quite ambitious, but sadly it has only one Canadian wine.
Open Tuesday to Saturday 5.30 pm to 10 pm. Closed on Sunday and Monday. Licensed. Amex, Master Card, Visa. Book ahead.

FOGO ISLAND, Newfoundland   MAP 64
FOGO ISLAND INN   ☆☆
210 Main Road   **$275**
Joe Batt's Arm
(709) 701-0764

It's possible to get to Fogo Island, spend a few hours there and get back to Twillingate the same day. But that would be a pity, because Fogo Island deserves a longer visit. It's just off the northeast shore of Newfoundland. It's windswept and wet and very beautiful. Caribou graze on the uplands in summer, humpback whales migrate along its shores in winter. Zita Cobb, a woman of enormous energy and substantial means, is determined to preserve the island through tourism. In 2013 she opened a multi-million-dollar hotel on Joe Batt's Arm, and it's the best place to stay on the Island. The food is remarkable, the service impeccable. The dining-room doesn't take non-residents except by reservation, and nobody will tell you the menu or the price. The figure at the top is an educated guess.

Open 5 pm to 9 pm. Licensed. Amex, Master Card, Visa. You must book ahead. &

FOGO ISLAND   **MAP 64**
NICOLE'S   ☆
Highway 334   **$125**
Joe Batt's Arm
(705) 658-3663

Not five minutes away from the Fogo Island Inn, Nicole Lattuga has opened a café at the edge of the sea. The kitchen is manned by local people and they do some surprising things. Their cod are caught in pots instead of nets and kept alive until they're ready to be used. There's cod chowder, of course, and even cod pizza, but the best dish is the cod with split peas and cabbage. The vegetables are all organic and grown on nearby farms and for once you can count on a really good green salad. They use partridge-berries to make their chutney. If bake-apples appear on the menu, be sure to order the dish, whatever it is. But you won't go wrong if you ask for the island-picked blueberry cobbler. The service is good, the prices low.

Open Monday to Saturday 10 am to 2 pm, 5 pm to 8.30 pm from early May until mid-October. Closed on Sunday. Licensed. All cards. Book ahead if you can. &

If you wish to improve the guide send us information about restaurants we have missed. Our mailing address is Oberon Press, 145 Spruce Street: Suite 205, Ottawa, Ontario K1R 6P1.

FREDERICTON, N.B.

MAP 66

BREWBAKERS
546 King Street   **$160**
(506) 459-0067

Brewbakers has a new chef this year, but the menu has changed very little. The place is on the third floor, up a steep set of stairs. If you can't climb stairs, call ahead and ask for a table on the ground floor, which is normally re-served for large parties. The regular menu has a longish list of dishes, including the highly-praised flat-iron steak encrusted with porcini mushrooms. There are also three set menus, priced between 35.00 and 50.00, each more elaborate than the last. The wine-list is extensive and there are some great beers on tap.
Open Monday 11.30 am to 9 pm, Tuesday to Thursday 11.30 am to 10 pm, Friday 11.30 am to 11 pm, Saturday 5 pm to 11 pm, Sunday 5 pm to 9 pm. Licensed. Amex, Master Card, Visa.

FREDERICTON

MAP 66

THE PALATE
462 Queen Street   **$100**
(506) 450-7911

The Palate is large, well served and remarkably cheap. They're at their best with their soups. Just try the cream-of-zucchini or the seafood chowder. There's a long list of pizzas, paninis, quesadillas and stir-fries. They make a very good club sandwich too and the molten-lava cake is known all over town. (Frankly, we prefer the sticky-tof-fee pudding.) There are precious few wines—six reds and six whites—but the house wines are from Banrock Sta-tion and they're both pretty good.
Open Monday to Friday 11 am to 3 pm, 5 pm to 9 pm, Saturday 5 pm to 9 pm. Closed on Sunday. Licensed. All cards. Book ahead.

If you use an out-of-date edition and find it inaccurate, don't blame us. Buy a new edition.

FREDERICTON

MAP 66

TERRACE ROOM
Lord Beaverbrook Hotel   **$130**
659 Queen Street
(506) 451-1804

The hotel (now called the Crowne Plaza) is right next door to the Beaverbrook Art Gallery and across the street from the theatre. The dining-room overlooks the river, and it's now one of the best restaurants in Fredericton. The same kitchen serves the Terrace and the Maverick. The Maverick concentrates on steak and is the more expensive of the two. The Terrace has a more general menu and offers an unusual variety of seafood as well as meats. The wine-list is sensible and fairly priced and, of course, you can expect linen on the tables and a pleasant sense of space. The kitchen buys local ingredients and grows its own herbs in its roof garden. (Bees are also kept on the roof and they provide the honey used downstairs.) A new chef took over both the Terrace and the Maverick last fall and plans to make some changes in the menus.
Open Monday to Friday 11 am to 2 pm, 5 pm to 10 pm, Saturday 5 pm to 10 pm, Sunday 10 am to 2 pm, 5 pm to 10 pm. Licensed. All cards. &

FREDERICTON

MAP 66
☆

WOLASTOQ WHARF
527 Union Street   **$125**
(506) 449-0100

Wolastoq Wharf is owned and operated by St. Mary's First Nation and right now it's as good as anything in Fredericton. It's clean and bright and sports a whole wall of running water. Seafood is the specialty of the house and the menu runs to such things as local Beau Soleil oysters (five for 10.00), scallops prepared in three ways, seafood chowder (better the scallops) and lobster rolls. The wine-list is very small and very cheap, and if you don't want the Santa Carolina chardonnay ask for the Masi pinot grigio. Almost everything is a good buy, and

they even have off-street parking at the front door.
Open Monday to Friday 11 am to 4 pm (lunch), 4 pm to 9 pm (dinner), Saturday and Sunday 9.30 am to 4 pm, 4 pm to 9 pm. Licensed. All cards. Free parking.

FREEPORT, N.S.   MAP 67
LAVENA'S CATCH   ☆
15 Highway 217 W   **$75**
(902) 839-2517

Freeport is at the southern end of Digby Neck and to get there from Digby you take a short ferry trip. The place was settled by Loyalists in 1784 and many of the original buildings are still standing. Overhead, during the spring and fall, migrating birds in their thousands travel the Atlantic Flyway. On the Fundy side there are minke and humpback whales, and you can get tickets to see them at Lavena's Catch, which is run by the captain's sister and is the only good place to eat anywhere near. Lavena makes everything from scratch and everything is special. People talk about the seafood chowder, which is full of scallops and haddock. The scallops all come from Digby and you won't get better. The greens and the vegetables come straight from Lavena's garden. As for the peanut-butter and coconut-cream pies, they're fabulous.
Open Friday and Saturday 4 pm to 9 pm from 1 April until 31 May, daily 11.30 am to 8 pm from 1 June until 15 October, Friday and Saturday 4 pm to 9 pm from 16 October until 30 November. Closed Sunday to Thursday in the spring and fall. Licensed. All cards.

FROBISHER BAY, Nunavut
See IQALUIT.

GALIANO ISLAND, B.C.   (MAP 211)
PILGRIMME   ☆☆
2806 Montague Road   **$165**
(250) 539-5392

Jesse McCleery worked at Noma in Denmark before

coming to Galiano as chef. Here he's been collecting awards. Pilgrimme has an established reputation among local people and well-to-do boaters moored in Montague Harbour and willing to make their way on foot through the woods to the restaurant. A couple should order three or four plates to get the feel of the place; everything is designed for sharing. There's seared albacore tuna with fresh greens and eggplant, beef-heart tartar, wild coho salmon with sea-asparagus, pan-seared breast of duck and oyama chorizo. There are only a couple of sweets— chocolate truffles and bergamot pot de crème with sea-salted caramel. We consider Pilgrimme as good as most of the Michelin two stars but at half the price.

Open Monday and Friday to Sunday 5 pm to 9 pm. Closed Tuesday to Thursday. Licensed. Master Card, Visa.

GANDER, Newfoundland
See BOTWOOD.

GASPE, Quebec   MAP 69
LA BRULERIE
101 rue de la Reine   **$70**
(418) 368-3366

This place is actually called Brûlerie du Café des Artistes to distinguish it from other Brûlerie bistros. But as it happens this is the only one in the guide. It's always a pleasure to stop here. The former C.N.R. telegraph office is now a cosy restaurant that's open winter and summer and has a chef who keeps the same menu all year. The same shrimps from Rivière-au-Renard appear in both the salads and the sandwiches. Home-smoked salmon comes by the plateful. They make their own sausages, their own pizzas and their own pasta. The helpings are generous, the prices low. A cream-of-mushroom soup and pork tourtière with sweet potatoes is yours for just 13.50. They roast their own coffee right here and serve it in all sorts of ways. Refills are free.

Open Monday to Friday 7 am to 10.30 pm, Saturday and Sunday 8 am to 10.30 pm. Licensed. Master Card, Visa.

GEORGETOWN, P.E.I. (MAP 37)
CLAMDIGGERS
7 West Street   **$120**
(902) 652-2466

Georgetown has become one of Prince Edward Island's liveliest places. It has the oldest live theatre on the Island; it has a golf-course; and it has Clamdiggers. Clamdiggers is a big place and it's right on the shore of Cardigan Bay. They buy all their fish every morning and fillet it by hand. Their clams are battered and deep-fried only if you want them that way. Everybody likes the snow crab and the seafood stew, which offers cod, salmon and haddock as well as mussels and clams. The clam chowder is thick and buttery and the fish and chips are outstanding. In season they also have lobster. The vegetables are fresh, but the sweets are still disappointing.

Open daily 11.30 am to 8 pm. Licensed. Amex, Master Card, Visa. Book ahead. ♿

GIBSONS, B.C. (MAP 209)
CHASTERS
Bonniebrook Lodge   **$130**
1532 Ocean Beach Esplanade
Sunshine Coast
(604) 886-8956

A reader wrote to us that the Bonniebrook Lodge was everything he had hoped for on the Sunshine Coast: good food, perfect service and magnificent sunsets. On the menu they say that two can dine for 69.00, plus wine and taxes. (They have a good cellar, featuring wines like See Ya Later and Burrowing Owl.) This may all still be true, but the Lodge was sold in the summer of 2015 to a couple from Vancouver. Further reports needed.

Open Tuesday to Sunday 5 pm to 9 pm. Closed on Monday. Licensed. Master Card, Visa.

Nobody can buy his way into this guide and nobody can buy his way out.

GLENVILLE, N.S.
GLENORA DISTILLERY
13727 Highway 19
Cape Breton
(800) 839-0491

(MAP 151)
☆
$145 ($350)

Most people find this place irresistible. The distillery occupies a 200-acre site. It's beautifully landscaped and produces the only single-malt whisky (called Glen Breton) in North America. There are several vintages: just remember, the older the better. The courtyard of the distillery houses several attractive (if simple) bedrooms, a pub and a dining-room. Here, all summer long, there's a ceilidh after lunch and another after dinner every day. Last year they featured ten different local performers and five (a mother and her four daughters) on Sunday. The cooking may not equal that of the glory days of John and Tracy Haines, but it's good to have Patrick MacIsaac back in the kitchen again. His seafood chowder is outstanding. So is his lobster and his lamb. The sticky-toffee pudding is still the best of his sweets. It comes with Glen Breton whisky in caramel sauce. The wine-list has recently been enlarged and now offers a number of bordeaux wines and several Scottish single malts.
Open daily 11 am to 3 pm (in the pub), 5 pm to 8.30 pm from 1 May until 24 October. Licensed. Amex, Master Card, Visa. Book ahead. ♿

GODERICH, Ontario
THYME ON 21
80 Hamilton Street
(519) 524-4171

MAP 73
☆☆
$140

Nothing will hurt Thyme on 21 unless Peter and Catherine King lose their long-time chef, Terry Kennedy, which doesn't seem likely. They've been together ever since this old Victorian house was turned into a restaurant. By now Kennedy has developed working relationships with most of the local suppliers, and he has a rare talent for cooking even the simplest dish. There's a different fish special every week, and whether it's perch or pickerel or salmon, you know it'll be correctly cooked. The beef all comes from Huron County, the pork from Metzger, and both beef and pork are always cooked *à point*. Kennedy is really at his best with vegetables and people usually start their meal with a spring-roll. In fact, the vegetable soufflé stuffed with goat-cheese, spinach and red peppers can't be taken off the menu. He makes all his own sweets, and at the moment the best of them is the flourless-chocolate cake with an orange ganache.

Open Tuesday to Sunday 11.30 am to 2 pm, 5 pm to 8 pm from the middle of June until Labour Day, Tuesday to Friday 11.30 am to 2 pm, 5 pm to 8 pm, Saturday 5 pm to 8 pm, Sunday 11.30 am to 2 pm (brunch), 5 pm to 8 pm from Labour Day until the middle of June. Closed on Monday. Licensed. Master Card, Visa.

GOLDEN, B.C.   MAP 74
THE CEDAR HOUSE   ★★
735 Hefti Road   **$185**
(250) 344-4679

The Cedar House may have new managers, but year after year the kitchen performs as well as ever. The old house has been lovingly restored. They have ten acres of wooded farmland where they grow organic fruits and vegetables. A menu that starts with parsnip, butternut squash and apple soup is obviously for real. You know that it will go on to offer Fraser Valley organic chicken, Pacific salmon, Brome Lake duck and Alberta beef. Corey Fraser is the chef now and Annie Clark the manager. Corey Fraser is looking for new ways to use local ingredients, making the most of modern techniques. He also knows the importance of a good sweet list, and he is regularly offering apple-and-pear tarte tatin and a dark-chocolate cake. They have a colourful list of local wines and craft beers.

Open daily 5 pm to 10 pm from early June until late September, Wednesday to Sunday 5 pm to 10 pm from late September until early June. Closed on Monday and Tuesday in winter. Licensed.

Amex, Master Card, Visa. Book ahead. ♿

GOLDEN   **MAP 74**
ELEVEN 22   ☆
1122 10 Avenue S   **$110**
(250) 344-2443

Konan Mar calls this place a restaurant, a grill and liquids.
The wine-list, to be sure, is very large and very cheap. So
is the menu, which changes all the time. They don't make
their own cannelloni any more, but what they do serve
is so good that few people seem to have noticed. Their
Asian dishes (nasi goreng and pad Thai) are attractive
takes on familiar dishes. There's always some fresh fish,
but the chef isn't as good with fish as with meat. He's at
his best with veal bratwurst, Kassler pork chops and, of
course, Black Angus beef with stilton and roasted garlic
or smoked paprika butter. Sweets are one of the specialties
of the house, and the chocolate truffles are very good too.
*Open daily 5 pm to 10 pm from mid-May until mid-October
and from mid-November until mid-April. Licensed. Master
Card, Visa.* ♿

GRAND MANAN, N.B.   **MAP 75**
THE INN AT WHALE COVE   ☆☆
26 Whale Cove Cottage Road, North Head   **$150 ($300)**
(506) 662-3181

Forbes magazine once named the Inn at Whale Cove one
of its five top world destinations. Actually, you don't
have to be rich to stay here. Dinner for two costs only
about 150.00. Now that fast car ferries make six round
trips a day, you should come to North Head before it
goes the way of so many precious places. Just remember
to book early—visitors have been coming here for more
than a century. The main house was built in 1816 and
Willa Cather once owned one of the cottages. The interior has been renovated and filled with old Shaker furniture and lots and lots of books. You can often see whales,
porpoises and seals from the front verandah. The ground

90

fish that used to be the backbone of the menu are gradu-
ally disappearing, but lobster is still plentiful, and you can
usually get salmon, haddock and halibut as well. There's
still local lamb, beef and pork, usually served with
rhubarb or sour cherries. Laura Buckley changes her
menu every day and at the moment her signature dish is
chicken Oscar, served with fresh fruit and fine fresh vegetables. Blueberries and strawberries are plentiful, but
there aren't many wines to be found in the local liquor
store.

*Open Saturday and Sunday 6 pm to 8 pm from Mother's Day
until late June, daily 6 pm to 8 pm from late June until mid-October. Closed Monday to Friday in the spring. Licensed. Master
Card, Visa. Book ahead.*

GRAND MANAN
See also CAMPOBELLO ISLAND.

GRAND PRE, N.S.   (MAP 222)
LE CAVEAU
Highway 1   **$150**
(902) 542-7177

Le Caveau is the winery restaurant of the Grand Pré vineyard and the château in which it operates is grand and
very beautiful. It overlooks the vineyard from a hilltop
site a short distance from the highway. Jason Lynch has
been in charge of the kitchen for eight years or more. He
has a small menu and changes it often. It's not safe to start
your meal with the lobster-and-scallop chowder. Better
the warm spaetzle salad. Both the partridge and the red
deer are usually better than the Arctic char, which is often
overcooked. The markups on their own Grand Pré wines
are much too high. Order a wine from away for the same
price—perhaps a better wine—and be thankful.

*Open Tuesday to Saturday 5 pm to 9 pm from early April until
mid-May, 11.30 am to 2 pm, 5 pm to 9 pm from mid-May until
late October, 5 pm to 9 pm from late October until the end of December. Closed on Sunday and Monday. Licensed. All cards.
Book ahead if you can.* ♿

GRAVENHURST, Ontario — MAP 77

BLUE WILLOW
900 Bay Street **$90**
(705) 687-2597

The Blue Willow may have started as a tea-shop—we can't remember. But it's certainly not a tea-shop any more. It's a brilliantly successful café and by far the best place for lunch in Gravenhurst. You can have a wedge of quiche Lorraine if you like, but if you want to save money ask for the mini-quiche, which comes with a green salad or a Caesar salad (take the Caesar) and a bowl of homemade soup. There's often a tourtière or meat-loaf as well, plus a number of sandwiches (take the grilled cheese). There's good gingerbread to follow and home-made fruit pies in season. They have a short wine-list and good coffee. High tea is served every day between 2 and 5 pm—so much for the tea-shop.

Open Monday to Thursday 11 am to 4 pm, Friday and Saturday 11 am to 8 pm, Sunday 11 am to 3 pm from 1 July until 31 August, Tuesday, to Thursday 11 am to 4 pm, Friday and Saturday 11 am to 8 pm, Sunday 11 am to 3 pm from 1 September until 30 June. Closed on Monday in winter. Licensed. Amex, Master Card, Visa. Book ahead if you can. &

GRAVENHURST

See also BRACEBRIDGE.

GUELPH, Ontario — MAP 78

ARTISANALE CAFE ☆☆
214 Woolwich Street **$140**
(519) 821-3359

The Artisanale Café restores your faith in restaurants. Yasser Qahawish and his wife were interested in fresh, local produce long before they became old hat for any aspiring new kitchen. Yasser spent eight years in charge of the dining-room at Osgoode Hall in Toronto before he bought this old limestone building in Guelph. Here he offers traditional French country cooking, the very dishes of his boyhood, simple but full of flavour. The menu is small, but it changes with the seasons. Spring brings asparagus, wild leeks, morels and rhubarb; summer brings green beans, heirloom tomatoes; fall apples, pears and squash; winter storage vegetables, preserved fruits and tomato sauces. At noon they have a two for twelve special—any soup, any sandwich and any salad, all for 12.00. You can also order, if you like, from the à la carte, where you'll find duck croquettes, roasted pears, organic blue cheese and a chicken-liver mousse. Duck is a favourite in these parts, so you'll usually find duck confit as well as baked haddock on the dinner menu. Keep an eye out for the *prix-fixe* menu, which costs only 25.00 for three courses. Yasser Qahawish never seems to lose his enthusiasm for cooking.

Open Tuesday 11.30 am to 3 pm, Wednesday to Saturday 11.30 am to 3 pm, 5 pm to 9.30 pm. Closed on Sunday and Monday. Licensed. Master Card, Visa. Book ahead if you can. &

GUELPH
See also MORRISTON.

GUYSBOROUGH, N.S.   MAP 79
DESBARRES MANOR   ☆
90 Church Street   **$175 ($425)**
(902) 533-2099

Guysborough is still very much as it always was, that is, a stretch of unspoiled country on Highway 16. The lovely DesBarres Manor was built in 1837 for W.F. DesBarres, who was a Supreme Court justice. It's been a hotel since 2003, winning awards of excellence every year. The ten bedrooms are spacious, with large bathrooms and enormous beds. It's a lovely place to stay, especially when there's a chef like Anna in the kitchen. She offers a seasonal four or five-course dinner every night, making full use of her organic garden. In season lobster is the main attraction. When lobster is not in season, there's salmon, haddock and pork tenderloin. For lunch they pack you a gourmet picnic basket. If you come in their off season (between 30 September and 1 May) and give them some notice, they'll take you in and give you dinner.

Open daily 6 pm to 8 pm by appointment only from 1 May until 30 September. Licensed. Master Card, Visa. You must book ahead.

HAIDA GWAII, B.C. MAP 80

Queen Charlotte City (it's really just a village) is a mile or so east of the ferry terminal on Graham Island. We really liked the Purple Onion here, but sadly it has closed. The best choice now is the Queen B at 3208 Wharf Street (telephone (250) 559-4463). It's a funky place that caters to vegans and vegetarians and to anyone who doesn't mind noise. The menu offers such things as fish and vegetables, but little shellfish, because it's too expensive. Dana Adams changes her menu every day and makes everything in her own kitchen. She's good with such things as soups, quiches and pasta and in season she has blackberries, salmon-berries and huckleberries. Wild raspberries grow right next door. They're open Monday to Saturday from 9 am to 5 pm (sometimes earlier) and take all cards. No liquor.

HAIDA GWAII MAP 80
BRADY'S BISTRO
Sandspit Airport **$35**
11 Airport Road
Moresby Island
(250) 637-2455

People come to Haida Gwaii to get to know the people who live there. Brady is one of them and you'll find her—she's not a man—right by the airport. She grinds her own coffee and sells it for 2.00 a cup (or two cups). She opens earlier these days (at 8 o'clock in the morning), because she finds that people don't want to wait for their coffee, or for some good company either. She makes everything herself, even the fish chowder. She makes a lot of sandwiches and does a lot of baking—bread, muffins, brownies and cinnamon buns. People speak of

her coffee and muffins as the best breakfast in the world—and probably one of the cheapest.
Open daily 8 am to 2 pm. No liquor. Master Card, Visa. &

HAIDA GWAII   MAP 80
CHARTERS   ☆☆
1650 Delkatla Street   **$85**
Masset
(250) 626-3377

Mike Picher and Kaylene MacGregor resurrected the Trout House a few years ago, then moved on, as people so often do in this part of the world. But Mike is a superlative chef, so it was good to hear that he had reappeared at Charters. His menu changes often, depending on what's fresh on the local market. His most successful dishes are the prawn ravioli and the baby back-ribs. Diners also speak highly of the Caesar salad, which comes with applewood bacon and fried parmesan crisps. (He actually candies his own bacon.) Everything is beautifully presented and there are wines from all over the world on the short wine-list. There aren't many tables, so you should call ahead to get one.
Open Wednesday to Sunday 5 pm to 9 pm. Closed on Monday and Tuesday. Licensed. Master Card, Visa. Book ahead. &

HAIDA GWAII   MAP 80
HAIDA HOUSE
2087 Beitush Road
Tlell
(250) 557-4600

Tlell is about 30 minutes from Queen Charlotte City. Look for it half a mile along the road that turns right just before you come to the bridge across the river. (Or book a trip with B.C. Ferries and let them get you there.) The Haida House is a new 34-room lodge on seven acres of land—a beautiful building in a beautiful setting. It's the best place to stay anywhere on the islands, which are about the closest thing this country has to the Galapagos.

Recently, the Gwaii Haanas National Park was named the best nature park in North America. Certainly the bird life is spectacular. The chefs prepare aboriginal dishes as well as regular Canadian fare. As for breakfast, it's a feast, offering such things as smoked-salmon omelettes, home-made jam and excellent coffee. Everything is made from scratch and the ingredients are all the real thing.
Open daily 5 pm to 7.30 pm from the beginning of May until the end of September. Licensed. Master Card, Visa. &

HALIFAX, N.S.   **MAP 81**
BISTRO LE COQ   ☆
1584 Argyle Street   **$150**
(802) 407-4564

We used to think that this place was like a Parisian bistro, but it no longer really has the feel of Paris. It's main-stream Canadian, offering such things as mussels, foie gras, snails, bone marrow and charcuterie. They're prob-ably at their best with sea-bass and mashed potatoes or steak tartar, but their table d'hôte at 37.00 for three courses is one of the best bargains in town. The wine-list starts with champagne by the glass, followed by vouvray, muscadet, Benjamin Bridge, Luckett and Willm. Surpris-ingly, the list rises to no fewer than four Pauillacs with a top price of several hundred dollars. Chances are they'll offer you a seat at the bar, but the seats there are uncom-fortable and the ambiance is poor. If necessary, go some-where else.
Open Monday to Thursday noon to 10 pm, Friday noon to 1 am, Saturday 11.30 am to 1 am, Sunday 11.30 am to 10 pm. Licensed. All cards. &

HALIFAX   **MAP 81**
CHIVES   ☆☆
1537 Barrington Street   **$160**
(902) 420-9626

Now that Dennis Johnson has gone, Craig Flinn is the leading exponent of the farm-to-table movement in Halifax. His menu keeps changing and some of the best things can disappear. You go to Chives today for the mushroom-and-gouda tartlet, the Digby scallops with gnocchi and the lamb pot roast. As always, dinners start memorably with the restaurant's signature tea biscuits served in a brown paper bag with butter and molasses on the side. And for special occasions there's a private table for four in The Vault, left over from the nineteen-fifties when the building was a branch of the Bank of Nova Scotia. The wines are few and familiar, and the service can be leisurely, but the staff will be happy to sell you one of the chef's cookbooks while you wait. Last year saw a third string added to Flinn's bow with the opening of Temple Bar, Cocktails & Kitchen at 1533 Barrington Street (telephone (902) 474-4380, open Tuesday to Saturday 4 pm to 12 am), right between Chives and 2 Doors Down (Flinn is tired of people trying to call the new venture 1 Door Down). At Temple Bar the focus is primarily on drinks, but there's also a small-plates menu featuring things like charcuterie, focaccia and tacos.

Open daily 5 pm to 9.30 pm. Licensed. All cards.

HALIFAX   MAP 81
EDNA
2053 Gottingen Street   **$135**
(902) 431-5683

People seem to like Edna, but it does have its disadvantages. You can't book a table, which means that you may have to sit at the bar. The menu is short and features things like Cowboy rib chop, confit of chicken and halloumi fritters. The seafood chowder is indifferent; better the soup of the day or even the pea-and-cauliflower pakoras. The Arctic char is nicely served with creamed corn and basil pesto, and if you admire Icelandic cod it's on the menu here. Edna is still a new restaurant and that shows.

Open Tuesday to Sunday 5 pm to 10 pm (later on weekends). Closed on Monday. Amex, Master Card, Visa. No reservations.

HALIFAX

MAP 81

ELEMENTS ON HOLLIS
Westin Hotel   **$110**
1181 Hollis Street
(902) 496-7960

The new chef at Elements, a man named Raj Gupta, has
created quite a stir in recent months. The Farmer's Market is located right next door and Gupta gets most of his
supplies from there. Two of his best dishes are currently
his salt-cod cake and his brioche in a can (a take on a traditional Acadian dish). One visitor wrote of these to say
that they were the best he'd ever eaten. All the seafood is
very fresh and well prepared—you can't go wrong with
anything. As for the wines, they're all sold at cost plus
5.00 a bottle, so most of us can afford everything on the
list.
*Open Monday to Friday 11.30 am to 2 pm, 5.30 pm to 10 pm,
Saturday 5.30 pm to 10 pm, Sunday 11.30 am to 2 pm
(brunch). Licensed. All cards.* ♿

HALIFAX   MAP 81
                                              ☆☆
EPICURIOUS MORSELS
5529 Young Street   **$110**
(902) 455-0955

Jim Hanusiak is shy and self-effacing. His restaurant has
an out-of-the way location. These factors make it easy to
overlook him. That would be a mistake, because Epicurious Morsels is one of the best restaurants in town.
Hanusiak is best known for his smoked salmon and his
gravlax. He does all his own smoking and curing and his
gravlax is as good as any we've ever had. There are always
some new dishes on the menu. Recently there have been
scallop-and-salmon cakes and a fine shrimp-and-avocado
salad with mango, and there are always one or two new
soups—curried parsnip or curried carrot, perhaps, with
sweet-mango chutney. In the evening there's an excellent
rack of lamb and roasted duck with honey and coriander.
For brunch, keep an eye out for the French toast stuffed

with banana and strawberries. And don't forget to take a
second look at the wine-list. It's getting better every year.
Open Tuesday to Friday 11.30 am to 3 pm, 5 pm to 8 pm, Sat-
urday 10.30 am to 2.30 pm, 5 pm to 9 pm, Sunday 10.30 am
to 2.30 pm, 5 pm to 8 pm. Closed on Monday. Licensed. All
cards. &

HALIFAX   MAP 81
FREDIE'S FANTASTIC FISH HOUSE
8 Oland Crescent   **$50**
(902) 450-3474

Fredie's seats twelve. It's on a side street in the Bayers Lake
Shopping Centre, within sight of the movie theatres.
They make the best fish and chips we've ever had—ever.
It's even better than John's Lunch was in its heyday.
Fredie (or Tammy Frederick) started in a truck parked
outside Peggy's Cove, where she developed a huge following. If you come a second time it's likely, no matter
how busy they are, that you'll be remembered. The fish
is never more than a day old and sometimes it was landed
that morning. It's first lightly prepped and then pan-fried
to order, a procedure that keeps the flesh moist. They use
no salt and no seasoning. Just the fish and the hand-cut
fries. They also have pan-fried clams and scallops, but the
fish and chips is better. Fredie's offers an authentic Maritime experience. Come and see.
Open Monday to Wednesday 11 am to 7 pm, Thursday to Sat-
urday 11 am to 7.30 pm. Closed on Sunday. No liquor. Master
Card, Visa. &

HALIFAX   MAP 81
DA MAURIZIO   ☆☆
Brewery Market   **$185**
1496 Lower Water Street
(902) 423-0859

The service is as good as ever at Da Maurizio, the cooking
almost better. Everything is good. The duck is impressive, the chicken is magic. Prices aren't low, but the

stuffed ravioli costs just 15.00. The foie gras is generously served and (contrary to expectation) goes beautifully with its fresh strawberries. The fried squid with lemon and garlic has few equals and the plate of medjool dates stuffed with goat-cheese is a lot better than it sounds. There are a number of good Canadian wines (Tawse chardonnay at 42.00 and Benjamin Bridge Tidal Bay at 38.00), but if you can afford it the best buy is probably the Querciabella chianti classico, which costs 75.00. For afters there's black and white sambuca and several excellent grappas.

Open Monday to Saturday 5.30 pm to 10 pm. Closed on Sunday. Licensed. All cards. Book ahead if you can. &

HALIFAX   **MAP 81**
STORIES   ☆☆
The Halliburton Inn   **$150**
5184 Morris Street
(902) 444-4400

Stories is as good as anything in Halifax, maybe better. Inside, it's small and elegant. The menu is distinguished, offering such things as house-made charcuterie, sea scallops wrapped in rice paper, carpaccio of bison (a magnificent dish), crab-cakes made with Queen crab, big-eye tuna and salmon from the Faroe Islands. The cooking is very accomplished and the wine-list is remarkable. They're probably at their best, however, with red meat.

Open daily in summer 5 pm to 9 pm. Closed on Monday in winter. Licensed. Amex, Master Card, Visa. Book ahead if you can. &

HALIFAX   **MAP 81**
TAKO SUSHI   ☆
480 Parkland Drive   **$80**
(902) 405-8855

It's hard to tell one sushi bar from another, but Tako is different. Kevin Chen has been a sushi chef for at least fifteen years. He makes all the usual curries, teriyakis and noodle dishes, but it's with his sushi, and especially with his special rolls, that he's made his name. The best of the special rolls are the Venus Roll, with its tuna, butterfish, hamachi and tobiko, all wrapped in a thin sheet of cucumber, and the Ginza Roll, with its tempura shrimp, chopped fish, avocado and mango. You can start, if you like, with an appetizer of rainbow pizza, which is stuffed with avocado, white tuna and flying-fish roe and served regular or spicy. Tako is located in a suburban shopping mall near Bedford, fifteen minutes by car from downtown Halifax. It looks like nothing from the outside, but it has sushi like you've never had it before.

Open Monday to Saturday 11 am to 10 pm, Sunday noon to 10 pm. Licensed. All cards. &

HALIFAX   MAP 81
TAREK'S
3045 Robie Street   **$80**
(902) 454-8723

Tarek's is in an out-of-the-way location in the north end of the city. They take no reservations and everyone just lines up at the door. Tarek is a Syrian who came to Canada when he was nineteen. He learned to cook in various hotels in Toronto and Vancouver before settling in Halifax, where he opened Tarek's in 2000. You can't go wrong no matter what you order. The combo dip offers an easy way to sample some of his special dips. Then there's half-and-half beef, chicken shawarma, lamb kebabs and steamed squid. They're all good. There's no liquor and the thing to drink is one of the juices on the juice bar.

Open Monday to Saturday 11.30 am to 7.30 pm. Closed on Sunday. No liquor, no cards. No reservations. &

This is a guide to Canadian restaurants from coast to coast—the first ever published and the only one of its kind on the market today. Every restaurant in the guide has been personally tested. Our reporters are not allowed to identify themselves or to accept free meals.

HALIFAX

MAP 81

2 DOORS DOWN
1533 Barrington Street   **$100**
(902) 422-4224

Since this place is two doors down from Chives, it's called
2 Doors Down. Craig Flinn is still the executive chef and
Andrew Farrell, his one-time chef at Chives, is chef de
cuisine. All the food is locally sourced; the menu changes
with the seasons, but usually speaks with more foreign
accents than the menu at Chives. Come here if you want
to keep in touch with Indian cuisine, or Thai for that
matter. Kung fu chicken is served with sweet-and-sour
kimchi, bok choy and soba noodles, and it may be even
better than the smoked pork chop with macaroni and
cheese. Our favourite sweet is still Flinn's mother's recipe
for cheesecake in a Mason jar.

Open daily 11 am to 10 pm. Licensed. All cards. No reserva-
tions.

HALIFAX

See also CHESTER.

HAMILTON, Ontario   MAP 82

LA CANTINA
60 Walnut Street S   **$125/$75**
(905) 521-8989

The cooking at Vicolo 54, the formal dining-room at La
Cantina, is delicate and refined. Try the grilled beef tenderloin, served with brandy and black peppercorns, or
the French-cut veal chop with caramelized onions. The
best of their pastas still has to be the risotto of porcini
and cremini mushrooms. This is a rich and wonderful
dish and it's full of flavour. La Spiga, the informal dining-room, has a wood-burning pizza oven where they
make nineteen varieties of pizza, all of which are now
excellent. Our favourites are the San Marco and the
Patate Rostini. The most interesting of their pastas is, in
our opinion, the ravioli alla ricotta, which is stuffed with

ricotta cheese and a dab of spinach. There's a well stocked wine-cellar and several good wines by the glass.

Open Tuesday to Thursday 11.30 am to 2.30 pm, 4 pm to 10 pm, Friday 11.30 am to 2.30 pm, 4 pm to 11 pm, Saturday 4 pm to 11 pm. Closed on Sunday and Monday. Licensed. Amex, Master Card, Visa.

HAMILTON   **MAP 82**
EARTH-TO-TABLE BREAD BAR   ☜
258 Locke Street S   **$85**
(905) 522-2999

The Bread Bar has developed quite a following in Hamilton. It's an artisanal bakery by day and a restaurant for lunch and dinner. They have some interesting salads as well as fried bread with burrata cheese, olive tapenade and sundried tomatoes. Then there are beef and pork burgers with mushrooms, truffled mayonnaise and umami sauce. The big attraction, however, is the pizzas. There are a dozen of them and they're all very good. Our favourite sweet is the apple pie with salted caramel. The spiked milkshakes are a pleasant surprise—try the raspberry mocha. Last year they opened a second location at 105 Gordon Street in Guelph (telephone (519) 767-2999).

Open daily 11 am to 4.30 pm, 5 pm to 10 pm. Licensed. Master Card, Visa. &

HAMILTON   **MAP 82**
LAKE ROAD
229 James Street N   **$145**
(289) 389-9525

Lake Road, which is the sister restaurant of the Twisted Lemon in Cayuga (see above), opened in 2015. It concentrates on Mediterranean cuisine. It has a cocktail bar and live entertainment. Dinners begin with tabouleh, cod fritters, pigs' ears and octopus three ways. Main courses are equally unusual—Moroccan hen, branzino with sugo puttanesca and flank steak marinated in red wine. Sweets

include baklava, tiramisu and fig tart in puff pastry. These are all excellent, even better, we think, than at the Twisted Lemon. Lake Road has made a very promising start.
Open daily 11.30 am to 2 pm, 4.30 pm to 10.30 pm. Licensed. Master Card, Visa.

HAMILTON
See also ANCASTER, BURLINGTON, DUNDAS.

HEDLEY, B.C.	**(MAP 161)**
THE HITCHING POST	☞
916 Scott Avenue	**$60**
(250) 292-8413	

The Hitching Post was the first permanent structure built in Hedley. It was opened in 1903 by a man called L.W. Shatford. At that time Hedley was the centre of the Simulkameen, a rich mining area. Originally a department store, it was developed as a restaurant by Moses Brown in the late seventies. In 2004 Wilson Wiley, a local chef, took over the kitchen. He serves breakfast till noon. Later in the day he serves lunch and an early dinner, starting with chicken wings, mussels, prawns and squid and going on to triple-A beef, a pizza and a variety of pasta. The best of the pizzas is probably the so-called Hedley Blast (chorizo, red onions and jalapeno peppers). Our favourite pasta is the homemade pesto with sundried tomatoes and pine-nuts. Fillet of cod can also be had, battered in beer for 8.95.
Open daily 8 am to noon, noon to 8 pm from early June until late October, Wednesday to Sunday 8 am to noon, noon to 8 pm from late October until early June. Closed on Monday and Tuesday in winter. Licensed. Master Card, Visa.

HOPE, B.C.	**MAP 84**
OWL STREET CAFE	☞
19855 Owl Street	**$60**
(604) 869-3181	

Things don't change much at the Owl Street Café, because Graeme and Sonia Blair are happy with everything the way it is. Sometimes the Café gets too crowded, but usually you don't have to wait long, considering that everything is cooked to order from scratch. They're no distance at all from Exit 168 on the Trans Canada; look for a raw-pine A-frame—it was made from trees killed by beetles in Manning Park. The inside walls are decorated with hundreds of owls donated by visitors and friends. You order your meal at the counter and they deliver it to your table, which you get to share with other guests. They have coin-operated washing-machines where you can take care of your laundry while you eat your soup and sandwich. There's a good chicken club, but the smoked-meat is even better.

Open Tuesday to Saturday 8.30 am to 11 am (breakfast), 11 am to 4 pm (lunch). Closed on Sunday and Monday. Licensed. Master Card, Visa. &

ILE D'ORLEANS, Quebec   (MAP 158)
LE CANARD HUPPE   ☆
2198 chemin Royal   **$180**
Saint-Laurent
(418) 828-2292

It's easy to forget that the Ile d'Orléans is only twenty minutes from the heart of Quebec City—it feels a world away. This is a small *hôtel champètre*, run by Philip Rae. He has a regional menu that every year makes more and more of duck and foie gras. There are some lovely things on the à la carte, but we prefer the table d'hôte, which costs about 50.00 a head. There's always foie gras to start with, then confit of duck with strawberries and cassis or filet mignon béarnaise. The wine-list now offers wines from both Australia and New Zealand, but little or nothing from Niagara or Prince Edward County.

Open daily 6 pm to 10 pm from late May until the middle of October. Licensed. Master Card, Visa.

Our website is at www.oberonpress.ca. Readers wishing to use e-mail should address us at oberon@sympatico.ca

ILE D'ORLEANS (MAP 158)
FERME AU GOUT D'AUTREFOIS ☆☆
4311 chemin Royal **$100**
Sainte-Famille
(418) 829-9888

Jacques Legros and his partner, Lise Marcotte, took this two-hundred-year-old farmhouse and ran with it. Then they spent years developing their organic garden and poultry farm, where they produce foie gras without force-feeding the ducks and geese. They grow greens and vegetables of all sorts and maintain breeding quarters where ducks, geese and wild turkeys are raised in the open air and on an all-natural diet. The government of Quebec declared the farm an official tourist destination. Legros and Marcotte cook well too and everything is full of flavour. Dinner costs 35.00 for three courses, 45.00 for four and 125.00 for twelve. All their dinners feature rillettes of duck and goose, breast of pheasant, guinea-fowl and wild turkey.

Open daily by appointment only. Bring your own bottle. Master Card, Visa. You must book ahead.

ILES DE LA MADELEINE, Quebec
See MAGDALEN ISLANDS.

INGONISH BEACH, N.S. MAP 86
THE PURPLE THISTLE ☆☆
Keltic Lodge **$165**
383 Middlehead Peninsula
(902) 285-2880

It must be forty years since we came around a curve on the Cabot Trail and got our first glimpse of the Keltic Lodge, high on its sea-girt peninsula. But the memory has lasted. Even when we failed to admire the cooking at the Lodge, we never missed an opportunity to walk to the end of the peninsula to enjoy the view. Others were quicker to praise the Highland Links golf course, which is one of Stanley Thompson's finest achievements. A couple of years ago for the first time they hired a chef who came from Cape Breton. Daryl MacDonnell has given new life to a kitchen that had begun to need it. Most people come here for the South Bay lobster, which you can have either with or without its shell, poached either in sea water or in beurre blanc. People also admire the croquettes of snow crab, the local oysters and the utterly fresh scallops with English peas. The pick of the sweets is the chocolate pâté, which is made with guanaja chocolate from valhrona. The kitchen may not be quite up to the sea-views, but they do have an outstanding wine-list and excellent service. The mattresses are new and the fiddlers in the bar are marvellous.

Open daily 6 pm to 9 pm from 15 May until 31 October. Licensed. All cards. &

IQALUIT, Nunavut   MAP 87
THE GALLERY
Frobisher Inn   **$195**
(867) 979-2222

You'll find the Gallery in the Frobisher Inn, which as it happens is the best place to stay in Iqaluit. Under Mylene LaChance, it's also the best place to eat in town. It gets its name from the wall of prints in the dining-room, which all come from the Pangnirtung Print Collection. The menu was changing as we went to press, but you can always count on fresh beef and lamb and fresh greens, no matter what the weather is like outside, because Iqaluit is on the great-circle route between the West Coast and Europe. Arctic char (here called maple char) is a perennial favourite, though elk and musk-ox are occasionally offered as well. Confit of duck is always a safe bet, and chocolate torte with Baileys whiskey costs only 9.95 a portion. If you come for Sunday brunch, be sure to ask for the waffles—they're great. The wine-list is a lot better than you'd expect, and the service is sometimes good, sometimes not.

Open Monday to Friday 11.30 am to 1.30 pm, 5 pm to 8.30

*pm, Saturday 5.30 pm to 8 pm, Sunday 11.30 am to 1.30 pm
(brunch), 5 pm to 8.30 pm. Licensed. All cards. Book ahead.*
&

IVY LEA, Ontario   **(MAP 92)**
THE IVY
61 Shipman's Lane   **$165**
Lansdowne
(613) 659-2486

The Ivy is part of the upscale Ivy Lea resort, which is just
off the Thousand Islands Parkway near Brockville. The
menu is shorter now and more conventional than it used
to be, but the ingredients are all locally sourced and carefully prepared. Dinner begins with Moroccan spiced
chicken en croûte or carpaccio of Korean beef. There are
usually about six main courses, among them boar chops
with Brussels sprouts and spicy braised short-ribs with
corn purée. The best of the sweets is either the lemon-
layer pie or the sticky-toffee pudding. There's a big wine-
list, as well as a number of draft beers. The patio
downstairs is open all day and offers flat breads and salads
at much lower prices.
*Open daily 5.30 pm to 9 pm from Victoria Day until Labour
Day, Friday and Saturday 5.30 pm to 9 pm from Labour Day
until Victoria Day. Closed Sunday to Thursday in winter. Licensed. All cards.*

JASPER, Alberta   **MAP 89**
BECKER'S
Highway 93   **$160**
(780) 852-3779

Becker's is situated on the Icefields Parkway about five
minutes south of the town of Jasper. It's a family-run
lodge opened as Becker's Cabins in the nineteen-forties.
We dropped it from the guide a few years ago because it
changed its chef. But, as someone remarked, the view is
so wonderful that the food is almost beside the point.
This year the food has been better. Over the years Triple-

A beef has been one of the chef's main interests. There were people who liked the fresh bison just as well as the beef, though others did not. But the Pacific salmon was always popular. They also serve elk tenderloin, marinated for 24 hours. Everything is prepared to order, even the silver-chocolate ganache. If you get up early, you'll find that breakfast is a great meal.

Open daily 8 am to 11 am, 5.30 pm to 9 pm from14 May until 11 October. Licensed. Amex, Master Card, Visa. Book ahead.

JASPER   **MAP 89**
KIMCHI   ☞⫟
407 Patricia Street   **$75**
(780) 852-5022

Monica An is proud of her seafood, especially her sautéed squid, but we suggest starting with the bin dae duk (a pancake made with ground pork and kimchee) or the gim bap (dried seaweed), or perhaps one of the hot-pot soups. The best of the main dishes (all Korean) are the bul-go-gi variations on marinated beef or pork, served on a sizzling stone plate. The meal ends with green-tea ice cream. The wine-list has little to offer but Jackson-Triggs chardonnay and Jackson-Triggs merlot. Go instead for the sake or a bottle of Japanese beer.

Open daily 11 am to 10 pm. Licensed. Master Card, Visa. ♿

JASPER   **MAP 89**
TEKARRA   ☆☆
Highway 93A S   **$190**
(780) 852-3058

Tekarra opened in 1952, a mile south of central Jasper, on what is now called Hazel Avenue. It's a beautiful setting and you should climb the cliff for the view before you leave. But people became aware of the kitchen only after the arrival of David George Husereau. Husereau had put in 25 years elsewhere before he returned to Jasper, and he still travels the world in search of new recipes. Everything he serves is made in the kitchen—the

smoking, the curing, the baking. We have particularly liked the dates soaked in port with serrano ham, the salt-roasted beef carpaccio, the oyster shooter with absolut, the rack of lamb rubbed with chutney. The wines are all cheap, even the best of them. In the morning there's a breakfast buffet that's as famous as the dinner.
Open daily 8 am to 11 am, 5.30 pm to 10 pm from early May until early October. Licensed. All cards. &

KAMLOOPS, B.C.   **MAP 90**
ACCOLADES   ☆☆
Thompson Rivers University   **$175**
900 McGill Road
(250) 828-5354

This has long been our favourite place to eat in Kamloops. They reopened late in 2015 after taking a year off to reimagine themselves, as they put it. They now offer a four-course *prix-fixe* dinner for 42.95. It starts with confit of duck with potato foam, smoked breast of chicken, tabouleh salad and sausage ravioli and continues with pan-seared spot prawns, scallops with horseradish, Campbell Lake trout, wild venison *sous vide*, triple-A New York steak and nose-to-tail lamb. After that students will bring the dessert trolley to your table.
Open daily (except in January and February) 11.30 am to 3 pm, 5.30 pm to 9 pm. Licensed. Amex, Master Card, Visa. Book ahead. &

KAMLOOPS   **MAP 90**
HELLO TOAST
428 Victoria Street   **$45**
(250) 372-9322

This cheery downtown café is an ideal place for breakfast or lunch. They have no air-conditioning, but on a hot summer day you can eat outside on the sidewalk. They do great eggs benedict and you can design your own omelette. At noon they have great chicken-curry soup and a good Thai-style corn chowder, as well as a number

110

of first-class sandwiches. The wrap filled with Swiss cheese, apples and dried cranberries is superb and so are the avocado cookies.

Open Monday to Saturday 7.30 am to 3 pm, Sunday 8 am to 3 pm. No liquor. Master Card, Visa.

KAMLOOPS   MAP 90
THE NOBLE PIG
650 Victoria Street   **$95**
(778) 471-5999

This place looks more like a sports bar than a restaurant, but the food will surprise you. The meal starts with squid alla puttanesca or crisp boneless chicken karaage, seasoned with togarashi spice and served with sriracha-lime mayonnaise. They do interesting things with pizza as well—we really like the duck pizza with mushrooms, mozzarella, goat feta and garlic. They make extensive use of pork, but they also do a good job with locally-raised bison. In fact, the best of the main courses, we think, is the bison korma with coconut curry. They have flights of craft beers that go well with almost everything on the menu.

Open Monday to Wednesday 11.30 am to 11 pm, Thursday to Saturday 11.30 am to midnight. Closed on Sunday. Licensed. Master Card, Visa.

KAMLOOPS   MAP 90
TERRA
326 Victoria Street   **$95**
(250) 374-2913

Terra has surpassed the Brownstone this year as the best restaurant in Kamloops. The owner, David Tombs, and his wife, Andrea, change their menu every month. "So there's no asparagus in November, no pumpkins in May and certainly no fava beans in January." The chefs work closely with local farmers and artisans who supply the kitchen with exceptional produce. Terra lacks visual charm, but the food makes up for that. You start with a

111

lovely beet salad on a bed of organic greens or slow-braised pork, house-made kimchee or sea scallops seared with black pearls. Follow that with roasted halibut served with seasonal vegetables (not asparagus in November) or loin of rabbit with mustard. Sticky-toffee pudding comes next, served with rum and raisin ice cream. It's remarkable.

Open Monday to Saturday 5 pm to 9 pm. Closed on Sunday. Licensed. Master Card, Visa.

KELOWNA, B.C.   MAP 91
BLARNEY STONE
Inn at Big White, 5340 Big White Road   **$90**
(250) 491-2009

Big White, an hour from Kelowna in the Monashee Mountains, is Canada's second-largest ski resort. The Blarney Stone, as it's called, is open only in winter, but they have outstanding pub food. Their soups are all excellent, especially the leek and potato with Guinness. There's also a steak-and-Guinness pie, an Irish lamb stew and whisky-braised ribs. Nothing is expensive. For example, a loaf of soda bread with sage butter costs only3.95. The service is friendly and the view from the patio is about the best in town.

Open daily 7.30 am to 10 pm from 21 November until 15 April. Licensed. Amex, Master Card, Visa. ♿

KELOWNA   MAP 91
BOUCHONS
1180 Sunset Drive: Unit 105   **$145**
(250) 763-6595

Bouchons is more traditional than either Raudz or the Waterfront and its menu is larger. In fact, it's too large. They offer crab and scallop ravioli, baked pear with roquefort, lingcod with a sweet-pepper coulis, bouillabaisse and a cassoulet Toulouse-style. There are almost as many mains, among them scallops en croûte, rabbit, lamb provençale and tenderloin of beef. The best of the sweets, we think, is the iced Okanagan lavender soufflé. They have a three-course table d'hôte, featuring escargots de bourgogne, breast of duck with raspberry vinegar and tarte tatin made with pears. The wine-list is big and quite ambitious.

Open daily 5.30 pm to 10.30 pm. Licensed. Amex, Master Card, Visa. ♿

KELOWNA   **MAP 91**
OLD VINES   ☆☆
Quail's Gate Winery   **$160**
3303 Boucherie Road
(800) 420-9463

Old Vines has fine views of Lake Okanagan from the heights of the Boucherie Mountain Bench. It also has an excellent kitchen. The chefs, Roger Sleiman and Nav Dhillon, have a seasonal menu with produce raised on neighbouring farms. They also have a splendid tapas menu that features cold-smoked breast of duck, rillettes of pork with anise and saltspring mussels in coconut-curry broth. The regular lunch menu offers duck ravioli and roasted breast of chicken with braised endive and sunchokes. Dinner offers steak tartar and torchon of foie gras, followed by goat-cheese soufflé and line-caught black cod from Haida Gwaii. The list of artisanal cheeses is very impressive and there are several outstanding sweets, among them apple cake and sticky-toffee pudding. Old Vines is also known for its Quail's Gate icewine.

Open Monday to Saturday 11.30 am to 2.30 pm, 5 pm to 9 pm, Sunday 10.30 am to 2.30 pm (brunch), 5 pm to 9 pm. Licensed. Amex, Master Card, Visa. ♿

KELOWNA   **MAP 91**
RAUDZ   ☆
1560 Water Street   **$150**
(250) 868-8805

Raudz is famous for its fresh-fruit martinis and its wine-list. Both, however, are expensive. They don't offer lunch, but dinner starts with a number of interesting appetizers, among them venison carpaccio, wild-boar meatballs and plums with blue cheese and walnuts. Main courses run to Arctic char, coq au vin, veal osso buco and steak. Rodney Butters is the chef and everything is well and carefully cooked. Parking nearby is a challenge, but there's free parking in the evening at the Chapman Parkade just across the street.

Open daily 5 pm to 10 pm (later on weekends). Licensed. Amex, Master Card, Visa. No reservations. &

KELOWNA   **MAP 91**
THE TERRACE   ☆☆
Mission Hill Winery   **$160**
1730 Mission Hill Road
(250) 768-6467

Matt Batey makes sure that the food here at the Terrace is every bit as good as the view. The ingredients are mostly local, though some come from as far away as Salt Spring Island or Vancouver Island. Visitors find themselves starting lunch with a tart of duck prosciutto or perhaps with a simple green salad made with heritage tomatoes and artisanal cheese. They may then move on to braised venison with figs or pan-seared sablefish. Or they may choose to sample dishes from Batey's *cuisine de terroir*. In the evening the meal starts with a torchon of foie gras with Martin's Lane pears, Sloping Hills pork belly or smoked Pacific tuna with preserved apple and a shiso lemon confit. The best of the main courses, we think, is the bison tenderloin with creamed cabbage and cranberry buckwheat. After that we usually ask for the glazed lemon tart.

Open daily 11 am to 3 pm, 5.30 pm to 8.45 pm from mid-May until mid-September. Licensed. Amex, Master Card, Visa. &

We accept no advertisements. We accept no payment for listings. We depend entirely on you. Recommend the book to your friends.

KELOWNA

THE WATERFRONT
1180 Sunset Drive: Unit 104
(250) 979-1222

MAP 91
☆
$145

Waterfront was enlarged last year, and a lot of its charm got lost. But Mark Filatow has kept his small menu essentially unchanged. He's still concentrating on such things as braised veal cheeks, ravioli carbonara and sweetbreads with handmade pappardelle. He also makes excellent squid chorizo, octopus with rosemary and ricotta cavatelli with grana padano and brown butter. And he still has his ambitious wine-list and his fine espresso. For seven years in a row, Waterfront has been called the best restaurant in the Okanagan by *Vancouver Magazine*.
Open daily 5 pm to 10 pm (later on weekends). Licensed. Amex, Master Card, Visa. Book ahead. ♿

KELOWNA
See also OKANAGAN CENTRE, OLIVER.

KINGSTON, Ontario   *MAP 92*

Woodenheads at 192 Ontario Street (telephone (613) 549-1812) has the best pizzas in town, though it's often crowded and always noisy. If you don't like any of the pizzas on offer, you can make your own. They also have wine and several draft beers. Olivea at 39 Brock Street (telephone (613) 547-5483) majors in Italian food Canadian-style (mainly pastas and risottos), washed down with one of a dozen wines by the glass or any one of a number of draft beers. If you aren't interested in Italian food Canadian-style, go to the Red House at 369 King Street E (telephone (613) 767-2558). The Red House is really a pub with some of the best fries in Kingston, as well as soups, sandwiches and two or three innovative dishes like cotechino sausages with lentils in red wine. Windmills (telephone (613) 544-3948) has been at 184 Princess Street for at least 25 years. It serves breakfast, lunch and dinner and cooks in a variety of styles (Italian, Thai, African). Their best dishes are the slow-roasted leg of lamb and the Thai black cod. Their sweets are good and they have some first-class draft beers. There are a number of sushi restaurants in Kingston and the best of them, in our opinion, is Ta-Ke at 120 Princess Street (telephone (613) 544-1376). Their sushi is all made to order and it goes well with their Japanese Sapporo beer.

KINGSTON   **MAP 92**
AQUATERRA
Delta Kingston Waterfront Hotel   **$135**
1 Johnson Street
(613) 549-6243

Clark Day left AquaTerra last year, but there have been few changes since his departure. The chef, Brent McAllister, is still in the kitchen and most of the waiters are still on the job. The *prix-fixe* dinner still costs only 40.00, for which they give you Seafood Waldorf (shrimps, apple chips, fennel, pistachio and cider aioli), followed by breast of chicken pan-roasted in duck fat and served with fingerling potatoes, leeks, carrots and turnips. The meal still ends with pumpkin panna cotta. The lunch menu is largely unchanged, as is the wine-list.
Open Monday to Saturday 11 am to 11 pm, Sunday 11 am to 10 pm. Licensed. All cards. &

KINGSTON   **MAP 92**
CASA DOMENICO
35 Brock Street   **$165**
(613) 542-0870

Italian restaurants—not counting pizza parlours—are rare in Kingston. The Casa Domenico is the oldest of them all. The prices are high, but they do have some innovative salads (greens with pears, gorgonzola and spicy cashews), as well as a big selection of pastas, the best of which is probably the duck linguine with mushrooms and truffled asparagus. The main courses—chicken with lemon and sage, braised lamb chops with smoked sausage and seared tuna with caramelized fennel and black pepper—are more conventional. If you can afford it, ask for the osso buco at 80.00 for two. There aren't many sweets (tiramisu, cannoli and gelato), but they do have a good limoncello cake and a likeable warm chocolate brownie. The wine-list is short and mostly Italian, but there are some interesting draft beers.

Open Monday to Thursday 11.30 am to 10.30 pm, Friday 11.30 am to 11.30 pm, Saturday noon to 11.30 pm, Sunday noon to 10 pm. Licensed. All cards.

KINGSTON   MAP 92
CHEZ PIGGY   ☆
68 (rear) Princess Street   **$150**
(613) 549-7673

Chez Piggy is an institution in Kingston. After 35 years it still manages to serve pretty good food at very reasonable prices. They like to begin with oxtail poutine with cheese curds, caramelized onions and red wine. Their main dishes are never the same two days running, but striploin of venison is usually on the menu. Recently they've added roasted breast of chicken and lamb crusted with garlic and mint. Their lunch is one of the best deals in town, offering a variety of small plates and pastas, as well as all the usual soups and sandwiches. The wine-list covers a lot of ground and is fairly priced, and they have a number of craft beers as well. The patio is a great place to have lunch or dinner on a hot day.

Open Monday to Saturday 11.30 am to midnight, Sunday 10 am to midnight. Licensed. All cards. ♿

KINGSTON   MAP 92
CHIEN NOIR
69 Brock Street   **$150**
(613) 549-5635

Chien Noir is the only restaurant in the Black Dog Hospitality Group that we recommend at the moment. It's always been popular with local people and visitors alike. Its style is that of a French bistro, though you wouldn't be likely to find snails in cream sauce or mac'n'cheese in Paris. But most of their dishes are more conservative than that. There's cassoulet, bouillabaisse, mussels and fries and steak and fries. These are all prepared just as they should be, and there's also a three-course *prix-fixe* menu for only 37.00. At noon they offer many of the same dishes in smaller portions, as well as sandwiches, salads, an omelette and a hamburger. There are only a few sweets, but they're all made in-house. The wine-list features two draft beers brewed especially for the restaurant.

Open Monday to Wednesday 11.30 am to 2.30 pm, 5 pm to 9.30 pm, Thursday and Friday 11.30 am to 2.30 pm, 5 pm to 10 pm, Saturday 11.30 am to 2.30 pm (brunch), 5 pm to 10 pm, Sunday 11.30 am to 2.30 pm (brunch), 5 pm to 9.30 pm. Licensed. All cards. Book ahead if you can.

KINGSTON   MAP 92
THE CURRY ORIGINAL
253A Ontario Street   **$70**
(613) 531-9376

The Curry Original is still about the best Indian (or Bangladeshi) restaurant in Kingston, or so we think. The place was opened by Ali and Weais Afzal more than twenty years ago and they're still in charge of the front of the house. They have all the traditional dishes—curries, kormas, vindaloos, dhansaks, saags, bhoonas and tandooris. Everything is fresh and carefully prepared, but, sad to say, the menu almost never changes. It's best to start with an onion bhaji, a samosa or daal, then go on to tandoori chicken (cooked in a traditional clay oven), chicken tikka, a korma, a vindaloo or dhansak, a bhoona or a biryani. They also offer a number of special dishes like kashmiri chicken, with peanuts, sultanas, coconut and homemade yogurt. Then try the barfi, which is homemade cottage cheese with coconut and pistachio nuts. On weekdays they offer a string of lunch dishes, all priced at less than 10.00. The wine-list majors in wines from Prince Edward County and draft beers from India.

Open Tuesday to Saturday 11.30 am to 2 pm, 5 pm to 9.30 pm, Sunday 5 pm to 9.30 pm. Closed on Monday. Licensed. All cards.

KINGSTON   MAP 92
DAYS ON FRONT
730 Front Road   **$150**
(613) 766-9000

Days on Front is in an unprepossessing strip mall a long
way from the centre of town, but it may be worth the
trip to sample a locally-sourced menu supervised by
Matthew Day. The chef is Jay Legere, who has worked
in several of the restaurants recommended in this guide.
It's a good idea to start with a beet salad or seared scallops
in a spinach purée, followed by breast of duck in a cranberry risotto. There are only a few sweets, the best of
which is probably the banana bread pudding. On the
wine-list they have (they claim) 40 wines that cost less
than 40.00 a bottle. Book ahead unless you come late.
*Open Monday to Thursday 11.30 am to 10 pm, Friday and
Saturday 11.30 am to midnight. Closed on Sunday. Licensed.
All cards.* &

KINGSTON   MAP 92
PAN CHANCHO
44 Princess Street   **$95**
(613) 544-7790

Pan Chancho was established years ago by Zal Yanovsky
to supply Chez Piggy with bread and pastries. Nowadays
it's an all-purpose deli with an upscale café at the rear.
You can get a good breakfast here from 7 o'clock—try
the French toast with apple-butter crème fraîche or (if
you feel up to it) the red-eye poutine with ham and eggs
and cheddar-cheese curds. At noon they have fine soups
and an exceptional Caesar salad with crisp pancetta and
grilled lemon. People swear by the cumin-spiced lamb
pita and the sweet-potato hash with mushrooms and red
peppers. You can get pain au chocolat or a lemon-currant
roll from the deli out front. In the café itself they always
have first-class coffee and good draft beer.
Open daily 7 am to 4 pm (5 pm on Sunday). Licensed. All cards.
&

KINGSTON
See also IVY LEA.

KINGSVILLE, Ontario   (MAP 220)
METTAWAS STATION
165 Lansdowne Avenue   **$110**
(519) 733-2459

Hiram Walker commissioned a noted architect to design
the Kingsville railway station several years before the line
from Windsor reached the town in the spring of 1889.
It's a handsome building, with stone walls and a slate
roof, fitted out with gas from the nearby gas fields. If
you're looking for the Jack Miner bird sanctuary or Point
Pelee National Park, you'll be happy to find the station,
which was taken over by Janet and Anthony Del Brocca
in 2008. Del Brocca's cooking is mostly Italian and it's
pretty good. He's at his best with pasta. Diners have spo-
ken highly of the Sicilian arancini. There are seven pizza
pies, all recommended; or you can rise to veal marsala,
rack of lamb or grilled sea-bass. Most of the wines come
from the Niagara Region.
*Open Tuesday to Saturday 11 am to 9 pm. Closed on Sunday
and Monday. Licensed. Master Card, Visa.*

KIPLING, Saskatchewan   **MAP 94**
PAPERCLIP COTTAGE   ☞
503 Main Street   **$40**
(306) 736-2182

Kyle MacDonald of Montreal traded one big red paperclip for this house and then turned it into a delicatessen
and bakery. All the meats are cooked on site, the cheesecakes are made from scratch and so are the cinnamon
buns. There are fresh-fruit pies and home-style sandwiches on home-baked bread. On Thursday and Friday
you can have supper between 5 o'clock and 7.30. You pay
only about 15.00 for a soup or a salad, roast beef and
Yorkshire pudding, roast pork, turkey or poached haddock, sweet and coffee. There's always a hot dish at noon.

You'll find Kipling about 90 minutes from Regina on Highway 48.
Open Monday to Wednesday 5.30 am to 4 pm, Thursday and Friday 5.30 am to 4 pm, 5 pm to 7.30 pm. Closed on Saturday and Sunday. No liquor. Master Card, Visa.

KITCHENER, Ontario
See WATERLOO.

LA HAVE, N.S.   (MAP 102)
LA HAVE BAKERY
3421 Highway 331   **$30**
(902) 688-2908

The La Have Bakery exudes character and charm. It operates in an old outfitters building, where for years they've baked and sold some of the best oatcakes in the world. The woman who baked them, however, has now retired. More recently, they've lost their long-time chef, though they still carry a variety of breads (among them Irish-style potato bread and Russian black bread) and make a number of first-class sandwiches—roast beef, ham and chicken. There's also an abundance of Nanaimo bars, Queen Elizabeth cakes and date squares. Their cappuccino machine makes double shots every time out. Each Sunday they put on a splendid brunch, and they serve—or will serve when a new chef arrives—themed dinners every second Thursday evening.
Open daily 8.30 am to 6.30 pm (shorter hours in winter). No liquor. Master Card, Visa.

LAKE LOUISE, Alberta   MAP 96
THE POST HOTEL   ★★★
200 Pipestone Road   **$325 ($625)**
(800) 661-1586

The Post Hotel is not, as you might expect, on Lake Louise. Drive to the lake to see it, but stay at the Post. It's one of the few remaining mountain lodges, built of the original rough-hewn logs and complete with a wood-burning fireplace in every room. George and André Schwartz bought the place in 1978, when it was little more than a ruin. Parking is free now and so is afternoon tea, if you're a resident. Hans Sauter has a fabulous menu. His six-course *prix-fixe* dinner costs 110.00 a head, but that's where you're likely to find the caribou and the bison. Next door there's a fondue restaurant, but none of the fondues are worth what they cost (which is staggering). The wine-cellar has 25,000 bottles and is the winner of one of only four Grand Awards given by the *Wine Spectator* in Canada. They have the best choice of burgundies in the country and a list of old barolos and super Tuscans that beggars belief.

Open daily 11.30 am to 2 pm, 6 pm and 8 pm (two sittings). Licensed. All cards. Book ahead. &

LAKE LOUISE
See also FIELD.

LANTZVILLE, B.C. (MAP 121)
RISO FOODS
7217 Lantzville Road **$115**
(250) 390-0777

Sarah Wallbank is the driving force behind Riso in Lantzville, which is a small hamlet just north of Nanaimo. The dining-room seats about 40 people and it's a bright, contemporary place. The menu is short and the big draw is the pizza. She went to Naples and worked in a Michelin-rated restaurant with three generations of chefs, and she learned. Our favourite is the calabrese sausage, topped with chilli, fennel, mozzarella and sundried tomatoes. The best of the mains are the braised lamb shanks and the chicken piccata with mushrooms and marsala. The sweets are wonderful. The best of them comes with roasted almonds, cracked caramel and apricots soaked in cointreau.

Open Wednesday to Sunday 11.30 am to 2 pm, 5 pm to 9 pm. Closed on Monday and Tuesday. Licensed. Master Card, Visa. &

122

LETHBRIDGE, Alberta   MAP 98
MIRO
212 5 Street S   **$130**
(403) 394-1961

Miro Kyjak trained in Europe and ran a successful restaurant in Calgary before he moved to Lethbridge. He learned everything from his father, who told him that simplicity is the mark of perfection. He makes everything from scratch, and that means the bread, the soups and the sweets. His wine-list has won an award of excellence from the Wine Spectator for ten straight years. Fresh fish is available every day and pasta is always on the menu, along with such dishes as hickory-smoked goulash with spaetzle. The pavlova is the best of the sweets—don't miss it if it's there to be had.
Open Tuesday 5 pm to 10 pm, Wednesday to Friday 11 am to 2 pm, 5 pm to 10 pm, Saturday 5 pm to 10 pm. Closed on Sunday and Monday. Licensed. All cards. &

LONDON, Ontario   MAP 99
DAVID'S
432 Richmond Street   **$135**
(519) 667-0535

David Chapman ran a seafood bistro for many years before he opened this place, where he's probably got the best kitchen in town. But he's always been at the top of his form with fish. Bay scallops have never been our favourite ingredients, but he does wonders with them here; his sauce is remarkable. He's also good with pan-roasted lake trout, pan-roasted sea-bass and pan-roasted skate, something that's seldom seen in Canadian restaurants. The obligatory filet mignon is on the dinner menu, where there's also duck confit, veal cheeks and osso buco with bone marrow and corn risotto. The vegetables are plain, but at the end of the meal there's sticky-toffee pudding—and a very good one at that. He has a fixed-price menu that changes every day and a special *du jour* at noon. David's is not expensive, and his *prix-fixe* costs only 26.00

123

for two courses and 30.00 for three. There's a short but sensibly-priced wine-list. One regular wrote to say that he'd gone to David's often and never been disappointed. *Open Monday and Tuesday 5 pm to 10 pm, Wednesday to Friday 11.30 am to 2.30 pm, 5 pm to 10 pm, Saturday and Sunday 5 pm to 10 pm. Licensed. Master Card, Visa.*

LONDON   **MAP 99**
TOOK
172 King Street   **$150**
(519) 936-2064

The Only on King has become TOOK, which is an acronym of the original name. Paul Harding is a first-class chef, but he's reached the age at which he has to conserve his energy. Elaborate dishes are now a thing of the past. Nothing on the menu nowadays costs more than 11.00 or 12.00 and no wine costs more than 45.00 a bottle. The restaurant is open all day for a snack and a glass of wine. Helpings are tapas-size and the menu is short and simple. He offers two fish dishes every day, but only one soup and one salad. The soup, however, may be shiitake and oyster mushroom and the salads come with a lovely house dressing. Harding has always been good with pork and his pork chops on a bed of red cabbage is still a specialty of the house. Short-ribs are served with a fine chimichurri sauce There are a couple of sweets every night and the wines are all well and carefully chosen.
Open Tuesday to Thursday 11 am to 10 pm, Friday 11 am to 1 am, Saturday 5 pm to 1 am. Closed on Sunday and Monday. Licensed. Master Card, Visa.

LORNEVILLE, N.S.   **MAP 100**
AMHERST SHORE COUNTRY INN   ☆
5091 Highway 366   **$160 ($260)**
(800) 661-2724

The Amherst Shore is run by a charming young couple, Rob Laceby and his wife, Mary. They have a huge garden where they grow most of their vegetables and all of their herbs. They also have three or four attractive chalets where you can spend the night (if you book ahead). Dinner is served in a handsome dining-room that overlooks Northumberland Strait. A recent dinner began with carrot-and-maple soup, followed by a marinated tomato-and-zucchini salad. Next came your choice of oven-steamed scallops and chicken wrapped in prosciutto (a good idea). The meal ended with molten-chocolate cake or pavlova, a dish made famous years ago by Rob's mother. The best of the wines is the Nova 7 from Benjamin Bridge.

Open daily at 7.30 pm by appointment only from early May until late October, Friday and Saturday at 7.30 pm by appointment only from late October until early May. Closed Sunday to Thursday in winter. Licensed. Master Card, Visa. &

LOUGHEED, *Alberta*   MAP 101
HAUS FALKENSTEIN
Lougheed Hotel   **$65**
4917 51 Avenue
(780) 386-2434

Despite its name, which is that of a former premier, Lougheed has never had a large population. (Today the population is just 273.) The owner of the Lougheed Hotel describes the place as "the middle of nowhere." Lougheed is about 55 miles southeast of Canmore on Highway 13. The proprietor hopes that you won't presume to cancel your reservation after 4.30 in the afternoon, and he feels free to tell you not to expect spaetzle with your schnitzel, since he doesn't come from the Schwaben area of Germany, where spaetzle was first made. The schnitzels are what people come here for. The proprietor used to say that he offered the largest variety of schnitzels in Canada (67), but, having found that most schnitzel makers sell frozen schnitzels, he's changed that claim. At the Haus Falkenstein fresh loin of pork is pounded, spiced, breaded and pan-fried, just as our grandmothers used to do. So they now say that they have the biggest variety of fresh schnitzels in the world. Start your meal with the gulyassuppe. It's good. The restaurant is open Tuesday to Friday for both lunch and dinner, Saturday for dinner only. They have a licence (and a beer garden) and take Master Card and Visa.

LUNENBURG, N.S.   MAP 102
FLEUR DE SEL   ☆☆
53 Montague Street   **$200**
(902) 640-2121

This exquisite restaurant is often compared with the best restaurants in Halifax, and rightly so. Martin Ruiz-Salvador regularly wins gold in cooking competitions (most recently in Halifax), and here in his own restaurant every detail speaks of perfection. Martin's wife, Sylvie, runs the front of the house with grace and style. Prices have risen in the last few years, but if you want a memorable meal this is it. The menu changes with the seasons according to what's available on the market. But normally, dinner begins with oysters on the half-shell and goes on to a charcuterie board of summer sausage, beef tongue, pig's ears and pickled garlic scapes. It costs only 18.00, which is considerably less than foie gras at 25.00. The tomato salad is typical of the restaurant at it best, with its yellow, beefsteak, cherry and grape tomatoes and stuffed zucchini blossoms in a gazpacho vinaigrette. The best of the main dishes is probably the butter-poached lobster with potato salad, bok choy and lobster-roe mayonnaise. The duck with mung beans and miso is cheaper, and so are the lamb, the beef tenderloin with hand-cut fries and even the halibut cheeks and the sweetbreads. All the sweets are made in house as a matter of course, but we usually ask for the superb cheese plate. Benjamin Bridge used to be the feature of the wine-list. If the 2010 vintage is still available, be sure to ask for a bottle. *Note:* Fleur de Sel is closed for the year 2016.
Open Wednesday to Sunday 5 pm to 9 pm from mid–April until late October. Closed on Monday and Tuesday. Licensed. Amex, Master Card, Visa. Book ahead. ♿

The map number assigned to each city, town or village gives the location of the centre on one or more of the maps at the start of the book.

LUNENBURG   **MAP 102**
LINCOLN STREET FOOD
200 Lincoln Street   **$100**
(902) 640-3002

Paolo Colbertaldo opened this small, sleek restaurant in
the summer of 2014 and they've been busy ever since.
They see themselves as a modern neighbourhood restaurant. Whatever that means, the food is good and everything is locally sourced. The menu is long and they offer
everything from Adams and Knickle scallops to beet
tartar. Their bouillabaisse is crammed with scallops, haddock, mussels and char and served in a tomato-
and-saffron broth. They're always crowded and noisy,
but they have a useful wine-list, local beers and a cider or
two. The service is friendly and efficient.
Open Wednesday to Saturday 5 pm to 9 pm from 1 May until
31 December. Closed Sunday to Tuesday. Licensed. All cards.

LUNENBURG   **MAP 102**
MAGNOLIA'S
128 Montague Street   **$95**
(902) 634-3287

Magnolia's is a Lunenburg institution. It's been on this
site for more than 25 years and now has a patio at the back
from which you can watch the boats in the harbour
below. The menu never changes, except for the daily specials. There's always a seafood chowder, as well as peanut
soup and French-onion soup. There's always haddock,
pan-fried scallops and Alma's vegetarian stew. The meal
always ends with key-lime pie. The wine-list is small,
perhaps too small. The service is hurried, but friendly,
even when the restaurant is packed.
Open Monday to Saturday 11 am to 9 pm from 1 April until 31
October. Closed on Sunday. Licensed. Amex, Master Card,
Visa. Book ahead if you can. &

If you use an out-of-date edition and find it inaccurate,
don't blame us. Buy a new edition.

LUNENBURG   MAP 102
SALT-SHAKER DELI
124 Montague Street   **$95**
(902) 640-3434

The Salt-Shaker Deli is just a block up from the harbour and it has lovely views of the sea below. Their seafood chowder has won all sorts of awards and so have their Adams & Knickle scallops and their traditional fishcakes, which are made with salt cod and salt pork. They make thin-crust pizzas too—14 varieties in all. Our favourite is the home-smoked salmon with dill, pickled onions and lemon.

Open daily 11 am to 9 pm from early May until mid-October, Tuesday to Saturday 11 am to 8 pm from mid-October until early May. Closed on Sunday and Monday in winter. Licensed. All cards. ♿

LUNENBURG   MAP 102
SOUTH SHORE FISH SHACK
108 Montague Street   **$80**
(902) 634-3232

Everybody loves the Fish Shack. It was opened in 2014 by Martin and Sylvie Ruiz-Salvador, the owners of Fleur de Sel and the Salt-Shaker Deli, and offers the freshest seafood in town. Fish and chips are the best seller, but they also have a superb lobster roll, scallops, clams and whole steamed lobsters. There's no table service. You simply place your order at the counter inside, pick it up when it's ready, and take a table on the deck overlooking the harbour. They have a couple of wines and local beer on tap.

Open daily noon to 8 pm from late May to early October. Licensed. No cards.

LUNENBURG
See also LA HAVE, MAHONE BAY, MARTIN'S BROOK.

There are sixteen islands in the 60-mile arc of the Magdalens. All but Entry Island are linked by sand dunes, and route 199 runs the whole length of the archipelago. More than half of the total population live on Ile Cap-aux-Meules. The next largest is Ile Havre-Aubert, which is at the southern end of the chain. Everywhere there's fine hiking, swimming and sailboarding. The Madelon Bakery at 355 chemin Petitpas on Cap-aux-Meules (telephone (418) 986-3409) has been here since 1964. It has a scattering of tables, inside and out, and offers a wealth of baked goods. We've also had good reports of the salmon pies, the Greek salads and the cold cuts. Big sandwiches are made to order, and if you're looking for a packed lunch, this is a good place to get it—they're open daily from 6 am to 9 pm. The Magdalens are known for their soft raw-milk cheese, which is like reblochon and is produced by the indigenous breed of cattle known as Canadienne. Gérémie Arsenault first came here in 1998 and fell in love with the raw-milk cream he saw everywhere. He returned with sixty head of cattle and is now turning out 25,000 wheels of cheese a year. He likes to say that the sea winds add a touch of salt to his recipe. You can buy some at the Fromagerie du Pied de Vent on Ile Havre-aux-Maisons (telephone (418) 969-9292). The ferry from Souris in Prince Edward Island takes five hours, but you can also get here by plane. Too few people come to the Magdalens, which is a shame.

MAGDALEN ISLANDS   MAP 103
CAFE DE LA GRAVE
969 route 199 $90
La Grave
Ile Havre-Aubert
(418) 937-5765

On the west side of Ile Havre-Aubert there's a village called La Grave, where a number of old fishing boats have been turned into restaurants and boutiques. The Café de la Grave, next door to the theatre, has always been our first choice for a sandwich or a custard cake. The place was filled with music all day long, because Sonia Painchaud, the daughter of the house, was a talented mu-

sician and nobody ever ventured to criticize the cooking. But a couple of years ago Sonia decided to sell the Café. A group of islanders, determined to maintain the tradition, bought it. The dining-room is small, but it's well appointed and comfortable. There's still live music and the chef is the best anybody can find. The café is open all day every day, has a licence and takes Master Card and Visa. Further reports needed.

MAGDALEN ISLANDS   MAP 103

LA REFECTOIRE
Hôtel Vieux Couvent   **$140 ($295)**
292 route 199
Ile Havre-aux-Maisons
(418) 969-2233

This old convent has always been one of the most attractive places to stay in the Magdalens. The bedrooms have been charmingly restored and the many-windowed seaviews are spectacular. For years Evangeline Gaudet was one of the best-known chefs in the Islands. Recently, however, she and her husband both retired and hired a chef from the mainland. Some things will never change. Mussels are cultivated in a lagoon nearby, and cod, clams, scallops, halibut, herring, mackerel, shrimps and lobster are all still available. People have always liked the seafood (especially the lobster); the veal stuffed with lobster and cheese also has a big reputation, but not the steaks. They still sell their raspberry vinaigrette by the bottle, and the house wheat beer is still on tap. This has always been a gay and lively place, but as for the future time alone will tell. *Open daily 5 pm to 9 pm from 25 February to 21 December. Licensed. Master Card, Visa.*

MAGDALEN ISLANDS   MAP 103
                                       ☆☆☆
LA TABLE DES ROY   **$250**
1188 route 199
Etang du Nord
(418) 986-3004

Johanne Vigneau has been the leading chef in the Magdalen Islands for 35 years. She's still as much in love with the Islands and their produce as ever. In recent years she's been spending a lot of time running a gourmet food store called Gourmande de Nature, where they sell a line of homemade jams made from local berries. Her restaurant, La Table des Roy, has always made much use of local produce. It was never cheap; a five-course seafood dinner now costs up to 90.00 a head. Keep an eye out for the lobster. She puts a whole half-lobster into her bouillabaisse and her lobster bisque is a dream. Scallops are prepared in five different ways and served as an appetizer, along with mussels and sometimes seal, which used to be common but is now rare. The meal ends with an exquisite maple soufflé that Johanne has been offering for many years. The wine-list has been expanded and there are now at least 200 labels on her list, many of them organic.

Open Tuesday to Saturday 6 pm to 9 pm by appointment only from the middle of June until late September. Closed on Sunday and Monday. Licensed. Amex, Master Card, Visa. Book ahead.

MAGDALEN ISLANDS   MAP 103
TAKA   ☆☆☆
Capitaine Gedeon   **$260**
1301 chemin de la Vernière
Etang du Nord
(418) 986-5341

Two years ago the Japanese artist Takanori Serikawa opened a full-service restaurant in this small bed-and-breakfast. He serves dinner at 7 o'clock by appointment only every night of the week. There's no printed menu. He'll prepare a seven-to nine-course dinner for you, for which he'll charge you 90.00 a head plus tip and taxes. Remember to bring your own bottle, because wine is not included. The dining-room holds a maximum of fourteen people, and you have to book your table at least three days in advance. (In winter he insists on having at least four people before he'll open.) Everybody thinks, however, that Taka is worth any amount of trouble, because Takanori Serikawa is a superb cook.

Open daily at 7 pm by appointment only from 15 July to 15 September and from 1 December to 15 March. Bring your own bottle. Master Card, Visa.

MAHONE BAY, N.S.
MATEUS
533 Main Street
(902) 531-3711

(MAP 102)
☆
$140

Matthew and Kira Krizan have run this bright and cheerful restaurant for several years now. They have sandwiches and burgers, of course, but they also serve such appetizers as three-cheese fondues and such mains as halibut risotto, lamb burgers and beef tenderloin with truffled mash. Weekend brunches feature a mushroom omelette or a smoked-duck benny. The wines are carefully chosen and favourably priced. People from away will be excited by such unfamiliar wines as Luckett's (ask for the Ortega) and Petite Rivière (ask for the Risser's Breeze). Both are well known locally, but are seldom seen elsewhere in the country. Likewise, few of us have ever tasted halibut with Lunenburg chow, which is made with onions soaked in brine. The brine is left to stand overnight and then served with tomatoes and purslane. Most nights they have live music.
Open Monday to Friday 11.30 am to 9 pm, Saturday and Sunday 10 am to 9 pm (shorter hours in winter). Licensed. Master Card, Visa. ♿

LA MALBAIE, Quebec
CHEZ TRUCHON
1065 rue Richelieu
Pointe-au-Pic
(888) 662-4622

MAP 105
☆☆
$175 ($295)

Dominique Truchon spent many years in the kitchen at the Auberge des Peupliers in Cap à l'Aigle, where he made a name for himself (see above). Two or three years ago he opened his own restaurant in a handsome old house on rue Richelieu in Pointe-au-Pic. Here he has a

darkly formal dining-room and several comfortable bedrooms. It didn't take him long to earn first place in an area
crammed with ambitious restaurants. Most of his best
dishes are essentially simple: Charlevoix lamb, roast beef
with potatoes fried in duck fat, halibut with red peppers
and quail marinated in Bordeaux wine. Before you leave,
be sure to ask for the pudding au chomeur with maple
cream. The wine-list is growing and the service is impeccable.

*Open daily 5.30 pm to 9 pm. Licensed. Amex, Master Card,
Visa. Book ahead if you can.*

LA MALBAIE
See also Cap a l'Aigle.

MANITOULIN ISLAND, Ontario   MAP 106
GARDEN'S GATE   ☆
Highway 542   **$95**
Tehkummah
(705) 859-2088

We've been writing about the Garden's Gate for fifteen
years now. When you arrive, you open a gate into a
pretty garden, beyond which is the restaurant, with a
split-rail fence in the middle distance. The garden is thick
with bird feeders and hummingbirds are everywhere.
Rosemary Diebolt is still making everything from
scratch. She grows all her vegetables and buys her blueberries, strawberries and raspberries from long time suppliers. She and her husband search every year for new
Niagara wines and local craft beers. There's a new abattoir
nearby, and so local lamb is back on the menu, served perhaps with apricots and Moroccan spices. She makes at
least ten different sweets every day and serves them with
fair-trade coffee and loose tea.

*Open Tuesday to Sunday noon to 8 pm from 1 May until 30
June, daily noon to 8 pm from 1 July until 31 August, Tuesday
to Sunday noon to 8 pm from 1 September until 31 October.
Closed on Monday in the spring and fall. Licensed. Master Card,
Visa. Book ahead if you can.* ♿

MANITOULIN ISLAND

MAP 106

THE SCHOOL HOUSE
☆

46 McNevin Street, Providence Bay
$120

(705) 377-4055

Lumber used to be plentiful and cheap in Providence Bay, so it's everywhere in the School House, which was built in 1898. Greg and Heather Niven came here in 1995 looking for a place to raise a family. And so it turned out to be. Niven trained in France and the quality of his cooking has never faltered. A neighbour brings him vegetables from his garden. Despite the new abattoir in town, most of his customers still expect whitefish. Niven does what he can with this rather tasteless fish. Luckily there are customers who ask for Atlantic salmon in a dill beurre blanc or rack of lamb with port. The meal ends well with a B52 crème brûlée or bread pudding with bourbon. Most of the wines come from the Niagara Region and Niven always buys the best he can find.

Open daily 5 pm to 9 pm from mid-May until mid-October. Licensed. Master Card, Visa. ♿

MAPLE BAY, B.C.

(MAP 56)

BAD HABITS

6701 Beaumont Avenue
$85

(250) 597-8089

Bad Habits is right on the water and offers breakfast and lunch all day every day but Monday and dinner on Friday and Saturday. The decor is edgy but comfortable. They serve soup and sandwiches at noon; the dinner menu is more elaborate. They have a licence and the cooking is good. Further reports still needed.

MARKHAM, Ontario

(MAP 204)

FOLCO'S
☆

42 Main Street N
$135

(905) 472-6336

Folco's has been around for a while and it just keeps on getting better and better. Some years ago the chef-owner turned his back on the rat-race in Toronto and went to Italy to study cooking. He eventually opened Folco's, where he now makes all the pasta on site. He likes to change his menu often, but regulars have been slow to trade in their pasta fagioli for squash and blood-orange soup, however well it's made. He makes everything to order and often flies in ingredients from Italy. Diners speak highly of the lamb and the chicken; we ourselves always seem to order ravioli, which is beautifully made here. The breads are baked in-house and the salads are all good. We also like the torta di nona, which is a lemon sponge-cake layered with mascarpone cheese.

Open Monday to Friday 11.30 am to 3 pm, 5 pm to 10 pm, Saturday 5 pm to 10 pm, Sunday 4.30 pm to 10 pm. Licensed. Master Card, Visa. Book ahead if you can.

MARKHAM (MAP 204)
INSPIRE
144 Main Street N **$130**
(905) 554-2889

Inspire is probably the most popular restaurant in Markham. It serves Asian fusion food. The menu is constantly changing, but they usually offer such things as duck-confit taco, a burger, pork three ways and Korean prime rib. The dinner menu features udon carbonara with Italian sausage, braised beef with mushrooms and a quail egg on top. The wine-list is quite short and, because the restaurant is crowded, the service is very slow.

Open Tuesday and Wednesday 11.30 am to 3 pm, 6 pm to 10 pm, Thursday to Saturday 11.30 am to 3 pm, 6 pm to 11 pm, Sunday 11.30 am to 3 pm, 6 pm to 10 pm. Closed on Monday. Licensed. All cards. Book ahead. &

MARTINS BROOK, N.S. (MAP 102)
OLD BLACK FOREST CAFE
10117 Highway 3 **$80**
(902) 634-3600

The Old Black Forest Café has first-class German food—

schnitzels with a sunflower-seed crust and maultaschen or house-made ravioli stuffed with ground beef and spinach. They also have some wonderfully fresh seafood. Their Black Forest cake is baked on the premises, and there's a beer soup on rye bread for almost nothing. We usually order the maultaschen—it's our favourite. In summer you can eat outside on the deck. Service is friendly and efficient.

Open Tuesday to Sunday 11.30 am to 9 pm from mid-April until mid-December. Closed on Monday. Licensed. Master Card, Visa. Book ahead if you can.

MASSEY, Ontario **MAP 110**
DRAGONFLY
205 Imperial Street **$65**
(705) 865-3456

This stretch of Highway 17 has scenery and a few gas-stations, but very little for anyone looking for good food. If you're travelling on Highway 17 you'll be happy to dis-cover the Dragonfly, a private home that's been turned into a restaurant. It has a big (too big) menu of interna-tional dishes. Burgers are the big seller, but you'll often be surprised to find a special or two on offer. First-class chicken soup costs almost nothing, but in fact everything is a bargain. The dining-room is usually packed, but the service is always patient and friendly.

Open Tuesday to Sunday 11 am to 9 pm. Closed on Monday. Licence pending. Master Card, Visa. Book ahead if you can. ♿

MATTAWA, Ontario **MAP 111**
MYRT'S
610 McConnell Street **$40**
(705) 744-2274

Mattawa is a friendly place and even in a dine-and-dash place like Myrt's the waiters quickly make you feel like a local. Scott Edworth serves comfort food and serves it fast all day long. He never lets you down; in fact, you'd have to go a long way to find a better cheeseburger with bacon or a better butter tart. He makes all his own soups, all his own pies and all his own pizzas. He makes all his own fish and chips too, using nothing but the freshest halibut. He grinds all his own beef for the hamburgers. And he puts on a hot special every day at noon. Bikers on the Temiskaming Loop are told to stop here, and everyone else should do the same.

Open daily 6 am to 8.30 pm. Licensed. Master Card, Visa. &

MEDICINE HAT, Alberta   MAP 112
THAI ORCHID ROOM   ☆
36 Strachan Court SE   **$95**
(403) 580-8210

Sounantha and Ken Boss migrated to Vancouver 38 years ago, and before long moved on to Medicine Hat. In all that time they've never wavered in their allegiance to Thai cooking. Their menu now is almost too long—they have ten vegetarian entrées in all. But everything is very fresh and very authentic. Start with the hot-and-sour soup or the fisherman's soup and go on to the yellow curry with chicken and coconut rice or the peanut curry (or the green curry or the red curry). They're all great. There's always chicken satay, spring asparagus with garlic and mussels with spicy black beans. Everybody asks for the white-chocolate crème brûlée at the end of the meal. There aren't many wines, but there are some interesting loose teas.

Open Tuesday to Thursday 11 am to 9 pm, Friday 11 am to 10 pm, Saturday 4.30 pm to 10 pm, Sunday noon to 9 pm. Closed on Monday. Licensed. Amex, Master Card, Visa. &

MEDICINE HAT   MAP 112
TWIST   ☆
531 3 Street SE   **$95**
(403) 528-2188

Twist was sold in 2012 to two sisters, Melissa and Cheryl-Lynn Whyte. So far they've kept most of the dishes that made Twist famous. Melissa used to work full-time here and she knows all the ropes. Our man on the spot recently ordered twelve of the tapas and now considers himself an expert on the subject. They've added some excellent salads to the list, and an all-day brunch on Saturday. They've also added live music on Thursday, Friday and Saturday nights. The paella and the triple-A beef tenderloin are still the backbone of the dinner menu, though there are some vegetarian options as well. Begin your meal with the coconut shrimp if it's offered. Melissa is only making the sweets now and they're all lovely.

Open Tuesday to Saturday 11 am to 10 pm. Closed on Sunday and Monday. Amex, Master Card, Visa. &

MIDDLE WEST PUBNICO, N.S.   (MAP 225)
RED CAP ☆
1034 Highway 335 **$95**
(902) 762-2112

The Red Cap has been in business for 70 years and it's changed hands only once in all that time. You'll find the village on the South Shore, about 30 miles east of Yarmouth, which makes it a two-hours' drive from the Digby ferry. The Pubnicos still have an active fishing fleet; in fact the dollar value of their catch is the highest east of Montreal. The kitchen has every kind of fish and shellfish at its disposal, and the fish on offer is always stunningly fresh. Nearly every ingredient they use is local. They grow their own herbs and buy their vegetables from local farmers. Everything is made from scratch—the sauces, the stocks, the soups and even the onion rings. Most of the wines come from Grand Pré or Peller, but if you like you can bring your own bottle. There's no corkage fee.

Open Monday to Saturday 11 am to 8 pm, Sunday 10 am to 7 pm from 1 May until 25 December. Licensed. Amex, Master Card, Visa. &

Every restaurant in this guide has been personally tested. Our reporters are not allowed to identify themselves or to accept free meals.

MONCTON, N.B.   MAP 115
THE WINDJAMMER   ☆
Hôtel Delta Beauséjour   **$200**
750 rue Principale
(506) 854-4344

The Windjammer is formal, dark, well served and extremely expensive. They have a tasting menu (five courses
for 78.00) and on the regular à la carte bison costs 65.00,
Wagyu beef 99.00. They have Beau Soleil oysters, pan-
seared foie gras with rhubarb and fig chutney, snails in
garlic butter, a shrimp-and-scallop stir-fry, rack of lamb
from Spring Brook Farm, fresh Atlantic salmon, Fundy
lobster and a variety of steaks. The best of the main
dishes is the Spring Brook lamb at 38.00, but actually you
may do better with the tasting menu, which starts with
wild sturgeon and goes on from there. Many of the wines
are sold in six-ounce and nine-ounce carafes, but on the
whole it's a good list, featuring wines from Oyster Bay,
Kim Crawford, Liberty School and Peter Lehmann. Valet
parking is free.
*Open Monday to Saturday 5.30 pm to 10 pm. Closed on Sun-
day. Licensed. All cards. Valet parking. Book ahead if you can.*

MONTAGUE, P.E.I.   (MAP 37)
WINDOWS ON THE WATER   ☆
106 Sackville Street   **$100**
(902) 838-2080

Lillian Dingwell has a lovely old house with a wrap-
around deck overlooking the Montague River. Her
cooking is old-fashioned, but she still gets awards for her
seafood chowder. Everything is perfectly fresh and the
prices are fair. The beef is expensive, but there's pan-
seared haddock with lemon-dill butter for only 24.00 and
grilled salmon with maple syrup for even less. We usually
order the blue mussels in a white-wine mirepoix, because
they're about the best thing the Island has to offer. Lillian's sweets are famous, especially the blueberry cake
with brown sugar. The wine-list is improving very

139

slowly.
Open daily 11.30 am to 9.30 pm from mid–May until mid–September. Licensed. All cards. Book ahead if you can. ♿

MONTREAL, Quebec   **MAP 117**
BOUILLON BILK   ☆☆
1595 boulevard St.–Laurent   **$160**
(514) 845-1595

Bilk overlooks a run-down stretch of the boulevard St.-Laurent. Inside it's all white on white, and at the back there's an open kitchen where they cook elegantly and extremely well. Dinner starts with raw hamachi, foie gras with apple and maple, ris de veau and oysters on the half-shell. The main courses are almost equally inviting. There's sea-bass with oyster mushrooms, scallops with cauliflower and shiitake, Cornish game hen with foie gras and venison with sunchokes and quinoa. Lunch is an ambitious meal too, with its beautifully tender calf's liver and its lovely chocolate cake with orange and grand marnier. There's a big list of bottled wines with many vintages from both the côte de Beaune and the côte de Nuits. Sixteen wines are also sold by the glass, including a dolcetto d'Alba for only 12.00.
Open Monday to Friday 11.30 am to 3 pm, 5.30 pm to 11 pm, Saturday 5.30 pm to 11 pm. Closed on Sunday. Licensed. Amex, Master Card, Visa. Book ahead.

MONTREAL   **MAP 117**
LA CHRONIQUE   ☆☆
104 avenue Laurier o   **$225**
(514) 271-3095

La Chronique has moved across the street and acquired a completely new interior, bright and very contemporary. Marc de Canck's cooking also seems brighter and more up-to-date, but that's probably an illusion. All that matters is that the cooking, whatever it used to be, is now very good indeed. Lunch begins well with lobster bisque, magret de canard, tartar of salmon and foie gras. The foie gras is foie gras, but the tartar of salmon is brilliant. Dinner is the same, except that one or two important dishes are added to the menu. The fondant au chocolat is a great dish, as is the gourmandise du sucre, which changes every day. There's a big wine-list with a Penfolds chardonnay and a côtes du rhône villages offered by the glass as well as the bottle. We used to say that Marc de Canck was no longer at his best. That is no longer true, if indeed it ever was.

Open Monday and Tuesday 6 pm to 9 pm, Wednesday to Friday 11.45 am to 1.45 pm, 6 pm to 9 pm, Saturday and Sunday 6 pm to 9 pm. Licensed. All cards. Book ahead if you can.

MONTREAL   MAP 117
LE CLUB CHASSE ET PECHE   ☆☆
423 rue St.-Claude   **$200**
(514) 861-1112

This is an amazing restaurant. The menu is inviting—hamachi tartar, bison ravioli, piglet risotto, wagyu tataki and foie gras with persimmon. The mains are more expensive and more traditional, but there's suckling pig with chestnuts as well as duck magret. The hamachi is delightful, the foie gras wonderful. Bison may be too substantial a meat for ravioli, but still, bison is bison. The so-called Ocean Delivery may be something like king salmon; venison comes with aged cheddar. The kitchen is endlessly inventive. The service is competent and well timed. The wine-list, it's true, is terribly expensive—the Antinori solaia costs more than 500.00 a bottle, but the list of open wines is remarkable for its quality. They actually have a premier-cru Saint-Aubin for 17.50. When did you last see a premier-cru wine by the glass?

Open Tuesday to Saturday 6 pm to 10.30 pm. Closed on Sunday and Monday. Licensed. Amex, Master Card, Visa. Book ahead.
&

We accept no advertisements. We accept no payment for listings. We depend entirely on you. Recommend the book to your friends.

141

LE COMPTOIR
4807 boulevard St.-Laurent   **$145**
(514) 844-8467

Le Comptoir has an unusual and interesting wine-list and
the dishes they offer are tapas-size and meant to go with
the wine. So choose your wine first, and you won't do
better than the Hautes-Côtes-de-Beaune by the bottle or
the glass. Then ask for the charcuterie board, which is
beautifully delicate. The octopus in white wine is very
tender and so are the beef cheeks with chimichurri and
balsamic vinegar. The loin of veal in a sage purée with
pickled radishes and the rainbow trout with green apple
and horseradish are both rather confused dishes—confu-
sion is never far away along the whole length of the
menu. That's why the best thing on the list is the charcuterie, which is a dish of clear and emphatic statements.
Open Monday 5 pm to 11 pm, Tuesday to Friday noon to 2 pm,
5 pm to 11 pm, Saturday and Sunday 10 am to 2 pm (brunch),
5 pm to 11 pm. Licensed. Master Card, Visa. Book ahead if you
can. &

MONTREAL   **MAP 117**
LES COUDES SUR LA TABLE
2275 rue Ste.-Catherine e   **$95**
(514) 521-0036

Elbows on the Table operates in a shabby district in the
east end of the city. The restaurant itself, however, is
brisk and attractive. The meal begins, surprisingly, with
a torchon of foie gras (for a *supplément* of 12.00) or, more
cheaply, with veal meatballs or a bowl of broccoli soup.
The tartar of salmon that follows is a bit disappointing,
and the fish of the day is apt to be mackerel. Ask instead
for the Cornish game hen with roasted thyme, lemon and
a hot basket of fries. The sweets are well conceived.
There's a moelleux of dates with caramel and salted butter and a lemon-meringue tart. Both are lively dishes.
There are a few wines by the glass and a full list of bottled

wines, which they tend to keep out of sight. Ask for it
and spend a few dollars.
*Open Tuesday and Wednesday 11.30 am to 2 pm, Thursday
and Friday 11.30 am to 2 pm, 5.30 pm to 10 pm, Saturday 5.30
pm to 10 pm. Closed on Sunday and Monday. Licensed. Master
Card, Visa. Book ahead if you can.*

MONTREAL   MAP 117
DOMINION SQUARE TAVERN
1243 Metcalfe Street $175
(514) 564-5056

The Dominion Square Tavern has been restored and now
looks much as it did when it opened in 1927. It serves
English-style pub food, though the chef, Eric Dupuis, is
certainly not an Englishman. The carte offers things like
bangers and mash, Cornish game hen, smoked trout and
striploin of beef. They also do pâté de campagne, house-
made charcuterie and, best of all, bone marrow—a gorgeous dish. Next door at 1237 Metcalfe Street (telephone
(514) 507-9207) there's a sister restaurant called the Balsam Inn. It has a table d'hôte for 21.00, featuring loin of
pork on Tuesday, pâté on Wednesday and catch of the
day on Thursday. Balsam is also owned by Eric Dupuis
and it's smaller, quieter and cheaper than Dominion
Square. They both have a number of on-tap beers and a
big wine-list.
Open daily 11.30 am to midnight. Licensed. All cards.

MONTREAL   MAP 117
LES 400 COUPS   ☆☆
400 rue Notre-Dame e   **$145**
(514) 985-0400

It's hard to get a table here, even if you book the day before. It's a small place and there just isn't much room, but
if you can't get a table you'll find that the bar is very well
served. If catfish is on the menu, be sure to ask for it. It's
a rare fish, but here it's beautifully prepared with buckwheat and mussels. If there's no catfish to be had, you can

settle for the suckling-pig sausage, which is no real hardship. There are three appetizers—liver mousse, rillettes of Arctic char and a soupe du jour. Everything on the menu is impeccable and the service would be worth two stars if the place had no other virtues. The wine-list is small—too small—but there's a nice sancerre from the Loire at quite an attractive price.

Open Tuesday and Wednesday 5.30 pm to 10.30 pm, Thursday and Friday 11.30 am to 1.30 pm, 5.30 pm to 10.30 pm, Saturday 5.30 pm to 10.30 pm. Closed on Sunday and Monday. Licensed. All cards. You must book ahead.

MONTREAL   MAP 117
HOTEL HERMAN   ☆
5171 boulevard St.-Laurent   **$130**
(514) 278-1000

This is a clever kitchen. The menu is clever, the cooking is clever. You sit down and they hand you a menu, which offers carrots, beets, celeriac, potato and trout. The chef plays variations on each of these, one after the other. Carrot, for instance, means carrots with coffee, quinoa and caraway. Beet means beets with juniper berries, celeriac means celeriac with soya and black garlic, trout means trout with onions and sumac, potato means potatoes with buttermilk and unripe elderberry. After all this excitement, the main course follows, with (marvellous) sweetbreads, terrine of foie gras and pork belly in brown butter. But every dish goes almost too far and the sweet tart is certainly way over the top. The goat's milk with sea buckthorne is safer. The wine-list is small and equally strange. There's a curious vintage from California called Love Red. Try it—it might work.

Open Monday and Wednesday to Sunday 5 pm to 11 pm. Closed on Tuesday. Licensed. Master Card, Visa. Book ahead.

Every restaurant in this guide has been personally tested. Our reporters are not allowed to identify themselves to the management or to accept free meals. We accept no payment for listings. We depend entirely on you.

MONTREAL   **MAP 117**
IKANOS
112 McGill Street   **$170**
(514) 842-0867

Ikanos is dressy and well served, but it's important to
know that it serves hardly any Greek food. Look in vain
for Greek lamb. What they serve is Atlantic salmon—
they're interested in seafood—sea-bass, squid and fishcakes. The specialty of the house is the seafood platter,
which actually costs 68.00. Apart from seafood, there's
little but beef carpaccio with truffled mushrooms and
grilled loin of pork. The wine-list, on the other hand, is
almost all Greek. There's a sauvignon blanc from San-
torini that's better than most; try it. The fishcakes and
the carpaccio are fine, complex dishes, and the rib-eye
steak is, well, rib-eye steak.
Open Monday to Friday 11.30 am to 2.30 pm, 5.30 pm to 9.30
pm, Saturday 5.30 pm to 9.30 pm. Closed on Sunday. Licensed.
Master Card, Visa.

MONTREAL   **MAP 117**
JOE BEEF   ☆
2491 rue Notre–Dame o   **$175**
(514) 935-6504

Joe Beef has its own vegetable garden and its own
smoker, designed and built by Frédéric Morin, David
McMillan's long-time partner. The restaurant itself takes
some getting used to. It's small and packed with people.
There's often a lineup at the door and if you have a booking (as you should), that doesn't seem to matter. There's
no printed menu or wine-list. The food and wines are
chalked up on big blackboards that are hard to read in the
dim light. Relax. They have oysters from the East and
West Coasts, and the best are from New Brunswick.
They have smelts, cod (on a bed of potato mash),
spaghetti with lobster (at a great price) and whole trout.
You won't be able to see any of these items on the wall,
but never mind, you have this guide in your hand. Any-

145

way, the trout is the thing to have. There's no use looking for a wine of your choice. Simply ask for the house white or the house red—they're both good, drinkable wines. Joe Beef is real Montreal and David McMillan probably knows more about food and wine than anyone else in the city. Talk to him if you can—he's the big man on the scene.

Open Tuesday to Saturday 6 pm to 10 pm. Closed on Sunday and Monday. Licensed. Master Card, Visa. You must book ahead. &

MONTREAL   **MAP 117**
LEMEAC   ☆
1045 avenue Laurier o   **$185**
(514) 270-0999

Leméac has an ample menu and a big wine-list. The wine-list starts with a sancerre from Henri Bourgeois and a pinot noir from the Willamette Valley and ends with a Château Saint-Emilion premier grand cru that costs almost 1100.00. The cooking is realistic and down-to-earth, featuring things like homemade blood pudding, wild-mushroom risotto and Icelandic wild cod. The restaurant is big, comfortable and well served. Everything is exactly as it should be.

Open Monday to Friday 11.45 am to midnight, Saturday and Sunday 10.45 am to 3 pm (brunch), 6 pm to midnight. Licensed. Amex, Master Card, Visa. &

MONTREAL   **MAP 117**
THE LIVERPOOL HOUSE   ☆
2501 rue Notre-Dame o   **$165**
(514) 313-6049

This is the second restaurant opened in this block by the Joe Beef group. In no time, the new restaurant was as crowded and noisy as Joe Beef itself. It has the same big helpings and the same chalkboards. The menu is broadly similar, but the atmosphere at the Liverpool House is more masculine than at Joe Beef, more gutsy. Not that the kitchen fails to score with its seafood, much of it raw. The lobster spaghetti is the most expensive dish on the menu. The oysters come from both the East Coast and the West. Everything appears to be prepared casually, but actually the kitchen cooks in high style, and everything has a lot of flavour. David McMillan will tell you that he has the most sophisticated customers in North America. They actually eat sweetbreads, tripe, cheeks, heart, ears and tails. As for the wine-list, it covers one whole wall. *Open Tuesday to Saturday 5 pm to 10 pm. Closed on Sunday and Monday. Licensed. Master Card, Visa. You must book ahead.* &

MONTREAL   MAP 117
MAISON BOULUD   ☆☆
Ritz–Carlton Hotel   **$195**
1228 Sherbrooke Street W
(514) 842-4224

The Maison Boulud is very splendid indeed. The best tables face a large open fireplace. The chairs are soft and luxurious. The service is formal and correct. The menu, however, is straightforward and plain, confining itself to such things as barley-and-mushroom soup, beef tartar, smoked salmon, ricotta ravioli and hanger steak. It's true, there are one or two unusual dishes—flounder gravlax is one; floating islands is another. And the cooking is always light-hearted and delicate. The smoked salmon, for instance, is wonderful and the floating islands is much more than a nursery pudding. The wine-list, of course, is stunning, though very expensive. There are four Bolgheri ornellaias, a Lafite premier cru for 2100.00 and a Latour premier cru for 2500.00. But don't be tempted to order the Petit Mouton from Rothschild; it's way overpriced at 650.00.
Open daily noon to 2.30 pm, 5 pm to 10 pm. Licensed. Amex, Master Card, Visa. Book ahead. &

Nobody can buy his way into this guide and nobody can buy his way out.

MIRCHI
365 place d' Youville   **$80**
(514) 282-0123

Mirchi is named for the green-chilli spice widely used in
India and Bangladesh. Here in Old Montreal Khaled
Rahman serves food from the Moghal north of India and
the Hindi south. He has a dozen appetizers, followed by
several biryanis and tandooris. If you aren't comfortable
with the cuisine, ask for an appetizer platter, with a combination dinner to follow. You can drink wine if you like,
but Indian beer goes better with the food. The cooking
may be cautious, but it's likeable. They have a table d'hôte
lunch for 12.00 and a table d'hôte dinner for 18.00.
Open Monday to Friday 11 am to 2 pm, 5 pm to 10.30 pm,
Saturday and Sunday 5 pm to 10.30 pm. Licensed for beer and
wine only. Visa. Book ahead if you can.

MONTREAL   **MAP 117**
TOQUE!   ✩✩✩
900 place Jean-Paul-Riopelle   **$225**
(514) 499-2084

Normand Laprise and Christian Lamarche still live in a
world of surprises, most of which are to be found among
their appetizers and amuse bouches. The most remarkable of these is the sea-urchin, adorned with oysters, ginger, soy, daikon and cucumber. (There are also scallops
with sumac and gin and carpaccio of venison with sea
snails.) It's a good idea to ask for two appetizers and pass
on the main courses, which, apart from the rack of suck-
ing pig, are more pedestrian. The wine-list too is full of
surprises. There are only half a dozen Canadian wines,
but at the other end of the list there's a grand-cru Saint-
Emilion and a Mouton-Rothschild for 2000.00 a bottle.
For ordinary people there's a sauvignon blanc from Naramata for 81.00 and a chardonnay from the Beamsville
Bench for 103.00. But Toque! is not really meant for ordinary people. It's for people who are able and willing to

pay for amazing delicacies presented in the most elegant surroundings.

Open Tuesday to Friday 11.30 am to 1.45 pm, 5.30 pm to 10 pm, Saturday and Sunday 5.30 pm to 10.30 pm. Closed on Monday. Licensed. Amex, Master Card, Visa. Book ahead. ♿

MONTREAL   **MAP 117**
VIN PAPILLON   ☆
2519 rue Notre–Dame o   **$140**

This tiny wine-bar is everything the Joe Beef group stands for. There are no reservations—they don't even have a telephone. The tables are packed so close together that it's hard to read the chalkboards—there's no printed menu. The sommelier has chosen a number of organic and bio-dynamic wines that nobody's ever heard of—just ask him to choose for you. This restaurant is much more interested in vegetables than either Joe Beef or the Liverpool House. People come back time and again for the whole cauliflower, spit-roasted with tarragon and charred lemon peel, for the gigantic fried zucchini flowers, above all for the smoked celery root. All the helpings are small, so you have room to try the wonderful herring, the chicken wings, the home-smoked ham. (The Papillon gets to use the Joe Beef smoker whenever they like.) The meal ends with your choice of one of their many French cheeses. You can stay as long as you like, unless you can't stand the noise.

Open Tuesday to Saturday 3 pm to midnight. Closed on Sunday and Monday. Licensed. Master Card, Visa. No reservations. ♿

MONT TREMBLANT, Quebec   **MAP 118**
LE CHEVAL DE JADE   ☆☆☆
688 rue de St.-Jovite   **$200**
St.-Jovite
(819) 425-5233

Olivier Tali and Frédérique Pironneau put all they had into this old farmhouse in St.-Jovite. Tali is the only Canadian winner of the Ordre des Canardières, which came to him for his caneton à la Rouennaise, the signature dish of the Tour d'Argent in Paris. It means pressed duck and it's on the menu at the Cheval de Jade every night of the week at a price of 99.00 for two. Tali aims to have the freshest and best fish to be had anywhere in the Laurentians and he probably does. He has a menu bouillabaisse for 53.95 that starts with an endive salad, followed by Mediterranean bouillabaisse served with rouille, croûtons and grated cheese. The discovery menu at 88.00 a head starts with duck foie gras, seared scallops with squid ink and green alder, followed by trout tartar, breast of duck with truffles and a palette of sweet surprises. The regular à la carte is, of course, less adventurous and less expensive. But it does offer feuilleté of snails, foie gras de canard and fish soup, followed by casserole of squid, fillet of kingfish, braised lamb shank and red deer steak. They buy all their supplies locally and we especially admire their truffled duck and their red deer. The presentation is always lovely, and the wine-list is splendid.

Open Tuesday to Saturday 5 pm to 10 pm. Closed on Sunday and Monday. Licensed. Amex, Master Card, Visa. Book ahead. &

MONT TREMBLANT   MAP 118
MILLE PATES
780 rue de St.-Jovite   **$95**
St.-Jovite
(819) 717-3830

Mille Pâtes is a small boutique that sells pasta. They also have a few tables where you can sit down and order what you like. They have a short list of house-made soups, salads and sweets for only a few dollars. In the evening they add shrimps on a skewer, gravlax of salmon with gin, pulled pork on columbine and spinach ricotta.

Open Monday and Tuesday 10.30 am to 6 pm, Wednesday to Sunday 10.30 am to 10 pm. Licensed. Master Card, Visa.

Nobody but nobody can buy his way into this guide.

MORRISTON, Ontario   **(MAP 78)**
ENVER'S
42 Queen Street   **$130**
(519) 821-2852

Morriston is a tiny village on Highway 6. You wouldn't
notice Enver's unless you were actually looking for it.
Keep an eye out for an old grey-brick storefront with
neo-Gothic windows. Enver was a one-man band, doing
almost everything himself. Terri Manolis, who bought
the place from Enver several years ago, was lucky enough
to sell a share of the business to Ken Hodgins, the chef.
Hodgins did what he could to cater to all comers. Just
about everything on his menu was local. His fish was always fresh. He made a superb duck-liver pâté. His wine-
list was greatly expanded. In the winter of 2014,
however, Hodgins sold up and left. His place has been
taken by his sous-chef, Lee Wilcock.
Open Tuesday to Friday 11.30 am to 2 pm, 5 pm to 8.30 pm,
Saturday 5 pm to 8.30 pm. Closed on Sunday and Monday. Li-
censed. Amex, Master Card, Visa. Book ahead if you can. ♿

MURRAY HARBOUR, P.E.I.   **(MAP 37)**
NO. 5   ★★
5 Church Street   **$75**
(902) 962-3668

No. 5 was opened in 2015 in a deconsecrated church by
Wade Little, a New Zealander. It quickly became extremely popular. They concentrate on what Wade Little
calls clean food. Until 4 o'clock he features sandwiches,
soups and salads. He makes his own bread and uses it for
all his sandwiches. Real maple syrup is big with him, and
so are fries, which you can have plain, salted or spiced.
The evening meal is more substantial than lunch, adding
barbecued chicken with walnut mustard and a number
of specials. People write to us about the hot chilli on
homemade toast and the Thai-style beef salad. The soups
are all wonderful and the sweets too. Everything is
cooked to order and the service is very attentive. This is

151

slow-cooked food at its best.
Open Wednesday to Saturday 11 am to 8 pm, Sunday 11.30
am to 6 pm. Closed on Monday and Tuesday. No liquor. Master
Card, Visa.

NANAIMO, B.C.   **MAP 121**
BISTRO AT WESTWOOD LAKE   ☆☆
2367 Arbot Road   **$145**
(250) 753-2866

Christina Paterson runs this place with artistry and skill.
Her tables are elegant and her dining-room is filled with
a sense of space. The cooking is of a piece with the setting. At noon she has a wonderful quiche, followed perhaps by breast of chicken stuffed with wild mushrooms.
In the evening she'll have oven-roasted breast of duck
with raspberries, loin of venison crusted with juniper
berries and pan-seared fillet of salmon in beurre blanc.
You can't go wrong with any of her sweets.
Open Tuesday to Friday 11.30 am to 2.30 pm, 5 pm to 10 pm,
Saturday and Sunday 5 pm to 10 pm. Closed on Monday. Li-
censed. Master Card, Visa.

NANAIMO   **MAP 121**
CROW AND GATE PUB
2313 Yellow Point Road   **$90**
(250) 722-3731

When you arrive at the Crow and Gate Pub you think
you're in Yorkshire. It has the same dark beams, the wide
plank floors, the low ceilings, the family portraits. They
make a fine shepherd's pie, pan-fried oysters with homemade tartar sauce and leek and stilton quiche, all traditional Old Country dishes. There's a different special
every day of the week—on Monday it's burgers, on
Tuesday bangers and mash, on Wednesday roast beef and
Yorkshire pudding, on Thursday bouillabaisse, on Friday
roast lamb, on Saturday roast beef again, on Sunday pork
schnitzel. The regulars, however, seem to go for the stilton quiche almost any day of the week. And no wonder.

Open daily 11 am to 11 pm. Licensed. All cards. &

NANAIMO   **MAP 121**
GATEWAY TO INDIA
202 4 Street   **$85**
(250) 755-4037

There are several Indian restaurants in Nanaimo now, but this is still the best of them. It doesn't look much from the outside, but inside it's another matter. To start with, they have such vegetarian dishes as bengan bartha, mashed eggplant sautéed in spicy tomatoes and aloo gobi of cauliflower, onions and garlic. They have the usual pakoras and panirs, tandoori chicken and all the familiar biryanis. There are a few Indian beers and a handful of wines. The service is warm and leisurely.
Open Monday to Friday 11 am to 9 pm, Saturday and Sunday 4 pm to 9 pm. Licensed. Master Card, Visa. &

NANAIMO   **MAP 121**
THE HILLTOP   ☆
5281 Rutherford Road: Unit 102   **$135**
(250) 585-5337

At the Hilltop we usually start with either the smoked-halibut croquettes served with crème fraîche, saffron and roasted tomatoes or the Humboldt calamari with grilled shishitos. After that we recommend the braised bison with spinach and oyster mushrooms, the roasted Arctic char with shrimps and mussels in a tomato broth and the Qualicum Bay scallops with braised organic chard, chorizo and horseradish. Ryan Zuvich has a rare talent and if you find yourself in Nanaimo you should come and see what he has to offer.
Open Wednesday to Sunday 5 pm to 11 pm. Closed on Monday and Tuesday. Licensed. Master Card, Visa. Book ahead if you can.

If you use an out-of-date edition and find it inaccurate, don't blame us. Buy a new edition.

NANAIMO   **MAP 121**
TWO CHEFS AFFAIR
123B Commercial Street   **$55**
(250) 591-4656

The Two Chefs closes in mid-afternoon, but they have a
very good breakfast, unless you want champagne with
your omelette. Most people order the eggs benedict with
a light and lemony hollandaise sauce, but we generally
find ourselves asking for the French toast, which is made
with rich egg bread, pumpkin and cinnamon topped with
real maple syrup. For lunch we suggest the pulled pork
with lettuce slaw or the local mussels steamed in apple
cider. We like both.
*Open Tuesday to Friday 8 am to 4.30 pm, Saturday and Sunday
8 am to 3 pm. Closed on Monday. No liquor. Master Card,
Visa.*

NANAIMO
See also CEDAR, LANTZVILLE.

NELSON, B.C.   **MAP 122**
ALL SEASONS CAFE   ☆
620 Herridge Lane   **$135**
(250) 352-0101

Nelson has been lovingly restored to the glory of its gold-
rush days, and it's an ideal base from which to explore the
Kootenays. At nearby Whitewater it also has some of the
best powder skiing in the country. We'll never forget the
excitement of discovering the All Seasons Café in a century-old house, hidden in a lane behind the main street,
with its tremendous list of Okanagan wines. Tracy Scan-
lon and Jonathan Langille couldn't put a foot wrong in
the kitchen. But in a few short years they were both gone.
Paul Archambault has owned the place for some time,
but the cooking rapidly became so inconsistent that we
dropped it from the guide. Since then, Amanda Skidmore
has put a whole new face on the kitchen. Her menu is
short, but everything seems to work. Her best dish is the

154

curried West Coast halibut. She also has several vegetarian dishes, some of them gluten-free. Her steak is expensive at 37.00, but her lamb shanks and duck breast, both raised on local farms, are perfectly prepared. Be sure to come early (with a booking).

Open daily 5 pm to 11 pm. Licensed. Master Card, Visa. Book ahead. &

NEW GLASGOW, N.S.   **MAP 123**
BaKED FOOD CAFE
209 Provost Street   **$60**
(902) 755-3107

This is a delightful little café that makes the most of the local, the seasonal, and the healthy. They have a great number of vegetarian dishes and make all their sandwiches on their own ciabatta bread. The daily special may be something like a chicken burger, served on an English muffin with a Thai sauce, tomato and green cabbage. The helpings are small and the sweets are really small. The coffee is made with freshly ground beans, one cup at a time. In the morning they serve a fine breakfast that starts with an omelette, made with a variety of fillings, among them ham, peppers, green onions, mushrooms and cheese.

Open Tuesday to Saturday 8 am to 5 pm. Closed on Sunday and Monday. Licensed. Master Card, Visa.

NEW GLASGOW   **MAP 123**
THE BISTRO   ☆☆
216 Archimedes Street   **$125**
(902) 752-4988

Robert Vinton bought the Bistro some fifteen years ago with his wife, Heather Poulin. During the first year, when the place was being renovated, the couple became involved with the local arts community. Every three months they still put on an exhibition of work in progress. There's always a public reception, with an abundance of appetizers supplied by the restaurant. This procedure hasn't changed since they opened in 2002. Nothing has, not even the staff. But Heather changes the wine-list every month to match changes in the menu. Vinton's meat is all organic and local, and you often see him in town shopping for one or more of the daily specials. He's usually at his best with fish, especially salmon, scallops and mussels. Salmon has been harder to get recently and so is more likely to appear as a daily special. The seafood paella is a better buy than the rack of lamb, which costs 36.00. The vegetables are all cooked to perfection and sticky-toffee pudding is almost always on offer.

Open Tuesday to Saturday 5 pm to 9 pm. Closed on Sunday and Monday. Licensed. All cards. Book ahead.

NEW GLASGOW   MAP 123
THE DOCK
130 George Street   **$90**
(902)752-0884

The Dock occupies an old stone house built in 1845. It's very inexpensive, offering seafood chowder for 5.25 and ginger chicken with orange for only a few dollars more. They're proud of their fresh haddock, served blackened Creole-style. Mussels they serve either straight or Thai-style, with Irish soda bread. They have a number of local craft beers and a couple of wines from Lindeman.

Open Monday to Wednesday 11.30 am to 10 pm, Thursday to Saturday 11.30 am to midnight, Sunday 11.30 am to 8 pm. Licensed. Amex, Master Card, Visa. &

NEW GLASGOW   MAP 123
WEST SIDE BISTRO
142 Stellarton Road   **$70**
(902) 755-9378

Phil Castle prepares everything here in an open kitchen. His wife, Darlene, runs the front of the house. The menu offers soup with salads or sandwiches. There's also pasta (penne with stir-fried rice), gluten-free dishes and daily specials like fishcakes and quiches. Darlene makes all the sweets, among them apple-and-cranberry pie, rhubarb pie and pumpkin cheesecake. The wines are few and far between. There are just two from Australia, one from Germany and one from Canada, plus half a dozen beers. *Open Tuesday to Friday 11.30 am to 2.30 pm, 5 pm to 8 pm, Saturday 5 pm to 8 pm. Closed on Sunday and Monday. Licensed. Visa.*

NEW GLASGOW
See also PICTOU, STELLARTON.

NEW GLASGOW, P.E.I. (MAP 37)
OLDE GLASGOW MILL ☆
5592 Highway 13 **$100**
(902) 964-3313

Emily Wells was the chef at the Dunes in Brackley Beach (see above) for many years before she left to open her own restaurant. This is it. Her cooking at the Olde Glasgow Mill is wonderful, perhaps even better than it used to be in Brackley Beach. The ribs are amazing and the haddock and the halibut are both beautifully cooked. The vegetables are all fresh and imaginative. And there's a takeout counter where you can buy baked goods and salads of all sorts.
Open daily 11.30 am to 4 pm, 5 pm to 9.30 pm from mid-May until mid-October. Licensed. Master Card, Visa. Book ahead if you can.

NIAGARA-ON-THE-LAKE, Ontario MAP 125
HOBNOB ☆
The Charles Inn **$150**
209 Queen Street
(866) 556-8883

The dining-room at the Charles Inn is now known as Hobnob, but Steve Sperling is still the chef and his meals still begin with scallops, potato gnocchi and seared foie gras. The foie gras is an interesting dish, marrying carrot purée and pickled carrots with shallot marmalade. Main

157

dishes run to pork and beef, chicken and salmon. The chicken and asparagus, the salmon with quinoa, bok choy and sunchokes. The wines are all grown in the Niagara Region. Most of them are fairly priced, though the Lailey reserve cabernet sauvignon is not. It costs 128.00 a bottle and the Tawse Robyn's Block only a little less at 92.00. Steam Whistle beer is on draft and there are two excellent half-bottles of local wine, one from Twenty Mile Bench at 27.00, the other from Tawse at 39.00. There are twelve comfortable bedrooms at the Charles Inn, which is a good place to stay.

Open daily noon to 2.30 pm, 4 pm to 8.30 pm from 1 May until 31 October, Monday to Friday 4 pm to 8.30 pm, Saturday and Sunday noon to 2.30 pm, 4 pm to 8.30 pm from 1 November until 30 April. Licensed. Amex, Master Card, Visa. Book ahead if you can.

NIAGARA–ON–THE–LAKE   MAP 125
RAVINE VINEYARD
1366 York Road   **$110**
St. David's
(905) 262-8463

Ravine is no longer open all day. Lunch is served from 11 to 3, dinner from 5 to 9. The appetizers—raw oysters, soup and a mixed salad with beets—are inviting and so are the main dishes. The menu is short but features such things as steamed mussels with ginger and cilantro and pan-roasted Arctic char with sorrel mayonnaise. The best of the sweets this year is, we think, the lemon mousse. The wines come from the Ravine vineyards and they're all modestly priced, costing about 40.00 a bottle or 10.00 a glass.

Open daily 11 am to 3 pm, 5 pm to 9 pm. Licensed. Master Card, Visa. &

The price rating shown opposite the headline of each entry indicates the average cost of dinner for two with a modest wine, tax and tip. The cost of dinner, bed and breakfast (if available) is shown in parentheses.

NIAGARA-ON-THE-LAKE   MAP 125
TREADWELL   ☆
114 Queen Street   **$120**
(905) 934-9797

Treadwell seems cheaper this year. The main dishes are all priced at little more than 20.00 at noon, appetizers at little more than 15.00. There's a selection of house-made charcuterie for only 23.00. Crisp-skinned mackerel costs no more than steamed mussels with chardonnay and rather less than Digby scallops and pork belly with cauliflower and honey. Cumbrae supplies the kitchen with beef, lamb and pork, Marc Eber with mushrooms, Whitty Farms with fruit and Monforte Dairy with goat's-milk and sheep's-milk cheeses. The wines are all local except for a vouvray and a few wines from Russian River. The best of the Niagara wines, in our opinion, are the Cave Spring riesling and the cabernet from Organized Crime.

Open Monday and Tuesday 5 pm to 10 pm, Wednesday to Saturday 11.30 am to 2.30 pm, 5 pm to 10 pm, Sunday 11.30 am to 2.30 pm (brunch). Amex, Master Card, Visa. ♿

NORANDA, Quebec
See ROUYN.

NORRIS POINT, Newfoundland   (MAP 164)
JUSTIN THYME
216 Main Street   **$105**
(709) 458-2326

Many travellers think this is the best place to eat in Norris Point, which is in the heart of Gros Morne National Park. Justin George and his wife, Lynn, spent sixteen years working in the hotel business before opening their own place here. The dining-room isn't large, the furnishings are plain and parking may be difficult. But Justin George could melt the hardest heart; he cooks well too and his prices are reasonable. The main dishes are chalked up on a blackboard every day, but there's also a printed menu.

The mussels are really remarkable. For that matter, all the fish and shellfish is superb, especially the cod and the seafood chowder. Justin serves meat and poultry as well, and in fact our favourite is the duck with ginger and orange. At noon he concentrates on sandwiches—Montreal smoked meat and chicken with brie. His coffee is outstanding.

Open Monday and Wednesday to Sunday 11 am to 9 pm from mid-May until mid-October. Closed on Tuesday. Licensed. No cards. Book ahead if you can. &

NORRIS POINT   (MAP 164)
THE BLACK SPRUCE
Neddie's Harbour Inn   **$160 ($395)**
7 Beach Road
(709) 458-3089

Neddie's Harbour Inn is a boutique hotel with stunning views of the bay and the mountains beyond. In the Black Spruce Jason Lynch offers a short but rather expensive menu that everyone seems to admire. Tenderloin of beef is the heart of the list, but you can also be sure of the market fish and the lobster-and-scallop platter. If you like you can start with the house pâté or the seafood chowder (the kitchen brings in fresh fish every day). Continue with potato gnocchi and finish with figgy duff and molasses. Everything is made from scratch and the presentation and service are fully professional.

Open Tuesday to Sunday 5 pm to 9 pm from mid May until mid-October. Closed on Monday. Licensed. All cards. &

NORTHEAST MARGAREE, N.S.   (MAP 151)
THE DANCING GOAT
6289 Cabot Trail   **$45**
Cape Breton
(902) 248-2727

The Dancing Goat is a real find. It's always full, though they've moved and have new owners. The kitchen staff hasn't changed and they still have no table service. You go up to the counter, choose what you want from the blackboard and take a number to your table. Every day they have two homemade soups—curried chicken, perhaps, or parsnip with apple. There's always a quiche and there are also a number of sandwiches, all made on thick, home-baked bread with crusts on. There's usually chicken with almonds and (our favourite) bacon with avocado. There's espresso and caffe latte to go with your sandwich and they're both good. You can take the oatcakes and the maple shortbread home with you if you like. There may be no liquor here, but there's just about everything else.

Open Monday to Wednesday 7.30 am to 5 pm, Thursday and Friday 7.30 am to 8 pm, Saturday 7.30 am to 5 pm, Sunday 8 am to 5 pm. No liquor. Master Card, Visa. &

OKANAGAN CENTRE, B.C.   (MAP 91)
GRAPEVINE
Gray Monk Estate Winery   **$140**
1055 Camp Road
(250) 766-3405

Here it's hard to choose between the venison meatloaf in a reduction of red wine with house-made pear chutney and the Fraser Valley duck confit with cranberry-onion marmalade and homemade spaetzle. Don't hesitate. Despite appearances, the venison meatloaf is much the better of the two. The sweets are all lovely, especially the cheesecake topped with fresh seasonal fruit. Grapevine is still run by Willi Franz and René Haudenschild, and they're as good as ever.

Open daily 11.30 am to 4 pm, 5 pm to 9 pm from 1 April until 31 October. Licensed. Master Card, Visa. &

Every restaurant in this guide has been personally tested. Our reporters are not allowed to identify themselves to the management or to accept free meals. We accept no advertisements. We accept no payment for listings. We depend entirely on you. Recommend the book to your friends.

OLIVER, B.C. (MAP 140)
MIRADORO
Tinhorn Creek Vineyard **$140**
32830 Tinhorn Creek Road
(250) 498-3742

This is probably the best of the winery restaurants in B.C. Jeff Van Geest makes skilful and abundant use of local organic produce in all his meals. The setting of the dining-room is elegant and the views of the Okanagan Valley are really impressive. The menu is Mediterranean in style, inspired by the cuisines of Italy, Spain and Portugal. Lunch is ambitious, featuring lingcod with brown butter and capers and braised duck with sage spaetzle and spiced wine gel. For dinner they offer bison carpaccio and beef and pork meatballs, followed by hand-made noodles with foraged mushrooms. The dry-aged grilled steak is said to be excellent, but we haven't yet tried it. The best of the sweets is the hazelnut cake with fruit preserves, birch syrup and vanilla-bean gelato.
Open daily 11 am to 3 pm, 5.30 pm to 9 pm. Licensed. Master Card, Visa. &

OLIVER (MAP 140)
TERRAFINA
Hester Creek Estate Winery
Road 8
(250) 498-2229

Terrafina's 47-seat restaurant on the Golden Mile Bench in the heart of wine country offers Tuscan-style food served with fresh local ingredients in an intimate, rustic environment. We like to start with a green salad flavoured with Poplar Grove cheese, followed by braised pork cheeks with roasted yam and parsnip or Fraser Valley breast of duck with green beans and white truffles. They also do nice wood-fired pizzas in the evening, and there's a potato-and-truffle pizza at noon. Their brunches are always excellent—Tuscan egg benedict with prosciutto di Parma, tomato jam and brown-butter hollandaise. If you want to enjoy a glass or two of one of the Hester Creek wines with your meal, there's a shuttle that runs regularly between Osoyoos and the vineyard.

Open Wednesday to Saturday 11.30 am to 9 pm, Sunday 10 am to 4 pm. Closed on Monday and Tuesday. Licensed. Master Card, Visa. &

ORANGEVILLE, Ontario   MAP 131
FORAGE
163 1 Street $95
Credit Creek Plaza
(519) 942-3388

Restaurant One 99 has both ambition and style, but right now it's being made over. Meanwhile, there's Forage. Forage is pretty noisy and you certainly have to book ahead, because Matthew Jamieson and his wife, Wendy, brought a lot of people with them when they moved here from the Hockley Valley. It's quieter at noon, when it seems casual and even comfortable. The cooking is simple, but everything is professionally plated, fresh and carefully foraged. The prices are fair and all the wines are sold by the glass as well as the bottle. They go out of their way to accommodate vegetarians. We keep ordering the crab-cakes, but others prefer the seafood stew. Admittedly, the kitchen is good with fish, even the squid and the tuna tataki. Wendy makes all the sweets, the best of which, we think, is the flourless-chocolate cake with salted caramel. There are six craft beers, as well as several wines.

Open Monday to Saturday 11 am to 9 pm. Closed on Sunday. Licensed. Amex, Master Card, Visa. Book ahead if you can. &

ORILLIA, Ontario   MAP 132
WEBERS
8844 Highway 11 N $25
(705) 325-3696

Webers opened in 1963. After all these years, there's still a feeling of excitement about the place. Rock music is playing loudly on the soundtrack. Nobody waits too long, nobody is disappointed. Children play, lovers touch each other, tired drivers sit down, at peace, under a tree, somebody goes to the bathroom. Everyone is happy. Webers now has countless flavours of ice cream, and if you want a real old-fashioned milkshake you can get it at the ice-cream counter. Each week in summer they process and sell more than three tons of ground beef—at least 50 tons a summer. Their burgers are now packaged and sold in Metro and Loblaws. Their fries all come from potatoes grown, cut and packed in Prince Edward Island. Teenagers take your order, make change and see that you get what you want within two minutes, no matter how long the lineup may be. There's free parking for hundreds of cars on both sides of the highway, with an overhead walkway that connects the southbound lot to the restaurant. Webers bought the walkway from the CN Tower and it's the only privately owned bridge over a highway in the province of Ontario.

Open daily 10.30 am to 7 pm from mid–March until the end of December (later on weekends). No liquor, no cards. &

OSHAWA, Ontario   **MAP 133**
CYRUS   ☞
563 Ritson Road S   **$30**
(905) 448-0892

The Gallery restaurant is long gone. The best place to eat in Oshawa now is Cyrus, just off the 401. Cyrus, as its name implies, is Persian, which means that they cook halal. They buy the best ingredients on the market and cook them to order. Their signature dish is chicken shawarma, which is slow-cooked on a spit and marinated in any number of spices. It's a remarkable dish, but you should also know about the falafel, the lamb kebabs and the satziki.

Open Tuesday to Friday 11 am to 8 pm, Saturday noon to 9 pm. Closed on Sunday and Monday. No liquor. Master Card, Visa. Book ahead if you can.

Nobody but nobody can buy his way into this guide.

OTTAWA, Ontario   **MAP 134**
ALLIUM
87 Holland Avenue   **$140**
(613) 792-1313

Lunch at Allium is simple and straightforward: chicken-fried snails, squid with pickled red onions, steak frites with smoked chilli, burgers with chipotle, shrimp wrap and roasted breast of duck. Dinner is more elaborate and on Monday they offer a big selection of tapas—pork belly with spinach and honey, scallops with quinoa and purple beets, tuna tataki with guacamole and lime and beef tartar with mustard mayonnaise. The wine-list is full of good buys, most of which come from the Niagara Region. Allium is at its best on Monday nights, but if you come on Monday you have to book ahead.
Open Monday 5 pm to 10 pm, Tuesday to Friday 11.30 am to 2 pm, 5 pm to 10 pm, Saturday 5 pm to 10 pm. Closed on Sunday. Licensed. Amex, Master Card, Visa.

OTTAWA   **MAP 134**
ATELIER   ☆
540 Rochester Street   **$325**
(613) 321 3537

From Tuesday to Saturday Mark Lepine is serving a twelve-course fixed-price menu of what he calls new Canadian food. His restaurant is at 540 Rochester Street; remember the number, because there's no other way of recognizing the place. The meal starts with a Chopin Waltz—coy names are part of the procedure—followed by a Shrimp Ring, Connect the Dots, You're Being Mighty Selfish, Winter Explosion and so on. The names become tiresome after a while. Each dish has a familiar ingredient (lingcod or shrimp, perhaps) attended by a variety of small tidbits (rutabaga or saffron, say). If you've come to celebrate a birthday or some other special occasion, they'll offer you a piece of cake in liquid nitrogen. Such a meal is expensive—dinner for two costs about 325.00 with a glass of wine. Is it worth it? That's for you

to decide.
Open Tuesday to Saturday 5 pm to 10 pm. Closed on Sunday and Monday. Licensed. All cards. You must book ahead.

OTTAWA   **MAP 134**
BECKTA   ☆
150 Elgin Street   **$225**
(613) 238-7063

Two years ago Beckta moved to the site of Friday's Roast Beef House on Elgin Street. The new setting is lovely, but the prices have risen dramatically. Dinner is now sold *prix-fixe* at 68.00 a head. For that you get three courses that start with torchon of foie gras or hamachi marinated in miso and go on to breast of chicken, triple-A steak or Alaska black cod with pomegranates. The meal ends with lemon upside-down cake or chocolate mud-pie. In the wine-bar, both lunch and dinner are served à la carte. As for the service, it's suave and very elegant.
Open Monday to Friday 11.30 am to 2 pm, 5.30 pm to 10 pm, Saturday and Sunday 5.30 pm to 10 pm. The wine-bar is open all day every day except Saturday and Sunday. Licensed. Amex, Master Card, Visa. Book ahead. ♿

OTTAWA   **MAP 134**
THE BLACK CAT   ☆
428 Preston Street   **$150**
(613) 569-9998

Patricia Larkin used nothing but the best ingredients in her kitchen and they, of course, are expensive. Richard Urquhart couldn't afford to keep her any longer, so she left, and was replaced by Michael Farber, who had closed Farbs some time before. The new menu features beef tartar, haddock, steelhead trout, rib-eye of beef and lamb shanks. We can no longer find the Frog's Leap or the Organized Crime on the wine-list, but the wines have all been chosen with real skill and care. Prices are reasonable and Richard Urquhart, who's been on the local scene longer than anyone else, never seems to get any older.

Open Tuesday to Thursday 5 pm to 9.30 pm, Friday and Saturday 5 pm to 10.30 pm. Closed on Sunday and Monday. Licensed. Amex, Master Card, Visa. Book ahead if you can. Free parking. ♿

OTTAWA   **MAP 134**
CARBEN
1100 Wellington Street W   **$145**
(613) 792-4000

Carben is a new restaurant in Hintonburg, just west of the city centre. It's named for its two founders, Kevin Benes and his wife, Caroline Ngo. Together they've built a short but interesting menu and an inexpensive wine-list. The menu starts with beet salad and runs through pork belly, wood-ear mushrooms, steak tartar and beef cheeks to Arctic char, duck, beef and rump of lamb. The cooking was awkward in their first summer, but has since settled down. Nothing is what you would expect. Wood-ear mushrooms, for instance, come with turmeric aioli and a miso glaze, beef cheeks with pickled cauliflower and wasabi, steak tartar with kimchee and taro-root crisps, scallops in a purée of edamame. Originality is simply an element (an important element) of Kevin Benes' style. The same is true of his choice of wines. There are no clichés on his wine-list, except perhaps the Appleby sauvignon blanc. When he wants a gewurztraminer he goes to Reif in Niagara; when he needs a good tempranillo he goes all the way to Spain.
Open Monday to Friday 5.30 pm to 10 pm, Saturday and Sunday 10.30 am to 2 pm (brunch), 5.30 pm to 10 pm. Licensed. Master Card, Visa.

OTTAWA   **MAP 134**
DATSUN   ☆
380 Elgin Street   **$125**
(613) 422-2800

This is where Matthew Carmichael has landed. Known as a brilliant chef at Eighteen, he hadn't really found him-

167

self again until now. Datsun has a good location at the foot of Elgin Street, right next door to El Camino, Carmichael's popular Mexican taco bar. It has a well-appointed interior, with bar stools that look like gigantic springs. It has an interesting menu, good presentation and good Asian cooking. Almost everything is hot and spicy. Start with spicy chicken wings, Japanese eggplant or tuna tartar furikake, wasabi and nori. If you can afford it, ask for the tuna sashimi with pickled ginger and yuzu ponzu. The most exciting of the big dishes is the green curry of pink shrimps and seared scallops. You can drink either sake or a craft beer. There are several of these, but we like Beau's best, which goes nicely with the deep-fried ice cream. Rumour has it that the Elgin Street restaurants are doing well enough for Carmichael and his partner Jordan Holley to expand up to the Sparks Street mall, where they are turning an old bank building into a more upscale dining-room tentatively called Riviera (both chefs have a passion for seventies cars).

Open Monday to Saturday 5.30 pm to 11 pm. Closed on Sunday. Licensed. Master Card, Visa. Book ahead. &

OTTAWA   **MAP 134**
EIGHTEEN   ☆
18 York Street   **$180**
(613) 244-1188

Meals come more quickly here than they used to and prices are lower. The menu has changed too and they now offer such things as raw oysters, corn chowder, Quebec foie gras and a brand-new version of albacore tuna. Black cod can still be had (with miso); roasted partridge, rib-eye steak and Ontario lamb are still on the menu. But the cooking has lost some of its former excitement, though the service is as impressive as ever. Once a two-star kitchen, this must now settle for one.

Open Monday to Saturday 5 pm to 10 pm. Closed on Sunday. Licensed. Amex, Master Card, Visa. Book ahead.

Every restaurant in this guide has been personally tested.

OTTAWA   **MAP 134**
FAUNA
425 Bank Street   **$100**
(613) 563-2862

Fauna is a late-night restaurant—the only one in Ottawa.
Not that you have to start your dinner after midnight. In
the early evening they offer marvellous bison tartar, followed by scallops with chorizo. Sausages don't go with
scallops, of course, but chorizo is all the fashion nowadays. The sweets too are daring and memorable. Try the
pear-and-apple tart with salted caramel—it's a rare and
exciting dish. Hours are long and prices are low. But the
service can be painfully slow. Fauna's owner Jon Svazas
recently took over the space occupied by George Mon-
sour's Back Lane Café at 1087 Wellington Street W in
Hintonburg, and he plans to open a wood-burning Spanish tapas bar there.
Open Monday to Wednesday 11.30 am to 2 pm, 5.30 pm to 10
pm, Thursday to Saturday 11.30 am to 2 pm, 5.30 pm to mid-
night, Sunday 5.30 pm to 10 pm. Licensed. Master Card, Visa.
Book ahead if you can.

OTTAWA   **MAP 134**
FRASER CAFE   ☆
7 Springfield Road   **$140**
(613) 749-1444

You can usually get a table here in the late evening, when
they offer cheese and charcuterie and oysters on the half-
shell from St.-Simon, impeccably cleaned, chilled and
served with horseradish. The menu changes with the seasons, but you can normally count on beef with fries,
salmon, Cornish game hen, halibut and tuna. In 2015
Fraser's opened a second restaurant called The Rowan at
915 Bank Street (telephone (613) 780-9292). It's similar
but cheaper. Fraser's has Ross and Simon Fraser and, for
that reason if for no other, is the better of the two.
Open Monday to Friday 11.30 am to 2 pm, 5.30 pm to 10 pm,
Saturday 10 am to 2 pm (brunch), 5.30 pm to 10 pm, Sunday

10 am to 2 pm (brunch). Licensed. Amex, Master Card, Visa.
Book ahead.

OTTAWA   **MAP 134**
NAVARRA   ☆
93 Murray Street   **$190**
(613) 241-5500

The cooking here is basically Mexican—with a difference. It's true that they still offer mole of pulled lamb
shank, but if you prefer something like tuna sashimi or
Iberico ham, just ask for it. The tuna sashimi comes with
parsnip jam and pickled sunchokes, but the Iberico ham
is disappointing. There's usually pan-roasted trout with
tarragon mayonnaise to follow, breast of duck with
Granny Smith apples and beef tartar with charred pepper.
We don't admire the crème brûlée; the chocolate terrine
with campari and strawberry ice cream is, we think, a better choice. The dining-room is as awkward as ever, but
that can't be helped. The service is always reliable.
Open Tuesday 4 pm to 10 pm, Wednesday to Saturday 5.30 pm
to 10 pm, Sunday 10.30 am to 2.30 pm. Closed on Monday.
Licensed. Amex, Master Card, Visa. Book ahead.

OTTAWA   **MAP 134**
THE POMEROY HOUSE   ☆
749 Bank Street   **$180**
(613) 237-1658

The Pomeroy House got its maîtrise d'hôtel, Lindsay
Gordon, from Fraser's. The chef, Richard Wilson, came
from Beckta, where he was the sous-chef. They have a
small menu, with seven appetizers and four main dishes.
Their strategy is to take a mainstream dish and quicken
it by adding a dissonant ingredient. The most spectacular
case is their torchon of foie gras, which is seasoned with
braised cherries, a daring and delightful manoeuvre.
Their parsnip soup is flavoured with pickled shiitake
mushrooms, their so-called grey owl with pickled pomegranates, their smoked mackerel with jalapeno, their

duck confit with rye berries, their fries with smoked salt,
their beef with chimichurri. Dissonance is an unusual
strategy, but it makes the Pomeroy House what it is.
Open Tuesday to Saturday 11.30 am to 2 pm, 5.30 pm to 10
pm, Sunday 5.30 pm to 9 pm. Closed on Monday. Licensed,
Master Card, Visa. Book ahead if you can.

OTTAWA   **MAP 134**
SIDEDOOR
18B York Street   **$125**
(613) 562-9331

Sidedoor was opened as a cheaper alternative to Eighteen.
Like Eighteen, it's all rough stone and glass. The menu is
basically Mexican, though the tacos aren't made with
corn. They're white and soft, and at noon there isn't
much else. In the evening there are five or six tacos,
served as appetizers, followed by salt-and-pepper squid
and poached lobster in green curry. For sweet there's
nothing but doughnuts, but there's an ambitious wine-
list as well as several sakes.
Open daily 11.15 am to 2 pm, 5 pm to 10 pm. Licensed. Amex,
Master Card, Visa.

OTTAWA   **MAP 134**
SIGNATURES
453 Laurier Avenue E   **$165**
(613) 236-2499

Signatures occupies a fine old house at the eastern end of
Laurier Avenue. It's an old-fashioned place and none of
the waiters wear T-shirts and none sport tattoos. The
dining-room is run by the Cordon Bleu school of cookery and the menu is thoroughly French. Meals start with
sautéed snails in a purée of celery or a terrine of black
trumpet mushrooms served country-style. Or you may
be lucky enough to be offered white-asparagus soup with
pancetta and green-asparagus foam. Best of all is the albacore tuna with miso hollandaise and marinated daikon.

171

The main dishes are on the whole less adventurous. There's loin of venison in a grand-veneur sauce, smoked sturgeon, breast of duck glazed with soya and maple syrup and fillet of white salmon with a grenaille of potato and spring cabbage. Dignity is everything at Signatures, dignity and tradition. Prices are quite modest, especially for wine.

Open Wednesday to Friday 11.30 am to 1 pm, 5.30 pm to 9 pm, Saturday 5.30 pm to 9 pm. Closed Sunday to Tuesday. Licensed. Amex, Master Card, Visa. Free parking. Book ahead. &

OTTAWA   **MAP 134**
WELLINGTON GASTROPUB
1325 Wellington Street W   **$135**
(613) 729-1315

The Wellington Gastropub may be simple, but it's very cheap. At noon they have beef short-ribs, sea scallops and pork meatballs. In the evening they add breast of duck, pan-seared salmon and grainy-mustard spaetzle. Most of these dishes come to the table with black beans or lentils. The ice creams are all first class and there are always some excellent artisanal cheeses. They actually make several of their own beers and one of them, the Eddie Double D, contains 9.2 percent alcohol, which is double what you get in the commercial product. They also have thirteen craft beers on tap, including two from Gravenhurst, two from Barrie and one from Calabogie. So far as we know, there's nothing else like this in Ottawa.

Open Monday to Friday 11.30 am to 2 pm, 5.30 pm to 10 pm. Saturday 5.30 pm to 10 pm Closed on Sunday. Licensed. Amex, Master Card, Visa. Book ahead if you can.

OTTAWA   **MAP 134**
WHALESBONE   ☆
430 Bank Street   **$195**
(613) 231-8569

Whalesbone may be crowded and noisy, but it also supplies fresh fish and shellfish to the whole city, keeping some of the best for themselves. A dinner here may start with raw oysters, albacore-tuna tataki with apple and ginger, clam chowder, mussels with coconut, garlic and lime and raw sea-bass with kimchee and sesame yuzu. Main dishes are equally exciting. There's mackerel with smoked tomato, salmon with eggplant and sage and yellowfin tuna with radishes. Wine is served in toothbrush glasses, but don't get the idea that Whalesbone is cheap. It's not. It's rough but it's not cheap. Joshua Bishop is about to open a second restaurant at 231 Elgin Street, with three times the capacity of the Bank Street location, and time will tell if he can do this well again.

Open Monday to Friday 11.30 am to 2 pm, 5 pm to 11 pm, Saturday and Sunday 5 pm to 11 pm. Licensed. Amex, Master Card, Visa. Book ahead.

OTTAWA
See also CHELSEA.

OWEN SOUND, Ontario   **MAP 135**
THE FLYING CHESTNUT
199 Pellisier Street   **$100**
Eugenia
(519) 924-1809

To get to Eugenia, turn off Highway 26 at Thornbury and drive south on Highway 13 almost as far as Highway 4. This is the heart of Blue Mountain country, where you can go fishing on Lake Eugenia or visit Eugenia Falls, second only in height to the falls at Niagara. Shawn Adler has installed a big wood-burning stove in his kitchen and dedicated it to regional, organic cooking—even his beer and wine are local. Every night three appetizers and three main dishes are written up on a blackboard. Usually there's one fish, one meat and a vegetarian dish. The menu changes every week, but dinner usually ends with bread pudding, butter tarts or a fruit crumble. The Sunday brunch offers omelettes, pancakes and waffles for about 15.00, and portions are very generous. The dinner on Sunday is *prix fixe* and costs 40.00.

*Open Thursday to Saturday 5 pm to 10 pm, Sunday 11 am to 2
pm (brunch), 5 pm to 10 pm. Closed Monday to Wednesday.
Licensed. No cards. Book ahead if you can.*

PARRSBORO, N.S.   MAP 137
THE PORCHLIGHT
138 Main Street   **$65**
(902) 728-3330

The PorchLight is small, intimate and friendly. It's owned
by Mitch and Kim White—he cooks, she serves (and
makes friends). Most of their ingredients are local, helpings are big and prices are low. They're renowned for
their hamburgers, which are huge and weigh about nine
ounces. The biggest is the so-called Grand Baby Burger.
It comes with two patties, two thick slices of cheddar
cheese and six rashers of bacon—and costs 12.00. But our
favourite is the Teddy Alexander, which has two grilled-
cheese sandwiches on a bun; it's made with four different
cheeses, sautéed mushrooms, onions and bacon. All the
pies and crisps are baked on the premises, and the apple
crisp is just as good as any your grandmother used to
make.
*Open Monday to Thursday 11 am to 7 pm, Friday and Saturday
7 am to 7 pm, Sunday 10 am to 7 pm. Licensed. Master Card,
Visa.* &

PEMBROKE, Ontario   MAP 138

*Most of the restaurants in Pembroke confine themselves to lunch.
The Nook Crêperie at 26 Pembroke Street W (telephone (613)
735-4800) serves ten savoury crêpes and thirteen sweet crêpes.
You can make a dinner out of one of these (the lox or the
Michelangelo). In season, we go for the Voltaire (marinated beef
with asparagus and goat-cheese), plus a soup or a salad, for just
24.00. It's open all day every day but Sunday, when it's open
only in the morning, and Monday, when it's closed all day. It has
a licence and takes most cards. Janna's Gallery Café at 20 Pembroke Street W (telephone (613) 631-0443) is known for its*

coffee and its sweets. It's open all day every day but Sunday, has a licence and takes most cards. Then there's Ullrich's on Main at 214 Pembroke Street W (telephone (613) 735-6025), which started out years ago as a butcher's shop, branched out first into groceries, then into a deli and finally into a lunchroom, open from 11 am to 2 pm every day but Sunday. They offer two soups, a chicken quesadilla and a number of salads and sandwiches. Their chocolate cake is very good indeed and the service is quick and friendly. They have a licence and take most cards. &

PENETANG, Ontario   **MAP 139**
FROTH CAFE   ☆
102 Main Street   **$60**
(705) 549-7199

The trouble with Froth is that it's not open in the evenings and takes no credit cards. But after all, the glory of the restaurant is in its baking. Altogether they make thirty different kinds of bread, and if you're lucky, your bread will still be warm from the oven when you eat it. Recently they added bagels and cheddar biscuits with jalapeno. Already they were making hazelnut bread with pears and figs, pumpkin bread and apple bread with pecans. Apart from bread, they offer a good breakfast and a very good lunch, with soups, sandwiches, burgers, quiches and some really remarkable salads, the best of which is the fresh berry-and-pecan salad with a poppy-seed dressing. Their coffee is made with soy, but we haven't yet tried it.
Open Tuesday to Saturday 8 am to 6 pm, Sunday 9 am to 4 pm. Closed on Monday. Licensed. No cards.

PENETANG
See also WYEBRIDGE.

This is a guide to Canadian restaurants from coast to coast—the first ever published and the only one of its kind on the market today. We accept no advertisements. Nobody can buy his way into this guide and nobody can buy his way out.

PENTICTON, B.C.   **MAP 140**
VANILLA POD
Poplar Grove Winery   **$180**
425 Middle Bench Road
(250) 493-9463

Poplar Grove has always been known for its fine white
wines and for its great cheeses. Now they've opened an
excellent restaurant as well. They start their dinners with
a pickled mushroom salad or mussels in a tomato-and-
fennel broth, followed by steelhead trout with a potato-
and-spinach salad. They're good with salmon and halibut
when either is available on the local market. When
they're not, ask for the rack of pork or the breast of duck.
There's also a four-course tasting menu for only 55.00.
Open Tuesday to Sunday 11.30 am to 2 pm, 5 pm to 9 pm.
Closed on Monday. Licensed. Amex, Master Card, Visa. Book
ahead.

PENTICTON
See also OLIVER.

PERCE, Quebec   **MAP 141**
AUBERGE LE COIN DU BANC
345 route 132 e   **$150**
(418) 645-2907

The Coin du Banc is not everyone's cup of tea. It's housed
in an old frame building four miles north of Percé on
route 132. Everything seems to need a fresh coat of paint.
The place is littered with hurricane lanterns, ships' models, wood stoves and primitive artwork. It's open all day
and has a wonderful breakfast that features pain doré,
fresh-squeezed orange-juice, foie de morue and the lightest of crêpes, served with real maple syrup. Every day
they put on a dinner featuring escargots de bourgogne,
smoked salmon and a shrimp omelette, followed by cod
three ways, scallops and steamed lobster.
Open daily 8 am to 10 pm from 1 June until 30 September. Li-
censed. Amex, Master Card, Visa.

PERCE   **MAP 141**
LA MAISON MATHILDE
Auberge les Trois Soeurs   **$120**
77 route 132
(800) 463-9700

La Maison Mathilde is a small, rather pretty house attached to a sixty-room hotel. Look for it at the east end
of the village, overlooking the beach, the sea and the
rock. They have a three-course menu specializing in fish
and shellfish (including lobster). Everything—the
poached salmon, the seafood pastry, even the tomato
soup—is beautifully presented and full of flavour, and
the whole meal costs less than 50.00 a head. The tables
tend to fill up quickly, so book ahead. We have found the
service brisk, but others have had long waits. Everyone
agrees, however, that the food should be served hotter.
*Open daily 7 am to 11.30 am, 4 pm to 10 pm from mid-June
until the end of September. Licensed. Visa. Book ahead.*

PERTH, Ontario   **MAP 142**
FIELD HOUSE   ☆
43 Herriott Street   **$40**
(613) 267-7474

It's almost ten years since we recommended a restaurant
in Perth. The Field House is basically a takeout. It has just
four bar-stools inside and a small patio outside, open only
in summer. It closes early, like the old Hungry Planet.
And like the Hungry Planet, it keeps a close eye on every
detail. People like to say that it has the best bakery in the
county. Actually, everything is good and everything is
cheap, perhaps because the chef got his start at Whalesbone in Ottawa (see above). The kitchen offers a great variety of sandwiches, all made on their own crusty bread.
The coffee is wonderful, but there's no liquor. Instead,
ask for a glass of old-fashioned soda or a bottle of root
beer.
*Open Tuesday to Friday 8 am to 4 pm, Saturday 10 am to 3 pm.
Closed on Sunday and Monday. No liquor. Master Card, Visa.*

PERTH-ANDOVER, N.B. MAP 143
WATERFRONT CAFE
878 Perth Main Street **$90**
(506) 273-2878

Perth-Andover meant York's for so many years that it
feels strange to start looking elsewhere. But the Waterfront Café gives pleasure to everyone who crosses its
doorstep—or would if only it kept longer hours. The
chef serves dishes that look as good as they taste. That
doesn't mean high prices and small helpings. A brunch
with a choice of eggs can be had for only 10.00. Diners
find the flavours amazing, whether it's salmon cakes with
a composed salad, jumbo shrimp with cranberry and
goat-cheese, prime rib of beef with red wine or Atlantic
salmon with hollandaise sauce. You can finish your meal
with poached pears or New York cheesecake. Either will
cost you just 5.00.
Open Wednesday and Thursday 9 am to 4 pm, Friday 8 am to
8 pm, Saturday and Sunday 9 am to 4 pm. Closed on Monday
and Tuesday. Licensed. Master Card, Visa. Book ahead if you
can.

PETERBOROUGH, Ontario MAP 144
☆☆
ELEMENTS
140 King Street **$140**
(705) 876-1116

Nothing is delivered at the door to Elements. They buy
most of their fresh produce from local farmers. What
they can't buy locally, Norman Howard, the owner, forages for himself. Their menu is seasonal, inspired by the
cuisine of Spain. That means a satsuma salad, terrine of
rabbit, venison carpaccio and pinchos—spicy lamb and
pork served on a salad of cucumber, apple and onion
dressed in kaffir milk. Main courses are almost equally
interesting. There's Moroccan chicken, pork tenderloin
pan-roasted with chestnuts, fresh sage and blood orange.
There's always a triple-A steak on the menu and also a
vegetarian croquette made with garbanzo, quinoa, leeks,

178

white turnips, local greens and oriental sprouts. The sweets are all made on the premises, even the Spanish crème caramel with honey and fresh figs. Most of the wines come from Spain or Portugal.
Open daily 11.30 am to 11 pm. Licensed. All cards. &

PICTON, Ontario　　　　　　　　　　**MAP 145**
BLUMEN GARDEN　　　　　　　　　　　☆
647 Highway 49　　　　　　　　　　**$140**
(613) 476-6841

The Blumen Garden is a few miles from Picton on Highway 49. It's owned and run by Andreas Feller, who has a short menu with five or six appetizers and eight or nine main courses. Start with pan-seared crab-cakes or walnut gnudi with merguez sausage, chanterelles, apricots and spinach and go on to any one of several familiar bistro dishes—pulled rabbit over house-made gnocchi, lightly-seared salmon with potato rostii or braised lamb shank in a barley risotto with savoy cabbage and garlic. There's at least one interesting sweet—dulce de leche bread pudding with passion-fruit ice cream. The wines are mostly local and there are several local beers and a local cider on tap.
Open Monday and Thursday to Sunday 11.30 am to 2 pm, 5 pm to 9.30 pm from 1 April until 15 October. Closed on Tuesday and Wednesday. Licensed. All cards. &

PICTON　　　　　　　　　　　　　**MAP 145**
GAZEBO
Waupoos Estate Winery　　　　　　　**$140**
3016 County Road 8
(613) 476-8338

The Gazebo was started with a view to displaying the Waupoos Estate wines, and it does just that. But it's also a restaurant able to stand on its own feet, and in recent years it's been expanded more than once. We've always liked the seared scallops with lime marmalade. The main dishes on the whole we find less inviting. There are lamb burgers, chicken panini, a couple of pastas, fresh fish and steak. The menu is more ambitious in the evening, offering pan-fried local pickerel, breast of duck with shiitake quinoa and an escalope of veal with wild mushrooms. There are some in-house sweets, but you may do better with the plate of local cheeses. The wines all come from the Waupoos vineyards, several of which are sold by the glass as well as the bottle.

Open Wednesday and Thursday 11.30 am to 3 pm, Friday to Sunday 11.30 am to 3 pm, 5 pm to 9 pm from mid–May until mid–October. Closed on Monday and Tuesday. Licensed. Master Card, Visa. Book ahead if you can.

PICTON   MAP 145

MERRILL INN
343 Main Street E   **$150**
(866) 567-5969

The Merrill Inn is a grand old mansion right on Highway 49. The restaurant is tucked way at the back and is open only for dinner. Amy and Edward Shubert came here with impressive credentials and before long they had hired an equally impressive chef named Michael Sullivan. His meals usually start with shrimp-and-scallop gratin, or sometimes with smoked trout and radish slaw. There's always some fish to follow, as well as rack of lamb, beef tenderloin and perhaps breast of duck. Our favourite sweet is the chocolate cake. The wines are mostly local, and they have four beers and a local cider on tap. The service is old-fashioned and very friendly.

Open Tuesday to Saturday 5.30 pm to 9 pm. Closed on Sunday and Monday. Licensed. Amex, Master Card, Visa.

PICTON

See also BLOOMFIELD, WELLINGTON.

Where an entry is printed in italics this indicates that the restaurant has been listed only because it serves the best food in its area or because it hasn't yet been adequately tested.

PICTOU, N.S. (MAP 123)
STONE-SOUP CAFE
41 Water Street $80
(902) 485-4949

The Stone-Soup Cafe has been in business for only about
five years, but already it's attracted a big local following.
Barry Rundle and Camille Davidson have a generous
menu that's served all day until 8 o'clock in the evening.
Everything is prepared in-house except the bread and
bread-rolls, which come in daily from a local bakery. For
breakfast there's eggs benedict and a waffle, prepared on
weekends by Barry and Camille's teen-age son. At
lunchtime there's always a good soup, often cream-of-
wild-mushroom. If there are no wild mushrooms to be
had, ask for the seafood chowder. Next comes a variety
of sandwiches—poached salmon on a bagel, perhaps, or
a Thai-style chicken wrap. For dinner (if you come early)
there's usually some fish and chips or a seafood bake.
Sweets change daily—just look in the case and see what
they have. They're all good, especially the lemon squares
and the chocolate-chip cookies with split cherries.
*Open daily 7 am to 8 pm from 1 May until 15 October (shorter
hours in winter). Licensed. Master Card, Visa.* &

PLANTAGENET, Ontario MAP 146
MARIPOSA FARM
6468 County Road 17 $120
(613) 673-5881

Nothing of importance has changed at Mariposa Farm in
the last couple of years. Suzanne Lavoie and Ian Walker
have been raising Embden geese and Barbary duck on
their 175-acre farm east of Ottawa for almost 20 years.
(Recently they've also been breeding a full complement
of pigs—Berkshire, Tamworth and Saddleback.) They've
converted an old barn into a small but charming dining-
room, complete with white-linen table-cloths and a
broad view of the surrounding countryside. Sad to say,
the dining-room is open only two hours a week, on Sun-

day from 11 am to 1 pm. The chef, Matthew Shepherd, has a small menu—three appetizers, three main courses and two sweets (or a cheese plate), three courses for 45.00. Foie gras is always on the menu, along with either duck or goose and home-baked bread. Unfortunately, Mariposa Farm is not licensed, so the char-grilled breast of duck is marinated in fruit juice. The farm store is in the same building and it sells everything from duck and geese to homemade preserves, jams, jellies and pâtés. Look for the Mariposa Farm sign outside of town, just east of Wendover.

Open Sunday 11 am to 1 pm. Closed Monday to Saturday. (The store is open Friday to Sunday 9 am to 4 pm.) Master Card, Visa. Book ahead. ♿

LA POCATIERE, Quebec   MAP 147
CAFE AZIMUT
309 4 avenue Painchaud   **$120**
(418) 856-2411

The Café Azimut occupies an old house on 4 avenue Painchaud in La Pocatière, a few minutes from Exit 439 on Highway 20 west of Rivière du Loup. They have a cheap lunch of soup or salad, cod or haddock and coffee. In the evening there's a regular à la carte and a number of daily specials. The carte will usually offer tartar of salmon with honey and lemon, home-smoked sturgeon, baked salmon, filet mignon with black peppercorns and (if you're lucky) a wonderful tarte au sucre. The wine-list is full of private imports, and among the open wines there's an R.H. Phillips cabernet sauvignon and a Kim Crawford sauvignon blanc. One could hardly hope for more.

Open daily 9 am to 3 pm, 4 pm to 10.30 pm. Licensed. All cards. ♿

If you wish to improve the guide send us information about restaurants we have missed. Our mailing address is Oberon Press, 145 Spruce Street: Suite 205, Ottawa, Ontario K1R 6P1.

POCOLOGAN, N.B. MAP 148
BAYBREEZE MOTEL
1475 Highway 175 **$55**
(506) 755-3850

Driving on the old Highway 1 could be a frightening experience—waves could break over your car. But the new
Highway 1 is so far inland that you may never get to see
the Fundy shore at all. And unless you go out of your
way, you won't get to know people like John and Maria
Lytras, owners of the Baybreeze Motel. As for their
cooking, it's just been getting better and better. The vegetables, once quite ordinary, are now always fresh and
seasonal. Their potato salad is remarkable. Their shellfish
is the best you'll get anywhere. We usually ask for the
lobster roll or the lobster stew. Others prefer the fine
grilled halibut. The pastries are all prepared with a light
hand and the olives come from olive trees that grow on
the Lytras property in Italy, where John and Maria spend
the winter. If you want to stay, there are three bedrooms
in the motel.
Open daily 7 am to 10 pm from 1 May until 31 October. Li-
censed. All cards.

PORT CARLING, Ontario MAP 149
LOONDOCKS
98 Joseph Street **$140**
(705) 765-5191

Loondocks is uphill from the small-boat lock in the heart
of Port Carling. They have a lovely open-air deck overlooking the water. Kevin Duynstee, the owner, grew up
in Muskoka and Muskoka still means a lot to him. At
Loondocks he has a few small plates—spring-rolls, gnocchi with chorizo and a trout salad. Among his large plates
there's macaroni and cheese, which is back in fashion
nowadays. There's also fillet of trout with maple and
merlot and an excellent beef tenderloin (from Morley
Stephen, Muskoka's best butcher) with mushrooms and
brandy. The meal will end, if you're lucky, with a big

wedge of flourless-chocolate cake. The wine-list has been enlarged and there are now several good wines from California, Australia and the Niagara Region, of which the best (we think) is the Tin Barn cabernet sauvignon from Sonoma.

Open daily 11 am to 8.30 pm from early May until late October, Friday to Sunday 5 pm to 8 pm from late October until early May. Closed Monday to Thursday in winter. Licensed. Master Card, Visa. Book ahead if you can. &

PORT CARLING
See also WINDERMERE.

PORT CREDIT, Ontario   (MAP 204)
BREAKWATER
Waterside Inn
15 Stavebank Road S   **$175**
(905) 891-6225

Breakwater is expensive. The menu is old-fashioned and the cooking variable. They're back in the guide this year for one reason only: they make the best roasted butternut soup we've ever had. It's thick and rich, its beautiful flavour heightened by the roasting. Forget the escargots, the risotto, the burger, the lobster Newburg and even the châteaubriand. Ask for the squash soup. As for the tiramisu, it's made with ladyfingers dipped in ice wine and served with fresh berries crowned with grapes and coconut flakes. Bizarre.

Open Monday to Friday 7 am to 11 pm, Saturday and Sunday 8 am to 11 pm. Licensed. Amex, Master Card, Visa. Book ahead if you can. Free parking. &

PORT ELGIN, N. B.   MAP 150
LE CHAT BLEU
342 Highway 970   **$90**
(506) 538-0110

Giselle Landry and William Ogilvie spent several years restoring this old place in Baie Verte, which is just a few

184

miles from Port Elgin. The building began life as a church in the eighteen-thirties and was converted into a general store 50 years later. The owners treated the place with love and respect, and filled the interior with treasures, among them a vintage motorcycle in the window. At first it housed a preserve company that made grape jelly and lime marmalade. Then in 2015 it became a restaurant. Most of the food is grown in the back yard, and the menu changes daily. One visitor we know of stopped here for a meal because the place smelled so good. Last year they offered prawns provençale, jerk pork, a black-bean quinoa burger, a seafood quesadilla, prawns with lobster and a butter-chicken curry. Somebody's mother makes the sweets, among them a rhubarb-and-strawberry pie and a pineapple carrot cake. The whipped cream is real and there are some local beers on tap.

Open Wednesday to Sunday 11 am to 8 pm from late April until Thanksgiving, Thursday to Sunday 11 am to 8 pm from Thanksgiving until late April. Closed on Monday and Tuesday in summer, Monday to Wednesday in winter. Licensed. Master Card, Visa.

PORT HOOD, N.S. MAP 151
HAUS TREUBURG
175 Main Street **$125 ($250)**
(902) 787-2116

Georg and Elvi Kargoll bought this old house in 1984 and restored it from top to bottom. Their menu seldom changes, their prices never do. Dinner comes in four courses unless you book the seven-course *menu surprise* in advance. Normally you start with house-smoked salmon or flammkuchen, an Alsatian version of pizza, followed by soup or a Caesar salad. Then there's a choice of meat, fish or a vegetarian dish. The meat might be beef stroganoff or a pork schnitzel, the vegetarian dish might be lasagne. We ourselves usually prefer the fish. The poached Atlantic salmon is about as good as it gets, though they also usually have some haddock or halibut or even fresh lobster. The meal ends with a fine apple strudel, made to an old family recipe and topped with real whipped cream. If you spend the night—the bedrooms are immaculate—you'll come down in the morning to what they call a German Sunday breakfast, which means farm-fresh eggs, homemade sausages, cereals, grains, hot buttered toast and homemade yogurt. The Haus Treuburg has its own sandy beach and some of the warmest water in Eastern Canada.

Open daily by appointment only from 1 June until 31 October. Licensed. Master Card, Visa. You must book ahead.

PORT HOOD
See also GLENVILLE, NORTHEAST MARGAREE.

PORT STANLEY, Ontario	**MAP 152**
WINDJAMMER INN	☆
324 Smith Street	**$125 ($250)**
(519) 782-4173	

Port Stanley is an attractive town and it has a fine beach within walking distance of the Inn. The Windjammer was built in 1854 by a local ship's captain called Sam Shepard. Kimberley Sanders has worked here for ten years and in all that time she's never sat down, or so it seems. She says that the tiredness comes and goes, and anyway she's determined to make the place a success. Before settling in Port Stanley, she worked in several important Toronto restaurants, and her dishes all look as they would in a big-city restaurant. Her menu changes every six or eight weeks and always makes the most of local ingredients. Perch and pickerel are usually on the menu, and beef and chicken are often available as well. Kimberley used to be a pastry chef, and she makes most of the sweets out of her head. The wonderful breakfast of former years has now given way to a brunch on Saturday and Sunday. You'll be surprised by the number of wines by the glass.

Open Tuesday to Sunday 8 am to 9 pm from early May until Thanksgiving. Closed on Monday (on Monday and Tuesday in winter). Licensed. Master Card, Visa.

PORTUGAL COVE, Newfoundland   **(MAP 174)**
FERRY LAST-STOP CAFE   ☆
2 Loop Drive   **$90**
(709) 895-3082

Paulette King used to run this place with the help of her
cherished mother, Mercedes. When her mother began
her last illness, she closed it. She's now decided that as a
memorial to her mother she'll reopen the café and keep
it the same. She can't hand out the scarves her mother
used to knit for every passing child, but she can offer
Mama's baked cod. The menu is now quite short, but it's
seductive. Everything is fresh and organically grown.
Bread is made in the kitchen each morning. The salads
are impeccable, the soups and the sweets are all made in-
house. There are fifteen to twenty wines on the list, most
of them sold by the glass as well as the bottle. The café is
right next to the ferry to Bell Island, which means that
you will want to know about the bedrooms upstairs. If
you stay here, you'll find that the breakfast is about as
good as the dinner.
Open Wednesday to Sunday 10 am to 3 pm, 6 pm to 9 pm from
early May until early December. Closed on Monday and Tues-
day. Licensed. Master Card, Visa.

PRINCE ALBERT, Saskatchewan   **MAP 154**
AMY'S ON SECOND   ☆
2990 2 Avenue W   **$140**
(306) 763-1515

Amy has been here for 28 years and it hasn't all been easy
sailing. She's always given a little more than she had to.
She talked to her customers and made allowances for
their preferences, but she's always kept to her standards.
She gets her vegetables from a local market gardener.
Once a week the only supplier of fresh seafood in the
province brings her mussels, wild salmon and Arctic char.
Pickerel comes from the river and it's a huge seller. The
striploin is all handcut triple-A Black Angus. Duck and
leg of lamb make regular appearances on the menu. The

pastry chef has been with Amy almost from the beginning, and every day she makes apple tart, lemon pie and at least eight varieties of cheesecake. The coffee is roasted locally. Amy was worried when her longtime chef, Klarke Dergoussoff, left for another career, but his sous chef (Kayla Kapacila) has turned out to be a breath of fresh air.

Open Monday to Saturday 11 am to 9 pm. Closed on Sunday. Licensed. All cards. Free parking. ♿

PRINCE GEORGE, B.C.
THE WHITE GOOSE
1205 3 Avenue
(250) 561-1002

MAP 155
☆
$165

Ryan Cyre loves what he's doing; in fact, he's passionate about it. He's felt that way ever since he arrived in Prince George in 2007. He now offers his magnificent five-course dinners seven nights a week and sells them for 60.00 a head. His express lunches, served six days a week, have gone up a dollar or two this year. He also has a regular à la carte and a food truck. Everything on his menus is the best he can find and everything is carefully and skilfully prepared. Every February he orders four whole truffles from France. The triple-cream baked brie with pears and roasted garlic and the duo of duck never leave the menu. For that matter, you'll still find most of the old favourites there—braised-beef short-ribs, crab-cakes, risotto of bison and polenta. The weekly menu surprise will be built around glazed salmon, goose or bison—not ostrich, since the nearby ostrich farm has closed. Cyre's mother still makes the chocolate cake, using an old family recipe, and she has no plans to stop. The wine pairings are all chosen with great care. The service is perfect.

Open Monday to Saturday 11 am to 2 pm, 5 pm to 9 pm, Sunday 5 pm to 9 pm. Licensed. Master Card, Visa. ♿

This is a guide to Canadian restaurants from coast to coast—the first ever published and the only one of its kind on the market today.

PRINCE RUPERT, B.C.
CARGO KITCHEN
101 1 Avenue E
(250) 624-8444

MAP 156
☆
$90

Cargo Kitchen is right next door to the wonderful Museum of Northern History, which means, if nothing else, plenty of free parking. In the last couple of years this place has become No. 1 in Prince Rupert. Its first chef, Avi Sternburg, spent years training in Japan, after which he laid out a shortish menu of classic dishes with an Asian kick. For instance, his karate chicken was his take on chicken karaage. His old sous chef, Angelo Octaviano, is now in charge. So far he hasn't made any important changes. His halibut and salmon are always exceptional, but you won't go wrong either with the Mayatta meatballs, the Moroccan chicken or the seafood risotto. A surprising number of people write to us about the grilled chicken on a bun, but we haven't yet tried it. They have the local Wheelhouse on tap; it's a nice pale ale and worth a try.

Open Monday to Friday noon to 2 pm, 5 pm to 9 pm, Saturday and Sunday noon to 9 pm (shorter hours in winter). Licensed. Amex, Master Card, Visa. Book ahead if you can. ♿

PRINCE RUPERT
COW BAY CAFE
205 Cow Bay Road
(250) 627-1212

MAP 156
☆
$85

We've been recommending this little café since 1992, the year Richard Davis opened it as a flyer from his main business in Terrace (see below). We liked it under Davis and we liked the very different restaurant under his successor, Adrienne Johnston. Since it has now been bought by the owners of Opa Sushi it has soared in the ratings, and you have to book ahead. The menu is built around fresh local seafood, and there's no better fish in the province. Look out for Prince Rupert's celebrated halibut. Diners praise everything, even the spaghetti bolognese. If you prefer beef tenderloin, it'll be correctly cooked and served with a nice barley risotto. They have a fine selection of imported wines and several craft beers. *Open Tuesday to Friday 11.30 am to 2 pm, 5 pm to 9 pm, Saturday 5 pm to 9 pm, Sunday noon to 3 pm. Closed on Monday. Licensed. Visa. Book ahead.*

PRINCE RUPERT   MAP 156
OPA SUSHI   ☆
34 Cow Bay Road   **$95**
(250) 627-4560

If you haven't tasted sushi made with really fresh seafood, come to Opa Sushi—they never have anything else in the kitchen. In season, they'll have salmon, squid, octopus, sweet shrimp and eel. Plus there are now four new specials, among them crab with avocado and tuna (called Firecracker) and crab with avocado, cucumber and curried honey (called Manila Vanilla). They have a sake bar, the only one in the Pacific Northwest. Opa Sushi is on the second floor of an old net loft, and it's one of the last of its kind. It seats just 35 people, so you should book ahead. If you ask for a table on the outside patio you may be able to watch the sea-eagles nesting overhead. *Open Tuesday to Friday 11.30 am to 2 pm, 5 pm to 9 pm, Saturday noon to 3 pm, 5 pm to 9 pm, Sunday 1 pm to 8 pm. Closed on Monday. Licensed. Visa. Book ahead.*

QUALICUM BEACH, B.C.   MAP 157
GIOVANNI'S
180 2 Avenue W: Unit 4   **$120**
(250) 752-6693

Giovanni's got new owners last year, but it's still, we think, the best place to eat in Qualicum Beach. At noon they serve soups, salads, pizzas and two or three traditional Italian chicken and veal dishes. In the evening they become more adventurous, starting with mussels in either white wine or tomato broth. The best of the pastas is a novel take on spaghetti puttanesca. (Others prefer the

ravioli stuffed with lobster and green onions, garlic and brandy.) The pick of the main courses is their marvellous rack of lamb with gorgonzola cheese. If you want a sweet, go for the crêpes stuffed with fruit and berries.
Open Tuesday and Wednesday 11.30 am to 2 pm, Thursday 11.30 am to 2 pm, 5 pm to 9 pm, Friday and Saturday 11.30 am to 2 pm, 5 pm to 10 pm, Sunday 5 pm to 9 pm. Closed on Monday. Licensed. Master Card, Visa.

QUALICUM BEACH
See also COOMBS.

QUEBEC, Quebec	**MAP 158**
APSARA	
71 rue d'Auteuil	**$85 ($175)**
(418) 694-0232	

The Apsara is now run by Chau Mouy Youk and her husband, a son of Beng an Khuong. Beng an Khuong escaped from Cambodia in 1975, leaving all his possessions behind. Within two years of his arrival in Canada he had bought this fine old house with his sixteen children, several of whom still work in the restaurant. Chau Mouy Youk has been in charge of the kitchen for at least thirty years and she makes a virtue of consistency. The menu includes several Thai and Vietnamese dishes as well as Cambodian, and it never changes. There are a number of vegetarian dishes, and they and everything else are surprisingly cheap. Some of the best dishes are the khemara soup, the mini lat and mou sati from Sangker, the oudong chicken and the Annam shrimp. The sorbets taste of real fruit and are all wonderful. The lunch menu, which changes daily, costs only 12.95. If you come with a companion, there are several dishes on offer for two or more, among them a starter of spicy pork with crisp noodles and a main course of stir-fried chicken with ginger. They have a few wines, but it's better, we think, to order a carafe of hakutsuru sake, which is sold on draft. It comes cold and clear and it's great.
Open Monday to Friday 11.30 am to 2 pm, 5.30 pm to 11 pm,

Saturday and Sunday 5.30 pm to 11 pm. Licensed. Amex, Master Card, Visa.

QUEBEC   **MAP 158**
INITIALE   ☆☆
54 rue St.-Pierre   **$215**
(418) 694-1918

Initiale has two menus, one headed sea, the other land. On the first of these, you can expect halibut with cauliflower or sole with hazelnuts; on the second breast of quail and roast loin of lamb with garlic and eggplant. Prices are high—the sole costs 49.00, the lamb 54.00. Sweets change daily and they too are expensive. The pétales from Osoyos is a rather disappointing wine, and it's better to choose one of the chablis or the pouilly fuissé. The kitchen is lively and inventive, especially at noon, and that's the best time to come, if only because the prices are much lower. The setting is dignified, the service impeccable.
Open Tuesday to Friday 11.30 am to 2 pm, 6 pm to 9 pm, Saturday 6 pm to 9 pm. Closed on Sunday and Monday. Licensed. All cards. Book ahead.

QUEBEC   **MAP 158**
LAURIE RAPHAEL   ☆☆
117 rue Dalhousie   **$190**
(418) 692-4555

Parking at Laurie Raphael is difficult, but if you can manage that the restaurant has many fine things to offer, the most spectacular of which is the orange soufflé. If you don't want the *menu vision* for 120.00, the à la carte starts with a seasonal soup (pumpkin in the fall), scallops or roasted apples (ask for the apples). Next comes superb Arctic char, cassoulet of guinea fowl and Boileau venison. Finally, there's the wonderful orange soufflé. The menu is quite small—so much the better—but the wine-list is tremendous. There aren't many good buys, but there's at least one—the macon villages from Jean Thévenet, which at 70.00 a bottle is a bargain in this company. There's also a fine, long list of grappas, among them a Jacopo Poli for 18.00.

Open Tuesday to Friday 11.30 am to 2 pm, 5.30 pm to 10 pm, Saturday 5.30 pm to 10 pm. Closed on Sunday and Monday. Licensed. All cards. You must book ahead. &

QUEBEC   **MAP 158**
LEGENDE   ☆☆
255 rue Saint-Paul   **$200**
(418) 614-2555

Légende is owned by Frédéric Laplante and Karen Therrien, formerly of La Tanière. Their menu here also has a lot of wild game. Look for buffalo tongue and elk carpaccio at noon, and pan-seared scallops, foie gras, pork belly, beef with bone marrow and breast of duck and partridge with oyster or shiitake mushrooms in the evening. If you never managed to get all the way out to La Tanière, you'll find the downtown location of Légende much more convenient. The cooking and service are essentially the same. *Open Monday to Wednesday 11.30 am to 10 pm, Thursday and Friday 11.30 am to 11 pm, Saturday 5 pm to 11 pm, Sunday 5 pm to 10 pm from mid-May until mid-October, Monday and Tuesday 5 pm to 10 pm, Wednesday 11.30 am to 10 pm, Thursday and Friday 11.30 am to 11 pm, Saturday 5 pm to 11 pm, Sunday 5 pm to 10 pm from mid-October until mid-May. Licensed. All cards. Book ahead.* &

QUEBEC   **MAP 158**
LE SAINT-AMOUR   ☆☆☆
48 rue Saint-Ursule   **$250**
(418) 694-0667

The interior of the dining-room at the Saint-Amour is now starting to look absurdly over the top. The menu is complicated and it's not easy to make sense of it. It's tempting to dismiss the place out of hand. The trouble is that, whether or not Jean-Luc Boulay himself is in the kitchen, the cooking on the table d'hôte—forget the à la carte—is amazing. In the evening, five courses cost 65.00; at noon three courses cost anywhere from 25.00 to 45.00, depending on what you choose. Both menus change every day. At noon look for such things as foie gras, confit of duck, brandade of halibut, Fundy salmon, blanquette of veal, scallops with wild ginger and grilled filet mignon. In the evening they add things like snow-crab ravioli, sea-bass, lamb and venison. The Fundy salmon is, quite simply, a miracle. The wine-list is long and sumptuous, offering three Latours, three Lafites and seven Rothschilds, all at prices that surpass belief—one Rothschild costs 9995.00 a bottle. Don't worry—there's a superb Tawse chardonnay for a few dollars a glass and an attractive Tawse riesling for even less. For all its splendid bordeaux, this is a list that makes a local wine like Tawse look very good indeed.

Open Monday to Friday 11.30 am to 2 pm, 6 pm to 10 pm, Saturday 5.30 pm to 10 pm, Sunday 6 pm to 10 pm. Licensed. All cards. Free valet parking. Book ahead.

QUEBEC　　　　　　　　　　　　　**MAP 158**
TOAST　　　　　　　　　　　　　　★★
17 Sault–au–Matelot　　　　　　　　**$200**
(418) 692-1334

Toast is no longer open for lunch. They have awnings and umbrellas for when they serve supper in the summer, but no more lunch. Christian Lemelin is still offering such things as bison tartar, torchon of foie gras, yellowfin tuna with chorizo and mushroom crostini, followed by monkfish with brown butter, gougères stuffed with gruyère cheese and mornay sauce and piglet with coco slaw and a gratin of pickles. The cooking is good, the presentation lovely. The wine-list is huge, starting with fifteen champagnes. There are many good buys, among them a hermitage from Tardieu-Laurent, a Duhart-Milon from Piedmont and six sauternes from Lur Saluces for 275.00 and up.

Open daily 6 pm to 10.30 pm (later on weekends). Licensed. All cards. ♿

QUEBEC
See also ILE D'ORLEANS, ST.-GEORGES-DE-BEAUCE.

RADIUM HOT SPRINGS, B.C.   **MAP 159**
HELNA'S STUBE
7547 Main Street W   **$160**
(250) 347-0047

Helna's is by far the best restaurant in Radium. The menu is German and offers an extraordinary variety of potato dishes. The cooking is essentially home-style, though there are always daily specials, which may be something unusual like elk with gin or venison with chanterelles. The kitchen is at its best, as you might expect, with wienerschnitzel, often served with cranberries. The restaurant seats 40 inside and 40 outside, but Radium is crowded in summer, so if you plan to come at that time of year be sure to book ahead.
Open Tuesday to Sunday 5 pm to 10 pm from 1 June until Thanksgiving, Tuesday to Saturday 5 pm to 10 pm from Thanksgiving until 31 May. Closed on Monday in summer, on Sunday and Monday in winter. Licensed. Master Card, Visa. Book ahead.

REGINA, Saskatchewan   **MAP 160**
LA BODEGA
2228 Albert Street   **$125**
(306) 546-3660

La Bodega is a tapas bar that claims to feature the best of native and foreign cuisine. With its three-level balcony extending into the overhead tree canopy, it's become a neighbourhood destination. There's a weekly fresh sheet that goes with the standard menu, and it lists most of Adam Sperling's latest ideas. That's where you'll find his jumbo shrimp in white wine, which has become a signature dish. Sometimes he's over the top, but his Sunday brunch is usually a success. He's strong on vegetarian dishes and he always keeps them on the menu. The first Monday of each month features a nine-course tasting menu, which at 35.00 a head has to be about the best deal in town. The wine-list has improved greatly over the past few years.

Open Tuesday to Friday 4 pm to 9 pm, Saturday 10.30 am to 9 pm, Sunday 10.30 am to 9 pm (brunch). Closed on Monday. Licensed. All cards. Book ahead if you can. ♿

REGINA   **MAP 160**
TANGERINE
2234 14 Avenue   **$45**
(306) 522-3500

Tangerine continues to turn out imaginative specials for their list of daily specials, which now covers a whole wall. The new pastry chef has turned out well, making several rich and wonderful sweets every day. Keep your eye out for her fruit crumbles, her fruit pies and her parfaits. The kitchen is committed to using local and seasonal produce whenever they can. Try one of their ricotta pancakes. They're a treat.

Open Monday to Friday 7 am to 6 pm, Saturday 8 am to 4 pm. Closed on Sunday. No liquor. Master Card, Visa. ♿

REGINA   **MAP 160**
WILLOW ON WASCANA   ☆
3000 Wascana Drive   **$160**
(306) 585-3663

With its lake-front balcony, Willow on Wascana has a better view than any other restaurant in Regina. It also has first-class cooking, which is all about local, fresh and seasonal. Order the six-course tasting menu and see them at their best. There's a substantial wine-list, but the service is not up to scratch.

Open Monday to Saturday 11.30 am to 9 pm. Closed on Sunday. Licensed. All cards. Book ahead. ♿

REGINA
See also VIBANK.

REVELSTOKE, B.C.   MAP 161
WOOLSEY CREEK CAFE   ☆
604 2 Street W   **$130**
(250) 837-5500

Revelstoke staggered in 2015, when the price of oil col-
lapsed. Now it has to rely on skiing and the low dollar.
Meanwhile, Sylvia Bisson is soldiering on at the Woolsey
Creek. She buys organic fruits and vegetables whenever
she can; she stocks wild salmon and wild black cod. We
considered her rack of venison too expensive at 42.00, so
she now offers loin of venison with a juniper rub for
33.00 and bison short-ribs for 25.00. Her dark-chocolate
flourless truffle cake is still on the menu and so is her five-
cheese plate with fresh figs. And she has a few wines that
you aren't likely to find in the liquor store.
*Open daily 5 pm to 9 pm. Licensed. Master Card, Visa. Book
ahead if you can.* ♿

REVELSTOKE
See also HEDLEY.

RIMOUSKI, Quebec   MAP 162
LE CREPE CHIGNON   ☜
140 avenue de la Cathédrale   **$90**
(418) 724-0400

This is one of the very few good places to eat in Rimouski. Basically, it's a crêperie with a conscience—
everything is either recyclable or bio-degradable. The
big, colourful menu offers fifteen or sixteen of their
favourite crêpes, as well as the crêpe Breton, for which
you choose your own filling from a list of several meats,
vegetables and cheeses. They make all their own jams and
their own yogurt and bake all their own bread. They also
make fine omelettes and several Mexican dishes, but
you're usually better with one of the crêpes. They have a
licence, and you can have a glass or two of Orpailleur if
you like, but we usually ask for the fresh-squeezed orange-juice or even a cup of the excellent coffee. The

Cathedral of Saint-Germain is just down the street and the dazzling white interior looks like a painting by Saenredam. It's worth a visit.

Open Monday 7 am to 9 pm, Tuesday to Thursday 7 am to 10 pm, Friday 7 am to 11 pm, Saturday 8 am to 10 pm, Sunday 8 am to 9 pm. Licensed. All cards. &

RIMOUSKI
See also LE BIC.

RIVIERE DU LOUP, Quebec	**MAP 163**
CHEZ ANTOINE	☆☆
433 rue Lafontaine	**$195**
(418) 862-6936	

Chez Antoine has an extraordinary wine-list, with its countless tignanellos, sassicaias, solaias and ornellaias. The cooking matches the wine. The feuilleté of escargots comes to the table with its snails in beautiful puff pastry. The carpaccio of beef is a delight and so is the ris de veau. The filet mignon is perfectly tender, the fillet of salmon is moist and very fresh. Even at noon the menu is amazing. There's rognons de veau, tartar of salmon, entrecôte of beef and bouillabaisse of pink shrimp. The service is perfect.

Open Monday to Friday 11 am to 2 pm, 5 pm to 9 pm, Saturday 5 pm to 9 pm. Closed on Sunday. Licensed. All cards. &

RIVIERE DU LOUP	**MAP 163**
AU PAIN GAMIN	
288-90 rue Lafontaine	**$35**
(418) 862-0650	

When this place opened ten or eleven years ago we thought it was special, and we were right. It's been fixed up since and you can now sit outside under a big umbrella. Their breads are still all made on the hearth from the finest available flour. If you order a ham sandwich you'll find that the ham comes from their own smokehouse. We always ask for the ham, but others speak highly of the smoked mackerel. Either sandwich, plus a bowl of homemade soup, costs only about 15.00.

Open Monday to Friday 8 am to 6 pm, Saturday 8 am to 5 pm from late June until Labour Day, Tuesday to Friday 9 am to 6 pm, Saturday 8 am to 5 pm from Labour Day until late June. Closed on Sunday in summer, on Sunday and Monday in winter. No liquor. Visa.

ROCKY HARBOUR, Newfoundland   MAP 164
JAVA JACK'S   ☆
88 Main Street N   **$135**
(709) 458-3004

It's been more than fifteen years since Jacqui Hunter opened this restaurant in Rocky Harbour, and after all that time it still has the best coffee and the best muffins in town. Java Jack's has been completely renovated and now has table-cloths and fresh flowers on every table and fresh paint on every wall. Jacqui grows fine fresh greens in her garden; her asparagus is always tender, her fish-cakes are the best in memory, her seafood chowder is full of fresh fish and her salmon is never overcooked. The wine-list is short, but it offers such unusual drinking as bake-apple liqueur and cocktails made with melting ice-bergs.

Open daily 9 am to 8 pm from 1 May until 30 June, daily 8 am to 9 pm from 1 July until 30 September. Licensed. All cards. No reservations.

ROCKY HARBOUR
See also NORRIS POINT, WOODY POINT.

ROUYN, Quebec   MAP 165
BISTRO JEZZ
44 Mgr. Rhéaume e   **$110**
(819) 764-5399

Bistro Jezz has moved to the centre of Rouyn, where it's hard to find. The restaurant is named for the owner, Jéz-abel Pilote, whose nickname is Jezz. She has an interesting selection of locally-sourced produce—fillet of pork with mushrooms and mustard, beef tartar and pavé of salmon with maple syrup—plus a good wine-list and a number of local beers. Things don't always go as they should, but at least everyone is friendly. *Note:* as this edition went to press, we received reports that the restaurant might be planning to close. Call before you go.

Open Monday to Friday 11 am to 2 pm, 5 pm to 10 pm, Saturday 5 pm to 10 pm, Sunday 8 am to 2 pm (brunch). Licensed. Master Card, Visa. Book ahead if you can.

ST. ANDREWS, N.B.   **MAP 166**
BRAXTON'S
Algonquin Hotel   **$225**
184 Adolphus Street
(503) 529-8823

The Algonquin Hotel, built in 1889, has been completely modernized and reopened as a Marriott, but the atmosphere has been little changed. The golf course hasn't lost its cachet, nor has the dining-room. (Braxton's is named for the first African-American chef of a major resort.) The menu is international. The Thai noodles, for instance, are perfectly spiced, and the seafood chowder and the smoked salmon, though familiar Canadian, are equally well prepared. On our last visit we were given one of the best Fundy halibut dishes within memory, as well as a memorable plate of local blueberries in a thin dark-chocolate sauce. They also make their own dulse sourdough bread.

Open daily 11 am to 10 pm. Licensed. All cards. &

ST. ANDREWS   **MAP 166**
ROSSMOUNT INN   ☆☆
4599 Highway 127   **$170**
(506) 529-3351

Times change. When the Aernis opened the Rossmount Inn a few years ago, it was essentially a restaurant with rooms—and brilliant cooking. Nowadays it's a summer resort with a swimming-pool and good (but no longer brilliant) cooking. Dinner begins with saffron-mussel soup, oysters on the half-shell, halibut ceviche with jalapeno and micro greens, watermelon with prosciutto, smoked salmon with avocado tartar and roasted elk with wild blueberries and foie gras. The seared yellowfin tuna you see everywhere, the gnocchi with naked lobster and arugula perhaps not. The lovely soufflés are rarely on the menu now, but the triple-chocolate truffle-cake is almost (though not quite) as good. The same is true of the warm apple tarte tatin. Chris Aerni (rhymes with Ernie) spares no expense in his choice of wine. If you want to drink champagne, there's plenty of Moet & Chandon, Veuve Clicquot and Pol Roger, and Aerni is one of the few people unwilling to settle for Caymus Conundrum, rightly preferring the cabernet sauvignon at twice the price. If you haven't got a hundred dollars to spare, ask for a bottle of Penfold's much cheaper Eden Valley.

Open daily 5.30 pm to 9.30 pm from 9 April until 31 December. Licensed. Amex, Master Card, Visa. Book ahead in season. &

ST. CATHARINES, Ontario   MAP 167
WELLINGTON COURT   ★★
11 Wellington Street   **$160**
(905) 682-5518

Wellington Court was opened by Claudia Peacock, who turned her father's little house on Wellington Street into a restaurant thirty years ago. Her son, Erik, who worked with his mother for some time, has been on his own for ten years, and is now a well-known chef. His menus are imaginative, even daring, offering things like fried shrimp-and-avocado salad with orange poblano and pâté of bone marrow with quince. He now has a second restaurant, this time at the Henry of Pelham winery at 1469 Pelham Road (telephone (905) 684-8423). At Wellington Court he changes the menu every couple of weeks. Fish is always a good choice, but you won't go wrong with the lamb, the duck or the fine rib-eye steak. The sweet might be a lemon mascarpone mousse or a

201

flourless-chocolate cake with preserved mango. Most of the wines come from Niagara, but you can bring your own bottle if you like; the corkage is only 15.00.
Open Tuesday to Saturday 11.30 am to 2.30 pm, 5 pm to 9.30 pm. Closed on Sunday and Monday. Licensed. All cards. Free parking. Book ahead in summer.

ST. CATHARINES
See also BEAMSVILLE.

STE.-FLAVIE, Quebec ***MAP 168***
LE GASPESIANA
460 rue de la Mer ***$95 ($210)***
(800) 404-8233

The cooking here may not be quite what it used to be, but the place is a godsend for anyone who comes to the Gaspé out of season. The bedrooms, all of which face the beach and the Gulf of St. Lawrence, are immaculate. The dining-room, which is open all year, is expansive and well served. The kitchen majors in fish and shellfish: clam chowder, shrimp bisque, cod meunière and bouillabaisse. They have a good sugar pie, but otherwise the cooking isn't distinguished. The wine-list, which is rather small and conventional, has two great buys: the Kim Crawford sauvignon blanc for 36.00 and the Liberty School cabernet sauvignon for 46.00. They're open Monday to Friday 11 am to 4 pm, 6 pm to 10 pm, Saturday and Sunday 6 pm to 10 pm (shorter hours in winter). Licensed. Amex, Master Card, Visa. ♿

ST.-GEORGES-DE-BEAUCE, Quebec (MAP 158)
MAISON VINOT ☆☆
11525 2 Avenue **$195**
(418) 227-5909

Raymonde Poulin and Philippe Vinot came here because they liked to cook. Luckily for us, after seven years on the job they still do. If you book ahead you'll get a table on the terrace, which in good weather is the best place to be. The chef works with locally-grown produce—which doesn't include fish. Bison is always on the menu, but beef

tenderloin must be ordered a day in advance. Beef is hard to get, and the kitchen is much happier to supply grain-fed local turkey. Dinners are all *prix fixe* and the price of the main course includes an appetizer, sweet and coffee. Beauce makes more maple syrup than anywhere else in the world, and it's hard to choose between one of their maple-syrup sweets and a plate of local cheeses. They've always been proud of their wine-list, however; it consists mainly of private imports. There's lovely country here-abouts and you should probably come and see it for your-self.
Open Tuesday to Friday 11.30 am to 1.30 pm, 6 pm to 9 pm, Saturday 6 pm to 9 pm. Closed on Sunday and Monday. Licensed. Master Card, Visa. Book ahead.

ST.-HYACINTHE, Quebec   MAP 171
LE PARVIS
1295 rue Girouard o   **$85**
(450) 774-0007

The Parvis occupies an abandoned church, built in 1878. Look in downtown St.-Hyacinthe for an old church painted brick red. Inside, it's very plain and one instinctively looks for the old box pews. But there are no box pews, only tables and chairs set out on a bare floor. Lunch is served five days a week, dinner six. Dinner starts with shrimps provençale or terrine of wapiti with cranberries in a peach coulis. A green soup comes next, then a bavette of beef, pavé of salmon with anise, chicken wings with green peppers or homemade pasta with sundried tomatoes and fresh pesto. Everything is table d'hôte and sweets are served buffet-style. Coffee comes with the meal.
Open Monday to Friday 11.30 am to 9 pm, Saturday 5 pm to 9 pm. Closed on Sunday. Licensed. Master Card, Visa.

This is a guide to Canadian restaurants from coast to coast—the first ever published and the only one of its kind on the market today. Every restaurant in the guide has been personally tested. Our reporters are not allowed to identify themselves or to accept free meals.

ST.-JEAN-PORT-JOLI, Quebec MAP 172
LA BOUSTIFAILLE
547 avenue de Gaspé e **$70**
(877) 598-7409

This small town of 3500 attracts a surprising number of tourists. Several of its woodcarvers have become famous. The parish church dates from 1779 and has some very fine sculptures. In 2005 the town was declared the cultural capital of Canada. There are several restaurants here, of which the Libellule at 17 place de l'Eglise (telephone (418) 598-9644) is one of the best. It has great atmosphere and a great location; the kitchen uses nothing but fresh produce and they're open for dinner year-round. Meanwhile, down the road east of town, the Boustifaille seems to have lost much of its old fire and spice, though it's never merely run-of-the-mill. It opened in 1965 with the intention of providing *habitant* cooking to all comers at a fair price. After 45 years, the kitchen is still preparing such dishes as split-pea soup, tourtière, ragoût de pattes et boulettes and, of course, sugar pie. But nowadays they take a lot of short cuts and the 20.00 table d'hôte is no longer always a good buy. They have a few wines and a couple of draft beers. And maple syrup is still sold in cans to take out.

Open daily 7 am to 11 pm from 1 June until 12 October (shorter hours in the spring and fall). Licensed for beer and wine only. Master Card, Visa. &

SAINT JOHN, N.B. MAP 173
THE ALE HOUSE
1 Market Square **$90**
(506) 657-2337

The Ale House is starting to get noticed right across the country. That's because Jesse Vergen is doing such a good job in the kitchen and behind the bar. He emphasizes local organic produce. His beef comes from Shipp Farms in Sussex; his fish mostly from New Brunswick. Some things are grown by Vergen himself in Quispamsis. Fish doesn't get any fresher than this and the beer-battered fish and chips is a steal at 9.45. The mussels, which come from Prince Edward Island, are also cooked with beer and the house-made pancetta and garlic are served with fries. Vergen has taken the bones out of his chicken but not the flavour, and his fried chicken fingers is one of the most popular items on the menu. Everything is cheap at the Ale House—everything, that is, but the lobster roll, which costs almost 40.00. They have the largest selection of beers in town, including drafts from Picaroon's in Fredericton and the Pump House in Moncton. Every Thursday Moosehead sends them a cask of real ale, and there are people who will drink nothing else. There's an all-Canadian wine-list that offers wines from Nova Scotia as well as Niagara and the Okanagan. You can sit upstairs in the formal dining-room if you like or downstairs in the pub.

Open Sunday to Thursday 11.30 am to 10.30 pm, Friday and Saturday 11.30 am to midnight. Licensed. All cards. No reservations. &

SAINT JOHN   MAP 173
BILLY'S
City Market   **$140**
49-51 Charlotte Street
(888) 933-3474

The menu at Billy's has changed slightly in the last year or two. Traditional dishes have become more sophisticated: bacon-wrapped scallops, for instance, have become scallops with bacon jam. Aside from the scallops, there are calamari with a curry dip and local Beausoleil oysters on the half-shell at 26.00 for a dozen. The best of the salads is the spinach-and-beet, the best of the main courses the fish and chips, which is now as good as any. There's also cedar-planked salmon with maple syrup and a seafood pie in puff pastry. This is a seafood restaurant, but you can ask, if you choose, for a striploin steak. Billy's is a supplier as well as a restaurant and Billy Grant himself can often be seen behind the counter cutting up

a whole halibut or a sashimi-grade tuna. He also has excellent sturgeon caviar—just ask.

*Open Monday to Thursday 11 am to 10 pm, Friday and Sat-
urday 11 am to 11 pm, Sunday (except in winter) 4 pm to 10
pm. Licensed. All cards.* &

SAINT JOHN   **MAP 173**
PORT CITY ROYAL   ☆
45 Grannan's Lane   **$95**
(506) 631-3714

The Port City premises used to house a sewing-machine
factory. The site has now been restored to look rough
luxe, as the architects call it, and it's true, the lighting fixtures look as if they had come from a coal mine. Jacob
Lutes, the chef, is a dedicated locavore and almost everything on the menu is local, which works well in summer
but not so well in winter. Keep an eye out for such Maritime specialties as hodge-podge or Jigg's dinner. Better
still are the cods' tongues, a delicacy that used to be plentiful but is now very rare. The roasted lamb, served with
chanterelles (another delicacy) is tender and full of
flavour, and the meal ends well with wild-blueberry tart.
The menu is short and there are only a couple of wines—
a white from Chile and a red from Argentina. There are
ten draft beers, however, and a cider from France.

*Open Tuesday to Friday 11.30 am to 2 pm, 5.30 pm to10 pm,
Saturday 5.30 pm to 1 am. Closed on Sunday and Monday. Licensed. Master Card, Visa. Book ahead.*

SAINT JOHN   **MAP 173**
THE URBAN DELI   ☆
68 King Street   **$50/$135**
(506) 652-3354

This place is a deli by day and an Italian trattoria by night.
The deli menu has changed very little over the years—it
hasn't needed to. They offer a broad selection of soups
and sandwiches. The soups include split-pea and a chowder, which costs 11.00 a bowl. They have smoked-meat

and corned-beef sandwiches, as well as a Reuben with dijon mustard. And they have beef burgers (with garlic), as well as fish and veggie burgers. There's both wine and beer to drink. At night the trattoria has a chef who knows all about antipasti, pasta, risotto and several authentic secondi like lamb osso buco and zuppe di pesce in a spicy tomato broth. The cooking is traditional in style, but occasionally the chef introduces a local specialty like maple syrup. They call the trattoria Italian by Night and offer a well-chosen list of Italian wines.

Open Monday to Saturday 11.30 am to 3 pm. Closed on Sunday. Italian by Night is open Wednesday to Saturday 5 pm to 9 pm. Closed on Monday, Tuesday and Sunday. Licensed. All cards. Book ahead.

ST. JOHN'S, Newfoundland　　　　MAP 174
ADELAIDE OYSTER HOUSE　　　　☆☆
334 Water Street　　　　**$150**
(709) 576-2782

People like to say that Stephen Vardy is having fun again. After wearing himself out working for others, he now has his own place, where he can do what he likes. The Adelaide Oyster House is what he likes. His best dish is probably the scallop ceviche with mango and passion fruit, but he also has a variety of raw oysters—Pickle Points from Prince Edward Island and Black Pearls from Quadra Island. He's tried all kinds of different toppings, but he's settled at last on mango for east-coast oysters and lime for west-coast oysters. Of course, he does much more than oysters. He does tuna taco, salt-and-pepper squid, pork belly and Korean chicken. Everybody orders three or four of these. The restaurant is noisy and tends to get noisier as the evening goes on, but the wine-list is excellent and there are some interesting craft beers as well.

Open Tuesday to Sunday 5 pm to 10 pm. Closed on Monday. Licensed. Master Card, Visa. No reservations.

Nobody but nobody can buy his way into this guide.

ST. JOHN'S   MAP 174
BACALAO   ☆
65 Lemarchant Road   **$140**
(709) 579-6565

Bacalao (which means salt-cod) occupies a lovely old
house well away from the downtown area. Each of the
four dining-rooms has an intimate feel, and each has its
own fireplace. Their salt-cod fishcakes are as good as any
in the province, if only because they come with cods'
tongues, which are now a rarity. Their Fogo Island cod
is also great—it's served with pork belly, smoky green
beans and barley risotto. The wine-list is outstanding.
Open Tuesday to Friday noon to 2.30 pm, 6 pm to 9 pm, Sat-
urday and Sunday 11 am to 2.30 pm (brunch), 6 pm to 9 pm.
Closed on Monday. Licensed. All cards. Book ahead if you can.

ST. JOHN'S   MAP 174
BASHO   ☆
283 Duckworth Street   **$160**
(709) 576-4600

Basho is a Japanese fusion restaurant. The sushi is all prepared upstairs by Tak Ishiwata, who began by working
for Nobu Matsuhisa in Tokyo. Tak brought many of
Nobu's recipes with him when he came to Canada. His
sushi is all superbly fresh, and he also has tuna tartar and
whitefish in season. Everyone likes the tuna tartar and the
whitefish too. The frozen goat-cheese cheesecake is great
and the martinis are all without parallel. People do say,
however, that some of the waiters suffer from an attitude
problem. We haven't noticed it.
Open Monday to Saturday 6 pm to 10 pm. Closed on Sunday.
Licensed. All cards. Book ahead. ♿

This is a guide to Canadian restaurants from coast to
coast—the first ever published and the only one of its
kind on the market today. We accept no advertisements.
Nobody can buy his way into this guide and nobody can
buy his way out.

ST. JOHN'S
BISTRO SOFIA
320 Water Street
(709) 738-2060

MAP 174
☆
$130

Bistro Sofia is a casual place in the heart of the city. The chefs pride themselves on their market-fresh produce. They cook with a strong Bulgarian accent and the most popular of their noon-hour dishes has always been either the shopska salad or the chicken schwarzwald sandwich. In the evening the cooking becomes more interesting and more expensive. You start with the spicy tomato soup with gin and go on to more substantial treatments of salmon (blackened with mango), lamb shanks (with a vegetable mirepoix) or filet mignon. The sweets are said to be the finest in St. John's. The gluten-free chocolate cake is about the best we've ever had, and they hope to have more gluten-free options in the future.
Open daily 9 am to 11 pm. Licensed. All cards. ♿

ST. JOHN'S
CHINCHED BISTRO
7 Queen Street
(709) 722-3100

MAP 174
☆
$150

Chinched Bistro is on the second floor of a building on Queen Street. Michelle LeBlanc is the hostess, Shaun Hussey the chef. Together they make an attractive pair. They have a charcuterie plate and fresh cod wrapped in potato and served on a panzanella salad in caper vinai-grette. But our favourite dish is the chicken wings with savoury waffles. For sweet there's olive-oil ice cream with a drizzle of balsamic vinegar and a squash blossom on the top. The wine-list is small and inexpensive.
Open Tuesday to Saturday 6 pm to 10 pm. Closed on Sunday and Monday. Licensed. Master Card, Visa. Book ahead.

We accept no advertisements. We accept no payment for listings. We depend entirely on you. Recommend the book to your friends.

ST. JOHN'S

THE DUKE OF DUCKWORTH

325 Duckworth Street
(709) 738-6344

MAP 174

$70

This place calls itself an Irish pub with a difference. The bottom line is that for 11.99 they'll give you some of the best fish and chips in the world, and for another 1.49 they'll give you the dressing and gravy that go with it. The menu runs from cod at one end to Ploughman's Lunch and steak-and-kidney pie at the other. (Ploughman's Lunch costs 9.99, steak-and-kidney pie 12.59.) The prices are unreal. The location is right in the heart of the city and the service is friendly and fast. The Duke of Duckworth is one of a kind; there's nothing else like it.
Open Sunday to Thursday noon to 1 am, Friday and Saturday noon to 3 am. Licensed. All cards. &

ST. JOHN'S

THE HUNGRY HEART

142 Military Road
(709) 738-6164

MAP 174

$50

The Hungry Heart is a perfect place for lunch and that's no secret, so be sure to book ahead. Carolyn Power turned on the heat when she took over from Maurice Boudreau as chef. Not that Boudreau cut any corners; on the contrary. But Carolyn Power has introduced traditional Newfoundland dishes as well as flavours from around the world. Beer and wine are now available for the first time. She prides herself on creating affordable meals that taste the way they should. She has a lot of baked goods that go well with the coffee, which is very good. Perhaps you should know that all profits from the Hungry Heart are used to help disadvantaged people with job training, housing and low-cost meals.
Open Monday to Saturday 9 am to 2 pm. Closed on Sunday. Licensed for beer and wine only. Master Card, Visa. Book ahead. &

ST. JOHN'S

MAP 174

INTERNATIONAL FLAVOURS
4 Quidi Vidi Road
(709) 738-4636

$45

This tiny, owner-operated restaurant never seems to change. If you're looking for a bargain, you'll find it here at the foot of Signal Hill. They make curries of all sorts, as well as dal, samosas and naan. And they sell spices, so you can make curries at home if you like. Everything is full of flavour and everything is very inexpensive.
Open Tuesday to Saturday noon to 7 pm. Closed on Sunday and Monday. No liquor. Master Card, Visa. No reservations.

ST. JOHN'S

MAP 174

MALLARD COTTAGE
Quidi Vidi Village
8 Barrows Road
(709) 237-7314

$130

Mallard Cottage is five minutes from St. John's in the charming village of Quidi Vidi. The wooden building has been restored with loving care by Todd Perrin, whose menu changes daily, always featuring seafood and wild game. Dried herbs hang from the walls and the tables are laid with mismatched china. All sorts of things are on the menu, from line-caught halibut to loin of lamb with braised kale and seared cod with salt pork and caramelized onions. They do a good brunch from Friday to Sunday and have live music on weekends.
Open Wednesday and Thursday 5.30 pm to 9 pm, Friday and Saturday 10.30 am to 2 pm (brunch), 5.30 pm to 9 pm, Sunday 10.30 am to 2 pm (brunch). Closed on Monday and Tuesday.

ST. JOHN'S

MAP 174
★★

RAYMONDS
95 Water Street
(709) 579-5800

$250

Raymond's is still the best restaurant in St. John's. Jeremy

Charles and Jeremy Bonia met when they were both working at Atlantica in Portugal Cove. When they came here, they set out to create a high-end restaurant supplied by local farmers and fishermen. Their menu is impressive, their service impeccable. But if you're looking for a really good meal, choose from the tasting menu. You can sit in either the formal dining-room or the bar. Either way, the menu will open with oysters on the half-shell and go on to such luxuries as veal cheeks, belly of lamb or sweet-breads. The wines are all expensive, and even the wine pairing costs upwards of 75.00.

Open Tuesday to Saturday 5.30 pm to 10 pm. Closed on Sunday and Monday. Licensed. All cards. Book ahead. &

ST. JOHN'S   MAP 174
THE SPROUT
364 Duckworth Street   **$50**
(709) 579-5485

When it opened, the Sprout was the only vegetarian restaurant in St. John's. It's small and doesn't take reservations. It's popular at noon, so if you want to be sure of a table it's a good idea to get there early. They have many vegan and several gluten-free items. There are lots of sandwiches, lots of burgers and lots of salads, the best of which is the so-called townie taco. The black-bean burrito is said to be excellent—it's made with black beans and sweet potatoes, all baked in a wholewheat tortilla. They're not really interested in sweets, which are still all out-sourced.

Open Monday to Friday 11.30 am to 9 pm, Saturday 10 am to 2 pm (brunch), 4 pm to 9 pm (shorter hours in winter). Closed on Sunday. Licensed. Master Card, Visa. No reservations.

ST. JOHN'S
See also PORTUGAL COVE.

The map number assigned to each city, town or village gives the location of the centre on one or more of the maps at the start of the book.

ST.-LUNAIRE-GRIQUET, (MAP 6)
Newfoundland
DAILY CATCH ☆
112 Main Street **$90**
(709) 623-2295

Global warming has brought more, not fewer, icebergs
to the bay at St.-Lunaire. The Daily Catch in the village
is close to the Viking settlement at Anse-aux-Meadows,
which is worth seeing. Terry Anderson comes from a
long line of fishermen, and a cousin or two still bring him
fish from their daily catch. Cod and lobster occur locally,
but salmon and halibut come in from Labrador. Crab-
cakes and crab au gratin are often on the menu. Cods'
tongues are also usually available, as are pan-fried cod and
scrunchions. The chips are always cut by hand and fried
in the kitchen. Christmas cake, made to an old family
recipe, is offered all summer long, along with apple crisp
and fresh-fruit pies. They have a wine-list, but most people seem to drink Iceberg beer or one of the local berry
wines.
Open daily 11 am to 9 pm from 1 June until 30 September. Li-
censed. All cards. ♿

ST. MARYS, Ontario (MAP 192)
LITTLE RED'S
159 Queen Street E **$130**
(226) 661-2233

Chris and Mary Woolf have a long history in the Stratford area. Having closed Woolfy's at Wildwood, they've
reappeared at this small (50-seat) pub and eatery right on
the main street of St. Mary's. Here they have a short
bistro-style menu and a large blackboard of daily specials,
with nearly everything coming from nearby suppliers.
People talk about the cheeseburger with bacon from a
bison farm just outside town, but one diner praises his
summer trout, which, he says, was beautifully cooked
and served with impeccable vegetables. Everything, even
the tomato ketchup, is made from scratch on the premises

213

and you'll be pleased with both the salads and the fries. Perth County pork might appear in a tourtière with Stonetown cheese as an appetizer. There are a number of traditional sweets, among them a pavlova made with real whipped cream and a crème brûlée made with local berries. The dining-room is noisy, but the service is calm and poised and the parking is ample. The wine-list is novel and interesting and there's a good selection of local craft beers.

Open Tuesday to Saturday 11 am to 2 pm, 4.45 pm to 9 pm. Closed on Sunday and Monday. Licensed. All cards. &

ST. MARYS   (MAP 192)
WESTOVER INN
300 Thomas Street   **$160 ($360)**
(519) 284-2977

This is a lovely place to stay and it makes an ideal base for the Stratford Festival. Stratford itself is only a few miles away and St. Marys is one of the finest small towns in Ontario. The Westover Inn occupies a wooded estate at the edge of town. The main house was built a hundred years ago of rough stone, and today the dining-room and lounge fill most of the ground floor. The dining-room is handsome and dignified and the service is friendly, but the cooking is no longer up to scratch. The pork tenderloin is probably the best choice, though they also have a good striploin of beef, a demi-glazed rack of lamb, seared scallops and an imposing rack of venison with cranberries. Meals begin rather well with a spinach salad or a ragoût of snails, but the wines are all expensive. Take refuge in a glass of Tin Roof chardonnay for 9.75.

Open daily 11.30 am to 2 pm, 5 pm to 8 pm. Licensed. All cards. Book ahead.

This is a guide to Canadian restaurants from coast to coast—the first ever published and the only one of its kind on the market today. Every restaurant in the guide has been personally tested. Our reporters are not allowed to identify themselves or to accept free meals.

ST. PETER'S, N.S.   MAP 177
BRAS D'OR LAKES INN   ☆
10095 Granville Street   **$140 ($295)**
(800) 818-5885

We never expected Jean-Pierre Gillet to retire, but this year the Inn has a new chef, Dean Pottie. Jean-Pierre is still very much involved and some of his dishes, such as the daily mussel creation (steamed in beer with lime and ginger) will probably never leave the menu. The dinner menu offers two courses for 25.00 and three for 30.00. Last year they introduced lunch until 4 o'clock and this year they plan to serve breakfast every day from 8 o'clock to 10. The new dinner menu will feature a seafood platter with mussels, clams, shrimps, scallops and crab, all from nearby waters. Breast of chicken has been joined by quail and the stuffed pork chops have been replaced by roast duck. Don't miss the scallops provençale or the local lamb. We still hanker for the apple pie with caramel, but others prefer the gâteau St.-Honoré. Most nights there's live gaelic music.

Open Monday to Saturday 8 am to 10 am, 11 am to 4 pm, 5 pm to 8 pm, Sunday 11 am to 2 pm (brunch), 5 pm to 8 pm from early May until mid-October, Wednesday to Saturday 8 am to 10 am, 11 am to 4 pm, 5 pm to 8 pm, Sunday 11 am to 2 pm (brunch), 5 pm to 8 pm from mid-October until mid-December. Closed on Monday and Tuesday in the fall. Licensed. Amex, Master Card, Visa.

ST. PETERS BAY, P.E.I.   (MAP 37)
THE INN AT ST. PETERS   ☆
1668 Greenwich Road   **$160 ($280)**
(800) 818-0925

The success of the Inn at St. Peters is largely due to the hostess, Karen Davey. She does everything, even arranging tee times for golfers. Most of the cottages overlook the sea and the view from the dining-room windows is amazing. The chef, Sarah Forrester Wendt is keen on whole foods and macro cooking. She grows most of her own vegetables and her brother-in-law has an organic farm. Breakfast means blueberry pancakes, your choice of eggs, a quiche and freshly-squeezed fruit juice. Dinner is equally remarkable. There are mussels from the Bay; there are local scallops. Oysters come from South Lake and the trout is smoked in-house. In season lobster is boiled in the traditional way; North Shore halibut is served with a jalapeno aioli. If you don't like seafood there's always pork, pheasant and duck. The kitchen makes all its own sorbets and all its own ice creams.

Open daily 5 pm to 8.30 pm from 28 May until 2 October. Licensed. All cards. &

ST.-PIERRE-JOLYS, Manitoba   MAP 179
OMA'S SCHNITZEL STUBE
601 Sabourin Street S   **$45**
(204) 433-7726

St.-Pierre-Jolys is half an hour by car south of Winnipeg and Oma's is right in the centre of town. People say that Oma's has the best German food to be had anywhere in Canada. There's a big buffet every Friday and Saturday night; on other evenings you order a schnitzel from the à la carte. The schnitzels are great, and as for the apple strudel it has few equals anywhere. The same is true of the coffee. Diners have left a trail of e-praise on the internet. Certainly, everything is a steal at 50.00 for two, but if you come on Friday or Saturday come early because the regulars clean out the weekend buffets in no time.

Open Wednesday to Sunday 11 am to 9 pm. Closed on Monday and Tuesday. Licensed. Master Card, Visa. &

SALTAIR, B.C.   (MAP 56)
DAYLINER CAFE
10445 Chemainus Road   **$115**
(250) 324-3777

The Dayliner Café is about halfway between Chemainus and Ladysmith at the north end of the Cowichan Valley.

They serve breakfast and lunch every day, so they can limit themselves to three dinners a week, on Friday, Saturday and Sunday. Breakfast is an ambitious meal, offering wraps filled with scrambled eggs or sausages with yam hash, cheddar cheese and chipotle mayonnaise. At noon there are salads, curries and more wraps (turkey and brie for one). Dinners are served *prix fixe* for about 30.00 a head and feature a Caesar salad, fresh halibut tacos, beef stroganoff on egg noodles, barbecued short-ribs with blueberries and ravioli stuffed with squash, ending with a lemon tart or white-chocolate panna cotta.

Open Monday to Thursday 8 am to 3 pm, Friday 8 am to 3 pm, 5 pm to 8.30 pm, Saturday and Sunday 9 am to 3 pm, 5 pm to 8.30 pm. Master Card, Visa. &

SALT SPRING ISLAND, B.C.   (MAP 211)

Salt Spring Island has always been known for its lamb and cheese and shellfish. More recently it's been known for its wineries, for its abundance of organic produce and for its bakeries. Try either Jana's Bake Shop at 149 Fulford Ganges Road (telephone (778) 353-2253) for fresh muffins, fabulous butter tarts and mini-quiches or the Embe Bakery at 174 Fulford Ganges Road (telephone (250) 537-5611) for great cookies and pies. David Wood's celebrated goat cheese and sheep's-milk cheese can be found at the Cheese Farm Shop at 285 Reynolds Road (telephone (250) 653-2300). The best way to get to know what's available on the Island is to visit the Farmer's Market in Ganges, which is held every Saturday morning from Easter until Thanksgiving. If you drive south out of Ganges you'll soon come across the Garry Oaks and Salt Spring Island wineries. Both offer tours and tastings. A third winery, Mistaken Identity, makes a number of certified organic wines. Smoked salmon and crab or salmon pâtés are both available right in Ganges itself from a shop called Sea Change. If you have to wait for the ferry to Swartz Bay, you can get something to eat close to the terminal at the Rock Salt Café at 2921 Fulford Ganges Road (telephone (250) 653-4833). It's under new ownership and now serves breakfast, lunch and dinner. The restaurant in Hastings House is, we think, too expensive for most of our readers. Piccolo at 108 Hereford Avenue (see below, telephone

217

(250) 537-1844) is closer to the mark and attracts visitors by the boatload.

SALT SPRING ISLAND   (MAP 211)
HOUSE PICCOLO   ☆☆
108 Hereford Avenue   **$130**
(250) 537-1844

We think this is now the best place to eat on Salt Spring Island. Piccolo Lyttikainen used to price his meals as if the House Piccolo were the Hastings House. Last year, however, he reduced his prices, which makes the restaurant accessible to the ordinary traveller. Piccolo has no sea view, no open-air deck. He has nothing to offer but good food. Our favourite appetizer is the lovely sautéed sea scallops with curried mango, though the chilled Scandinavian gravlax cured in sea-salt and brandy is an impressive dish too. When it comes to the main course, diners have to choose between Grand Veneur venison with juniper and lingonberries and pan-fried wild sablefish with brown butter—we usually ask for the venison. Piccolo is good with pastry and his Alsatian pear-and-almond tart is still the best of the sweets. Some of the most interesting of the wines are private imports.
Open Wednesday to Sunday 5 pm to 9 pm. Closed on Monday and Tuesday. Licensed. Master Card, Visa.

SASKATOON, Saskatchewan   MAP 182
AYDEN   ☆☆
265 3 Avenue   **$140**
(306) 954-2590

Dale MacKay has named his restaurant after his son. It's housed in a graceful downtown building, where he practises his innovative urban style of cooking six nights a week, usually playing to a full house. Snacks are offered at noon and that means house-made charcuterie, popcorn prawns and Thai-style chicken wings. In the evening they have a rib-eye steak and freshly-ground hamburgers. These two are always on the menu, while the chicken, pork, fish and pasta change every day. Dinner ends with a soufflé and one or two of Proust's madeleines. Take them both.

Open Monday to Friday 11.30 am to 2 pm, 5.30 pm to 10 pm, Saturday 5.30 pm to 10 pm. Closed on Sunday. Licensed. You must book ahead. &

SASKATOON   MAP 182
THE ODD COUPLE
228 20 Street W   **$75**
(306) 668-8889

Saskatoon is booming, and people are now making money even in the once-neglected Riversdale district. Andy Yuen has joined his father in an effort to create an upscale but affordable Asian-style restaurant. The interior of the Odd Couple, inspired by the Chinese film, *In the Mood for Love,* is stylish and comfortable. Outside there's a Double Happiness symbol; inside the message is just eat together. The food is simple but fresh and well prepared. There are several dishes to share and a number of vegetarian options. Traditional dishes like won-ton soup, fried rice, chicken and gailan are somehow made to seem exciting. Not that they don't have innovative dishes as well, dishes like eggplant with ground pork, chicken with shimeji and oyster mushrooms, sweet chilli chicken and, for sweet, sesame rice with chocolate. They have a good wine-list, as well as Sapporo beer on tap.

Open Monday to Thursday 11.30 am to 2 pm, 4.30 pm to 11 pm, Friday and Saturday 11.30 am to midnight. Closed on Sunday. Licensed. Master Card, Visa. &

SASKATOON   MAP 182
ST. TROPEZ
238 2 Avenue S   **$150**
(306) 652-1250

Regulars come here because they know exactly what they'll get. After all, the same chef has been in charge for twenty years, and his son has been here for at least ten.

The shrimps with garlic are still on the menu. There's always filet mignon and curried lamb. The beef is local, the lamb often not. But everything is correctly cooked; the vegetables are fresh, the saskatoons hand picked every summer. At the end of the meal, crème caramel is always available. There are at least 70 labels on the wine-list. Most of them cost 100.00 a bottle or more, but if you pay cash they give you a 10% discount on your next meal. If you have tickets for the theatre around the corner, they'll make sure you get there on time.
Open Wednesday to Sunday 5 pm to 10 pm. Closed on Monday and Tuesday. Licensed. All cards. &

SASKATOON   **MAP 182**
SUSHIRO   ☆
737 Broadway Avenue   **$75**
(306) 665-5557

Megan Macdonald moved to Vancouver two years ago and sold two thirds of the restaurant to her employees. That didn't sound like good news, but so far there haven't been any important changes. The fish is still beautifully fresh, and the sushi is the best in town. The yam tempura is still a magical dish and so are the chilli squid and the seared tuna tataki with avocado and orange. They have Hakutsuru sake on draft, as well as two or three premium sakes by the bottle.
Open Monday to Saturday 5 pm to 10 pm. Closed on Sunday. Licensed. All cards. &

SASKATOON   **MAP 182**
TRUFFLES   ☆
230 21 Street E   **$140**
(306) 373-7779

Truffles is located in the old Birks building in downtown Saskatoon. Inside it's bright and *au courant*. This is one place where the table d'hôte could be regarded as the specialty of the house. There's almost always a first-rate eight-ounce striploin with wonderful truffled fries on it, or perhaps steelhead trout from Diefenbaker Lake. But Lee Helman is a trained French chef and there are those who think that it would be a mistake to stick to such things as steak or steelhead trout, even if they are cheap. If you feel that way, ask for the breast of duck or perhaps the house-made ravioli. Everything is made from scratch, even the tomato ketchup. He makes all his own bread and all his own sweets. His soups are exquisite. But he could still use more wines by the glass.

Open Monday to Friday 5 pm to 10 pm, Saturday 10 am to 2.30 pm (brunch), 5 pm to 10 pm, Sunday 10 am to 2 pm (brunch). Licensed. All cards. ♿

SAULT STE.-MARIE, Ontario   **MAP 183**
ARTURO'S   ☆
515 Queen Street E   **$185**
(705) 253-0002

Arturo Comegna came from Abruzzo in Italy and established one of the best of the many Italian restaurants in the Sault. That was at least 25 years ago. Now his sons, Thomas and Christopher, run the place. He himself has opened a new restaurant called Antico at 6 Village Court (telephone (705) 575-0455) on the other side of town. He took his sous-chef, Dino, with him and they make a great pair. Go to Village Court and see for yourself. Meanwhile, at the original location on Queen Street, Thomas and Christopher still have a good kitchen. The veal is all milkfed, the seafood all fresh. There's a daily catch every day, and often it's salmon or sea-bass, both perfectly cooked. Christopher (the chef) uses an old family recipe for his seafood risotto. We like it and we also like the gnocchi and the rack of lamb. Most of the wines of course, come from Italy.

Open Tuesday to Saturday 5 pm to 10 pm. Closed on Sunday and Monday. Licensed. All cards. ♿

Every restaurant in this guide has been personally tested. Our reporters are not allowed to identify themselves or to accept free meals.

LA SCIE, Newfoundland
THE OUTPORT TEAROOM
Highway 414
(709) 675-2720

MAP 184
$45

There were no roads to the outports in the old days. There's a road to La Scie now, but a visit to the Outport Tearoom will give you an idea of what Newfoundland was once like. Valerie Whalen has said that she and her husband, Larry, would feed anyone who came to their door, no matter what time of day it was. And that was true. She did all the cooking while Larry played old Newfoundland songs on his accordion or guitar. The Whalens converted their family home into a museum and then opened a tearoom on the verandah that runs the length of the house. At first they just served fruit tarts, tea-buns and rhubarb crumbles. Later they added such traditional dishes as crab-au-gratin, pea soup with dumplings and jiggs dinner. Salmon has often been hard to get, so they've filled in with cod. La Scie is special; don't miss it.

Open Monday to Saturday 8 am to 8 pm, Sunday 10 am to 6 pm from 1 June until 15 September. No liquor. Master Card, Visa.

SHAUNAVON, Saskatchewan
HARVEST
492 Centre Street
(306) 297-3315

MAP 185
☆
$120

Shaunavon is a picturesque town 70 miles south of Swift Current. Already Harvest is changing the face of gourmet cooking in the heart of cattle country. Garrett Thienes, the chef, focuses on fresh local ingredients. He slow-cooks brisket and hand-carves well-aged strip-loins. He has an open kitchen and if you take a nearby table you're welcome to talk to him while he prepares your meal. Kristy Thienes is in charge of the front of the house, which is perfectly run. Most people ask for the deconstructed flapper pie or the crème brûlée. The wines

have been carefully chosen and the coffee, which is from
Costa Rica, is freshly ground to order.
*Open Tuesday and Wednesday 11 am to 4 pm, Thursday and
Friday 11 am to 11 pm, Saturday 4 pm to 11 pm. Closed on
Sunday and Monday. Licensed. All cards. Book ahead.* ♿

SHELBURNE, N.S.   MAP 186
CHARLOTTE LANE CAFE   ☆
13 Charlotte Lane   **$135**
(902) 875-3314

Kathleen and Roland Glauser have been operating this
colourful little restaurant for many years now, and in
2013 it was named the best small restaurant in the
province. The cooking is innovative and the kitchen
makes much use of such local ingredients as garden
greens, red cabbage and asiago cheese. Lunch is essentially
the same as dinner, though it also includes soups, salads
and sandwiches. They do several theme nights during the
season, of which the burger night is probably the most
successful. Roland cooks rich but he's also adept with
spices (scallops with pesto, salads with dill and tandoori
peanuts). The service is professional but very friendly.
*Open Tuesday to Saturday 11.30 am to 2.30 pm, 5 pm to 8 pm
from early May until late December. Closed on Sunday and
Monday. Licensed. Master Card, Visa. Book ahead if you can.*

SHELBURNE
See also CLARK'S HARBOUR.

SIDNEY, B.C.   (MAP 211)
DEEP COVE CHALET   ☆☆☆
11190 Chalet Road   **$160**
(250) 656-3541

The Deep Cove Chalet was built in 1913 by the B.C.
Electric Company, and for many years has served as a
restaurant, where Pierre Koffel has worked for 43 years.
His lunch now starts at 40.00, for which you get lobster
bisque, a cheese soufflé and a beautifully ripe avocado

with curried prawns. In the evening his menu is larger and more expensive, offering black cod, beef tenderloin, steamed clams, rabbit and salmon. Everything is perfect and the slice of chocolate cake, offered as a sweet course, is a marvel. The wine-list has few equals anywhere. There are seventeen Mouton-Rothschilds, five Lafites and five Latours, all listed at staggering prices. If you want something cheaper, there are many fine wines from the Okanagan, wines like Poplar Grove, Wild Goose, Blue Mountain and Burrowing Owl, none of which costs more than 100.00 a bottle, many much less. It takes an hour to get to Deep Cove from Victoria by Highway 17. Start on Blanshard Street and turn left at Swartz Bay on Land's End Road. The fact is that, at the moment, Pierre Koffel is cooking as well as anyone on Vancouver Island, probably better.

Open Wednesday to Sunday noon to 2 pm, 5.30 pm to 9 pm. Closed on Monday and Tuesday. Licensed. All cards. Book ahead. ♿

SINGHAMPTON, Ontario   MAP 188
EIGENSINN FARM   ☆☆☆
449357 Townline 10   **$800**
(519) 922-3128

Michael Stadtländer and his wife, Nobuyo, have been running Eigensinn Farm for 21 years. This year they plan to be open only on Friday and Saturday, and since there are only twelve seats in the dining-room you should book at least three months in advance and pay when you book. It's a long way to go from almost anywhere, even for an eight-course dinner. The price of a meal is 300.00 a head, plus tip and tax. As for wine, you must bring your own bottle. Michael Stadtländer ranks with the best chefs in the world. He was born the son of a farmer, and here he has a vegetable garden so big that he has had to employ a full-time gardener. He has two farm ponds, where he raises speckled trout and crayfish. He breeds ducks and sheep. He grows fruit trees. All these things eventually find their way onto his table. To get to Eigensinn Farm,

head west from Singhampton on Townline 10 and remember, if you bring your own bottle there's no charge
for corkage.

Open Friday and Saturday at 7 pm by appointment only from 1
May until 15 October. Closed Sunday to Thursday. Bring your
own bottle. No cards. You must book ahead.

SINGHAMPTON   MAP 188
HAISAI   ☆☆
794079 County Road 124   **$100**
(705) 445-2748

Haisai is currently operating year-round on weekends,
with Michael Stadtländer's son, Hermann, as manager
and his Japanese protégé, Min Young Lee, as chef. This
is very much a family enterprise—once a dinner was actually cooked by Michael himself. Everything in the place
is made by hand, even the wine glasses and the furniture.
Eigensinn Farm supplies Haisai with most of its ingredients, which means that both restaurants use nothing but
organic produce. Haisai has a limited menu, concentrating on small plates and wood-fired pizzas. Sometimes
they offer their own smoked ham and pork as well as a
small à la carte featuring fresh fish from the Georgian
Bay, local asparagus and stinging-nettle-and-potato soup.
At night there's a tasting menu for between 70.00 and
80.00, as well as the à la carte. The adjoining bakery,
which makes the breads and the sweets, is open only at
noon.

Open Friday and Saturday 1 pm to 3 pm, 5.30 pm to 9 pm,
Sunday 11 am to 4 pm. Closed Monday to Thursday. Licensed.
No cards. Book ahead.

SOOKE, B.C.   (MAP 211)
WILD MOUNTAIN   ☞
1831 Maple Avenue S   **$50**
(250) 642-3556

Oliver Kienast and his wife, Brooke Fader, are both
keenly interested in locally foraged produce, prepared

and slow-cooked in their restaurant in Sooke. You can come here for a glass of wine and a snack of smoked and marinated olives with polenta and a dip of nasturtium and lemon—all for less than the price of the cheapest appetizer at the once-great Sooke Harbour House. Apart from the smoked olives, they make two superb appetizers, one of pan-fried sweetbreads with wild mushrooms and a second of duck rillettes with hazelnut toast, red onion jam and pickles. Or you can try the endive salad with pears and almonds, dressed with quince and honey. They have a good number of craft beers, ciders and Okanagan wines. The menu may be small, but everything on it is perfect.

Open Tuesday to Saturday 5 pm to 9 pm. Closed on Sunday and Monday. Licensed. Master Card, Visa

SOURIS, P.E.I. (MAP 37)
21 BREAKWATER
21 Breakwater Street **$85**
(902) 687-2556

21 Breakwater is unassuming, comfortable and inexpensive. In fact it's probably one of the best places to eat fish on the Island. More than once we've had scallops that were caught earlier the same day—their fish is that fresh. Everybody likes the fish and chips. Fresh haddock is to be had everywhere, but seldom cooked this well. The menu is fairly small, because Pedro Pereira and Betty MacDonald limit themselves to general favourites, plus a daily special or two—perhaps a fish chowder full of mussels, clams and hake. Not that you have to eat fish. The beefsteak is just as good. The helpings are very generous, and you may not have room for the blueberry cobbler or the bread pudding. The view from the restaurant is lovely and most people are in no hurry to leave. In fact, lunch is so crowded that you'll be lucky to get in the door unless you have a reservation.

Open Monday to Thursday 11.30 am to 8 pm, Friday and Saturday 11.30 am to 9 pm from 1 June until 30 September, Wednesday to Saturday 11.30 am to 9 pm from 1 October until

31 May. Closed on Sunday in summer, from Sunday to Tuesday in winter. Licensed. Master Card, Visa. ♿

STELLARTON, N.S.   (MAP 123)
ANDRE'S SEATS   ☞
245 Foord Street   **$75**
(902) 752-2700

André started out with a pizza takeout at 243 Foord Street, where business was so good that he expanded next door and opened a full-service restaurant with seats. At noon you just ask for a slice of pizza and some salad. The pizza will probably be a pepperoni and the salad a Caesar. The dinner menu is enormous. There are always a lot of pizzas and a number of salads, but every evening they bring on salmon, haddock, several steaks and a brand-new dish. The Italian burger is so new that it isn't even on the menu. It comes with pesto aioli, sundried tomatoes and mozzarella cheese. Most of the sweets are made in the kitchen, and the best of them, in our opinion, is the three-layer carrot cake with real whipped cream. There are one or two good Canadian wines, as well as numerous imports. The walls are lined with posters from the eras of Neil Young, Elvis Presley and the Dave Clark Five. The glass-topped tables are covered with ticket stubs from concerts of the time, and there's a real jukebox on the floor.

Open Monday and Tuesday 11 am to 8 pm, Wednesday and Thursday 11 am to 9 pm, Friday and Saturday 11 am to 10 pm, Sunday 4 pm to 8 pm. Licensed. All cards. ♿

STRATFORD, Ontario   MAP 192
THE PRUNE   ☆☆
151 Albert Street   **$225**
(519) 271-5052

Scarcely a year goes by that there aren't rumours of the Prune's closing. And yet, whenever we ask for a table we get one and find that Bryan Steele is still in charge of the kitchen, his cooking as good as ever. The appetizers are much as one would expect: albacore tuna, chicken-liver mousse, goat-cheese tart and pickled rainbow trout. The main courses show the kitchen at its best. There's sirloin steak, salmon (slow-cooked with cilantro), pickerel (with steamed chard) and seared duck (with honey). After that there are raspberries, local wild blueberries (with blueberry ice cream) and frozen chocolate mousse. The wines are all fairly priced. The sauvignon blanc from Big Head on the Twenty-Mile Bench and the chardonnay from Margaret River both cost only 55.00 a bottle. There's also an unusual list of craft beers from Granville Brewery in Vancouver, Great Lakes in Etobicoke, Kensington in Toronto and Wellington in Guelph.

Open Tuesday to Saturday 5 pm to 8 pm from late May until mid-October. Closed on Sunday and Monday. Licensed. Amex, Master Card, Visa. Free parking. Book ahead.

STRATFORD	**MAP 192**
RUNDLES	☆☆☆
9 Cobourg Street	**$325**
(519) 271-6442	

Neil Baxter has been cooking at Rundles for more than thirty years, and he's still as good as he was when he first came to Canada in 1981. In that time, of course, his prices have risen, and a three-course dinner now costs 99.50 a head. The meal starts with side-stripe shrimp in sea-urchin butter, wild sockeye salmon with white asparagus, yuzu jelly and tangerine vinaigrette or rabbit with pickled cherries, pistachio yogurt and violet mustard. Main dishes are rather less adventurous and run to pan-fried pickerel, braised shoulder of pork, roast leg of rabbit, glazed rib-eye of lamb and bone-in rib steak of beef. All these dishes are brought to you in a calm white room by young waiters who move softly from one table to the next as the meal ripens. Dinner will end with a double-lemon tart, a passion-fruit baba or a blueberry crumble. Rundles is expensive, but the wines are not. There are six whites and six reds, all priced at just 54.50 a bottle or 14.50 a glass. Three of the wines are Canadian

(Cattail Creek, Red Tractor and Rosehall Run). They're all carefully chosen and only the champagnes are less than excellent. If you want to spend the night, there's stunning accommodation right next door. You won't do better anywhere in Stratford.

Open Thursday to Saturday 5 pm to 7.30 pm from late May until late October. Closed Sunday to Wednesday. Licensed. Amex, Master Card, Visa. Book ahead. &

STRATFORD
See also ST. MARYS.

SUMMERSIDE, P.E.I.   **(MAP 37)**
SAMUEL'S COFFEE HOUSE
4 Queen Street   **$60**
(902) 724-2300

This is a new café that offers specialty coffees and teas and a small lunch menu. Home-baked goods like cinnamon rolls and scones are made each morning, and so are their noon-hour specials, which are usually soups, vegetarian chillies and a variety of homemade sandwiches.

Open Monday to Thursday 7.30 am to 5 pm, Friday 7.30 am to 9 pm, Saturday 8 am to 4 pm, Sunday 9 am to 4 pm. Licensed. Master Card, Visa.

SUMMERVILLE BEACH, N.S.   *MAP 194*
QUARTERDECK GRILL
(800) 565-1119   *$115*

The Quarterdeck Grill is situated on a mile-long white-sand beach. It's a spectacular setting and they make good use of it. They offer everything a traveller could want: seafood chowder, mussels by the bucket, bacon–wrapped scallops, burgers and fish and chips. For 22.00 you can have a lobster roll; planked salmon costs 24.00, stuffed lobster tail 26.00. There are also one or two attractive sweets. One is blueberry crisp, the other bread pudding with cinnamon. The Quarterdeck is open all day every day from early May until the middle of October. They have a licence and take all cards. &

SUNDRIDGE, Ontario   MAP 195
DANNY'S JUSTA PASTA   ☆
367 Valleyview Road   **$125**
(705) 384-5542

There are those who don't agree with us when we say that Danny Galekovic makes the best pastas in the province. They should just come and take a look at the lineups at the door. Highway 11 may have been altered to leave Danny's out in the cold, but no matter, the world still beats a path to his door. Danny opened Justa Pasta in 1983, so he's been here for more than thirty years. Thirty years is nothing to the Galekovic family—Danny's parents ran the Sundridge Steak House far longer than that. We've always liked Danny's chicken penne and we still do, but this year we're recommending his linguine, which comes with your choice of smoked salmon or fresh Atlantic salmon with onions, tomatoes and leeks in a dill cream sauce. The helpings are certainly big, but everything on the plate is so light that you wouldn't notice it. Start your meal with pâté maison and warm herb bread. As for sweets, they change almost daily. Outside, Justa Pasta looks pretty plain and prices have certainly risen, but what do you expect? Do you want him to cut corners and lower his standards?

Open Monday to Thursday 11 am to 8 pm, Friday and Saturday 11 am to 9 pm, Sunday 11 am to 8 pm from 1 April until 31 October, Thursday 11 am to 8 pm, Friday and Saturday 11 am to 9 pm, Sunday 11 am to 8 pm from 1 November until 31 March. Closed Monday to Wednesday in winter. Licensed. All cards. No reservations. Free parking.

SYDNEY, N.S.   MAP 196
GOVERNORS
233 Esplanade   **$165**
Cape Breton
(902) 562-7646

This is now about the best place to eat in Sydney. They have first-class filet mignon and excellent Atlantic salmon with maple sugar. Everything is cheap—the fish and chips battered with beer costs an incredible 14.00 and the filet mignon itself costs only 35.00. For rather more than that—they don't give the price—they'll bring you a fresh naked lobster. Dinners begin well with crab-cakes, or with shrimps or mussels. The wine-list is small (seven labels) but choice. They have Tidal Bay from Grand Pré and Nova 7 from Benjamin Bridge. The reds are less exciting, but there is a Leon Millet from Grand Pré, and it's one of their best.

Open daily 11 am to 11 pm. Licensed. Master Card, Visa. &

SYDNEY   **MAP 196**
THE OLIVE TREE
137 Victoria Road   **$80**
Cape Breton
(902) 539-1553

The Olive Tree was redecorated inside and out a couple of years ago. There's colour everywhere you turn. Even the artificial plants have been arranged to look their colourful best. The menu is still too long and the prices are still too low. This used to be a pizzeria, but there's no longer a pizza in the place. They'll tell you that the Olive Tree is now a Mediterranean bistro. The Blue Plate special, which is the thing to have, changes daily. It might be chicken fettuccine with tomato, basil and lemon. There are also a number of wraps, sandwiches and salads, as well as things like Maltese haddock and lamb souvlaki. Everything is attractively presented and the service is extremely friendly. They may go back to pizzas any day, but until they do, chances are you'll be happy here, especially if you like a quiet soundtrack.

Open Monday to Saturday 11 am to 9 pm. Closed on Sunday. Licensed. Amex, Master Card, Visa. No reservations.

This is a guide to Canadian restaurants from coast to coast—the first ever published and the only one of its kind on the market today. Nobody can buy his way into this guide and nobody can buy his way out.

TATAMAGOUCHE, N.S.   MAP 197
TRAIN STATION INN
21 Station Road   **$150 ($250)**
(902) 657-3222

Years ago Jimmie and Shelley LaFrense came across an old C.N.R. dining-car in Winnipeg and brought it to Tatamagouche, where for 25 years it's served as a dining-room just off Station Road. There it stands on a track with several similar cars, now used as bedroom suites. The menu is quite ambitious and features such things as gravlax, lobster pot-pie, lemon-dill salmon, scallops gratin and stuffed pork loin. To drink, they have good local beer from the Tatamagouche Brewing Company and a few wines from Jost. After dinner you can if you like spend the night in one of the comfortable rail-car suites.

Open daily 11 am to 2.30 pm, 5 pm to 9 pm from 1 May until 31 October. Licensed. Master Card, Visa. Book ahead if you can.

TEMISCOUATA–SUR–LE–LAC, Quebec MAP 198
AUBERGE DU CHEMIN FAISANT   ✩✩✩
12 rue Vieux Chemin   **$225**
Cabano
(418) 854-9342

Cabano has now merged with Notre-Dame-du-Lac and become Témiscouata-sur-le-Lac. The Chemin Faisant has six bedrooms, all different and all decorated in the *art-déco* style. Every evening the chef, Hughes Massey, offers an eight-course *menu de dégustation,* featuring products of the Bas St.-Laurent: red-tuna tartar, saddle of rabbit with sautéed chanterelles and date purée, and grilled trout with sour cream and garlic. At noon the menu is simpler and smaller, offering little but fruit salad, poached egg with hollandaise sauce and tapioca with lemon and laven-der. From time to time he brings in crab from the Mag-dalens and regularly buys red deer, scallops and foie gras wherever he can find them. There are about 150 labels in his cellar and they're all constantly changing. Meanwhile, he likes to play the piano, which he does most evenings after dinner.

Open daily 6 pm to 8 pm from 1 June until Labour Day, Sunday 6 pm to 8 pm from Labour Day until 31 May. Closed Monday to Saturday in winter. Licensed. All cards. &

TEMISCOUATA-SUR-LE-LAC   MAP 198
AUBERGE MARIE-BLANC
2629 rue Commerciale s   **$150**
Notre-Dame-du-Lac
(418) 899-6747

The Auberge Marie-Blanc was built in 1905 by a New York lawyer for his mistress, Mlle. Marie-Blanc Charlier, who lived here until her death in 1949. Guy Sirois and his wife, Jeannine, bought the place in 1960 and ran it for more than 40 years. Many people thought it was the only dependable place to break a journey from Fredericton to New York. The motel units were plain but tidy, and everybody had breakfast on their porch overlooking Lake Témiscouata. The evening menu was simple in its early days, but it grew over the years into a four-course table d'hôte. Finally Guy's daughter took charge of the kitchen. She had never heard of sweetbreads, but her father lived just long enough to teach her. Guy Sirois may be gone now, but his kitchen is still there, turning out raw oysters, seafood salads—and sweetbreads. Main courses include tuna niçoise, magret de canard, fillet of beef béarnaise and, an unusual dish, young wild boar. For a few dollars extra, they give you a wedge of local cheese, a fruit sorbet and a cup of filter coffee.

Open Monday 8 am to 10 am, Tuesday to Saturday 8 am to 10 am, 5.30 pm to 8.30 pm, Sunday 8 am to 10 am from early June until mid-October. Licensed. Master Card, Visa.

The price rating shown opposite the headline of each entry indicates the average cost of dinner for two with a modest wine, tax and tip. The cost of dinner, bed and breakfast (if available) is shown in parentheses.

TERRACE, B.C.
DON DIEGO'S
3212 Kalum Street
(250) 635-2307

MAP 199
☆
$85

Don Diego's flirts with Mexican cuisine, but it could never be described as a Mexican restaurant. (A Mexican restaurant wouldn't have lasted long in Terrace.) They do offer margaritas, but the menu as a whole offers whatever has worked well over the years. They do a lot of seafood, which is brought in from Prince Rupert. Shrimp is scarce on the Pacific coast, but keep an eye out for it, usually with chipotle and lime. Fresh fruit and vegetables are plentiful in Terrace, and stirling beef comes in from Alberta. The baby back-ribs are fall-off-the-bone tender. Sweets have always been a big thing here. At the moment the winner is the chocolate-and-peanut-butter pie. The recipes may be unusual, but they work, and the helpings are generous. The dining-room is small and it can be very noisy. Some people like it that way; others don't.
Open Monday to Saturday 11 am to 2 pm, 4.30 pm to 9 pm. Closed on Sunday. Licensed. Amex, Master Card, Visa. Book ahead if you can. &

THORNBURY, Ontario
SIMPLICITY BISTRO
81 King Street E
(519) 599-5550

(MAP 47)
☆
$145

This is an endearing little restaurant, decorated to match the season and offering fresh food cooked to order. That means that if you come in summer they'll give you sunchoke soup and seared pickerel with quinoa and brown butter. In winter it'll be bean-and-kale soup and seared scallops in a cauliflower purée. Beef short-ribs are served with mashed potatoes and a bordelaise sauce, rack of lamb with mustard and crushed cranberries. Their crabcakes actually taste of crab and their pumpkin tart is served with real whipped cream and pumpkinseed brittle. Everything—the cooking, the presentation and the serv-

234

ice—is top-notch. If you want wine, ask for Georgian Hills, a local winery that's not in the liquor store.
Open Monday to Thursday 11 am to 4 pm (lunch), 4 pm to 9 pm (dinner), Friday and Saturday 11 am to 4 pm, 4 pm to 10 pm, Sunday 11 am to 4 pm (brunch). Licensed. All cards. ♿

THUNDER BAY, Ontario   MAP 201
BISTRO ONE   ☆
555 Dunlop Street   **$170**
(807) 622-2478

We always feel sure of ourselves when we write about Bistro One. Jean Robillard never lets us down. Nor do any of his staff. The chef de cuisine has been with him for 21 years, and so has Maria Costanzo, his patissière. Their menu touches all the bases. They even offer pan-roasted fillets of Alberta veal, which is rare in Canada. Nothing is ever overstated or overcooked. The rack of lamb is imported fresh from New Zealand and served with gorgonzola butter. If you're looking for beef, the Angus filet mignon is wonderfully tender, though we find it hard not to ask for the breast of duck flavoured with brandy. Everybody speaks highly of the amazing list of cheeses, and many diners praise Maria's molten-chocolate cake. The wine-list offers several wines that no-body else seems to carry. They're expensive but they're very good drinking.
Open Tuesday to Saturday 5 pm to 10 pm. Closed on Sunday and Monday. Licensed. All cards. ♿

THUNDER BAY   MAP 201
THE SILVER BIRCH   ☆
28 Cumberland Street N   **$150**
(807) 345-0597

Darlene Green was born and raised in Thunder Bay and is fiercely attached to the area. She ran a respected cater-ing business for 25 years before she opened the Silver Birch. She calls her food Northern Inspired Cuisine and specializes in fish from Lake Superior, as well as local beef and rabbit and local mushrooms. Everybody likes her wild-mushroom tart, which is made with puff pastry and aged local gouda. And everybody likes her seafood chowder, which she calls bouillabaisse and serves in a tomato broth with fennel and fresh mussels. One of her best (and cheapest) dishes is the so-called Shore Dinner, which is made with northern pike and costs just 18.00, or 38.00 if you ask for pickerel instead of northern pike. Walleye is a great fish and it appears all over the menu, but Northern pike is a great fish too. Darlene makes all the sweets herself, and we particularly like her saskatoon-berry tart. *Open Tuesday to Saturday 5 pm to 10 pm. Closed on Sunday and Monday. Licensed. All cards.* ♿

THUNDER BAY   MAP 201
THE SOVEREIGN ROOM
220 Red River Road   **$110**
(807) 343-9277

Thunder Bay has needed a good gastropub for years. Nowadays you really have to book a table before 5 pm at the Sovereign Room to be sure of a seat, and that's not just for a drink. It's true, they do carry dozens of imported beers, including important things like Innis & Gunn and Southern Tier. Sleeping Giant and Lake of the Woods are on tap—there are beers here that most people have never even heard of. We used to scorn their stone-baked pizzas, but the fact is that they're all models of their kind. We especially admire the fig pizza with prosciutto, gorgonzola and honey. If you don't want a pizza you should start with buttermilk-fried chicken with chipotle mayonnaise, or, if you come with a large party, the charcuterie board, which costs 28.00. They do beef short-ribs with polenta, and the vegetable burgers are about as good as it gets. All the food is regional and the prices are very reasonable.
Open Tuesday to Thursday 4 pm to 11 pm, Friday 4 pm to midnight, Saturday and Sunday 11 am to 2 pm (brunch), 4 pm to 11 pm. Closed on Monday. Licensed. Master Card, Visa. No reservations.

236

THUNDER BAY MAP 201
TOMLIN ☆☆
202 Red River Road **$150**
(807) 346-4447

Tomlin is pretty well at the top of the heap in Thunder
Bay. It's small and takes no reservations. But Steve Simpson is a creative chef and his menu evolves with the seasons. There are two menus, one large and one small. It's
customary to order two small dishes and one large. They
buy locally and when they buy a pig they eat every part
of it. They have an excellent charcuterie board and two
kinds of pasta. We like the juicy roast chicken with barley; we like the salmon too. Everyone loves the coffee.
Most of the wines come from the Niagara Region and
that's a good thing.
*Open Tuesday to Thursday 5 pm to 10 pm, Friday and Saturday
5 pm to 11 pm. Closed on Sunday and Monday. Licensed. All
cards. No reservations.* ♿

TOBERMORY, Ontario MAP 202
GRANDVIEW INN
11 Earl Street **$140**
(519) 596-2220

The Grandview Inn may not give you the best dinner
you've ever had, but on a fine night it will give you about
the finest sunset you've ever seen. They've always kept a
good kitchen here. People write to us about their high
prices, but you'll be lucky to find better food for less.
They've been in business for almost half a century and
their menu doesn't change much. Seafood is usually your
best bet. Georgian Bay whitefish is prepared in several
different ways, but most people ask for their whitefish
blackened Cajun-style. The salmon with orange and ginger is, however, an attractive alternative, as is the trout.
They buy most of their fish and most of their vegetables
from organic suppliers, and they never overcook either.
The Grandview is directly opposite the Chi Cheemaun
ferry terminal, which connects Tobermory to Mani-

toulin Island. A short walk along the lakeside boardwalk will also take you to the north end of the Bruce Trail. *Open daily 5 pm to 8 pm from 1 May until Thanksgiving. Licensed. Master Card, Visa. Book ahead if you can.*

TOBERMORY   MAP 202
MOLINARI
57 Bay Street   **$125**
(226) 668-0512

Molinari went through a bad patch a few years ago, but now it has some of the best food in town. The chef has a tiny menu of what he calls (with justice) lovely Italian dishes. The pasta is house-made and the spaghetti bolognese tastes as good as it looks. There are usually three sweets, among them a first-class tiramisu. The Italian gelato is no longer on the menu and neither is the ravioli. But Molinari is a warm and very satisfying restaurant. *Open daily noon to 9.30 pm from early May until mid-September. Licensed. Master Card, Visa.* ♿

TOFINO, B.C.   MAP 203
SHELTER
601 Campbell Street   **$150**
(250) 725-3353

When is a pub not a pub? Shelter is a restaurant in pub's clothing. They use local, organic produce whenever they can. Their salmon and halibut are caught locally and the shellfish comes from the Gulf Islands, the poultry from the Cowichan Valley, the greens from a nearby farm. The chef, Matty Kane, makes a fine lunch every day of Cortes Island mussels in a broth of sautéed chorizo, red peppers and basil or albacore-tuna tartar with ginger and soy. Every evening the kitchen rises to wild salmon, side-stripe shrimps and Peace River sirloin of lamb with capers and mustard in a purée of cauliflower. They still offer their wonderful warm chèvre salad with goat cheese, caramelized onions, garlic and apple-cider vinaigrette, and it's as good as ever.

238

Open daily 11.30 am to 5 pm (lunch), 5 pm to 11pm (dinner).
Licensed. Amex, Master Card, Visa. Book ahead if you can.

TOFINO   **MAP 203**
SOBO   ☆
311 Neill Street   **$145**
(250) 725-2341

Sobo stands for Sophisticated Bohemian, and it's come a
long way from the days when it was located in a chip-
wagon parked by the side of the road. It now occupies
one floor of an austere but elegant building that overlooks the harbour—thanks to the energy and skill of the
chef, Lisa Ahier. At noon we usually ask for the seared
scallops with pea-shoots and mint or the garlicky Caesar
salad with asiago croutons. After that we go for the
seafood stew, which is full of mussels, clams, scallops,
humpback shrimps and cod in a tomato broth or a
seafood taco with spiced wild fish in a corn tortilla and
fruit salsa. They do nice pizzas here too. Try either the
ricotta spinach with caramelized onions and kale or the
shiitake mushroom with pesto and mozzarella cheese.
Open daily 5 pm to 9.30 pm from early February until mid-
April, daily 11 am to 9.30 pm from mid-April until the end of
December. Licensed. Amex, Master Card, Visa. ꕔ

TOFINO   **MAP 203**
THE SPOTTED BEAR
120 4 Street: Unit 101   **$90**
(250) 725-2215

The Spotted Bear closed at the end of 2014. The good
news is that it's been sold to Rob Leadley and Mitsumi
Kawai, who will turn it into a Japanese restaurant called
Kuma (Japanese for Bear) under Simon Burch, the former
chef. Kuma will be a restaurant with 28 seats and a small
menu offering things like osake-style okonomiyaki,
chicken karaage, tuna tataki and noodle bowls "to warm
the soul." They'll have local beer and hot and cold sake.
Open daily 5.30 pm to 11 pm. Licensed, Master Card, Visa.

TOFINO   **MAP 203**
TACOFINO CANTINA   ☆
1134 Pacific Rim Highway   **$35**
(250) 726-8288

If you really miss Sobo's old purple truck, look for the
bright-orange van of Tacofino Cantina. It's parked right
next to the Wildside Grill. Kaeli Robinsong is offering
what she calls "fast slow food, made from scratch with
no wait." There are picnic tables around the truck and
lots of sand and surf. They have huge burritos for 10.00,
and they're really good. But what makes Tacofino famous
is its Baja-style tacos. They have sustainable-tuna tacos,
beef tacos and halibut tacos. They're all great and bring
people from all over the province.
Open Monday to Thursday 11 am to 5 pm, Friday and Saturday
11 am to 6 pm, Sunday 11 am to 5 pm. No liquor. Master Card,
Visa.

TOFINO   **MAP 203**
WICKANINNISH INN
500 Osprey Lane   **$140**
(250) 725-3106

The Wickaninnish Inn may have lost some of its most
talented kitchen staff to Wolf in the Fog, but it's still
known for elegant dining. The kitchen uses everything
it can from the Pacific Rim National Park, foraging locally for evergreen huckleberries, wild mushrooms, sea
truffles and gooseneck barnacles. Dinner is offered from
a seasonal à la carte, but if you want the best of the best,
ask for David Sider's tasting menu, paired with local and
imported wines. Meals start with a pork torchon from
Sloping Hills Farm or an oyster risotto with foie gras and
sourdough bread. They're equally good. For the main
course they offer at least two great dishes—poached
Camelina sablefish and striploin of venison with smoked
pears and caramelized parsnips—both cost 42.00. After
that there's Earl Grey crème brûlée and a baked-apple
crumble. Sadly, however, all the best tables are kept

for residents.
Open daily 8 am to 9 pm. Licensed. All cards. Book ahead if you can. &

TOFINO   MAP 203
WOLF IN THE FOG
150 4 Street   **$90**
(250) 725-9653

Wolf in the Fog was the best new restaurant of the year in 2014. It's a two-storey facility, serving breakfast and lunch on the ground floor and dinner upstairs. The upstairs dining-room is dramatic, if crowded and noisy, and it has a spectacular bar that quickly established a reputation for exotic cocktails. The best way to experience the place is to order a sharing plate. There are several of these, including the Mighty Duck (a whole duck with blood orange and gorgonzola lasagne), the Arabian Nights (lamb shank, pomegranates, bulgur and goat-cheese), the Block Party (fried chicken, barbecued ribs and pulled pork) and the French Bombshell (scallops, black cod and endive). They're all good.
Open daily 9 am to midnight. Licensed. Amex, Master Card, Visa. Book ahead. &

TOFINO
See also UCLUELET.

TORONTO, Ontario   MAP 204
ALO   ★★★
163 Spadina Avenue: Floor 3   **$275**
(416) 260-2222

Last year Patrick Kriss opened what has to be the best restaurant in Toronto. Here he offers a five-course tasting menu priced at 89.00 a person. With wine, service and taxes an evening at Alo costs almost 300.00—and it's worth every penny. The critics all say, and it's true, that what makes Alo is Kriss himself. His cooking is superlative. He begins with a corn sorbet with buttermilk and amaranth, foie gras with king oysters and veal trotters, dungeness crab with lime and spices, hamachi with barese cucumbers and continues, without taking a breath, with rack of Yorkshire pork and Dorset shoulder of lamb and ends with a dark chocolate ganache or a yellow-plum sorbet with bulgur and bitter almond. It's hard to pick and choose among these pleasures, but our favourites are the pain au lait (made with butter churned in-house and a glass of madeira) and the dungeness crab with Carolina-gold rice and lime. All these dishes are meticulously thought out and prepared in classical Parisian style. The wine-list is spectacular; the service superb.

Open Tuesday to Saturday 5.30 pm to 10.30 pm. Closed on Sunday and Monday. Licensed. Amex, Master Card, Visa. Book ahead. &

TORONTO   **MAP 204**
ARIA   ☆
Maple Leaf Square   **$175**
25 York Street
(416) 363-2742

Aria has stunning looks and the cooking almost matches the appearance of the place. The kitchen puts on a table d'hôte of grilled Humboldt squid, albacore tuna and tiramisu for just 45.00 a head. On the à la carte you pay more, of course. The menu starts with yellow gazpacho, carpaccio of beef or mushroom ravioli and continues with a veal chop milanese or organic salmon. There are no fewer than twenty-two barolos priced from 125.00 to 550.00 and nine chiantis with a top price of 380.00. They offer a couple of solaias and a couple of sassicaias at the usual prices, but for a lot less you can drink a bottle of dolcetto d'Alba or go Canadian with a chardonnay from Norman Hardie at 75.00. No hardship there.

Open Monday to Friday 11.30 am to 3 pm, 5 pm to 11 pm (later on Friday), Saturday 5 pm to 10 pm. Closed on Sunday. Licensed. Amex, Master Card, Visa. Book ahead if you can. &

Every restaurant in this guide has been personally tested.

TORONTO MAP 204
BAR BUCA
75 Portland Street **$100**
(416) 599-2822

This is the third Buca in Toronto. They started on King Street, then opened a second in Yorkville (see below). This one is deliberately uncomfortable in the best modern style. They take no reservations and, once you get a table, you climb onto a high chair to sit down. The staff are all friendly and relaxed, however, and they're quick to offer you a glass of Italian wine. There are twenty reds and ten whites. The menu is short and the best thing on it is either the bianchetti (small fried smelts) or, if you come in on a weekend, the nova rossa, which combines egg yolk with crisp potatoes and scallions. The critics also admire the focaccia with roast pork and farm-fresh eggs, but there's too much focaccia for our taste and too little pork. The best of the sweets is the bombolone with vanilla cream and lemon, and it's famous all over town. *Open Monday to Friday 7 am to 2 pm, Saturday and Sunday 10 am to 4 pm. Licensed. Master Card, Visa. No reservations.* &

TORONTO MAP 204
BAR ISABEL ☆
797 College Street **$170**
(416) 532-2222

Bar Isabel is crowded and unbearably noisy. Talk is out of the question. It's also expensive. Iberico ham costs 50.00 a portion or 25.00 for a half-portion. If you can't afford that (and who can?), they have fine smoked sweetbreads, grilled mussels and ceviche of Pacific halibut. Grant van Gameren is a clever cook. For instance, he makes a very good cake basquaise. One critic calls the cake erotic, but of course it's not anything of the sort. All the wines on the long list are Spanish, which to most people means rioja or nothing. (A glass of rioja costs 20.00.) As we said, Bar Isabel is expensive. Clever but expensive.

Open daily 6 pm to 2 am. Licensed. Amex, Master Card, Visa.
You must book ahead.

TORONTO   MAP 204
THE BLACK HOOF   ☆
928 Dundas Street W   **$120**
(416) 551-8854

At the Black Hoof the menu concentrates, without apology, on meat. Jowl, bone marrow, tongue and even ears appear all over the place. Don't think of this as a place that serves bison or beefsteak. It's a sophisticated restaurant that deals in all parts of the animal. The house charcuterie features things like horse and beef heart with dill, served with whipped chicken fat. The smoked pork jowl makes pork belly seem tame by comparison. Cut through the richness with a glass of West Avenue cider and go on to layers of wafer-thin tongue held in place between two pieces of brioche by a skewer. Or maybe you prefer some pig's-ear slaw, which is surprisingly light and likeable. The kitchen can be heavy-handed at times—the sweetbreads, for instance, are thickly breaded and fried longer than necessary. But after all, you're meant to be reminded of the last days of Rome. And a meal like this will cost less than 40.00, which is pretty hard to beat. The winelist is small—there are only three or four reds by the bottle and three or four whites, most of which cost about 80.00. We for our part usually drink cider.

Open Thursday to Saturday 6 pm to 1 am, Sunday and Monday
6 pm to 11.30 pm. Closed on Tuesday and Wednesday. Licensed.
No cards. No reservations.

TORONTO   MAP 204
BORALIA
59 Ossington Avenue   **$145**
(647) 351-5100

Boralia is all about Canadian food—things like smoked mussels. They're big, tender and sweet, brought to your table under a glass dome with smoke from burning pine needles swirling around, and flavoured with broth scented with pine ash. They also have scallops crudo with wild ginger, pickled chanterelles and fermented chilli, bison tartar with fennel and garlic aioli, and pork with apple and potato croquettes. We find the pork too dry, and the hot chocolate beignets offered as a sweet course too heavy. But those are exceptions. Everything on the menu is prepared from old Canadian recipes and every dish has its date of first use attached, which makes for an interesting meal. Five small plates are a complete dinner, but order a second portion of the smoked mussels, because you won't want to share them. Most of the wines come from Niagara, but there are several from both Tuscany and Piedmont and one from Blue Mountain, a lovely Pinot Noir from the Okanagan.

Open Wednesday to Sunday 5.30 pm to 9.30 pm. Closed on Monday and Tuesday. Licensed. Master Card, Visa.

TORONTO   **MAP 204**
BUCA   ☆
53 Scollard Street   **$200**
(416) 962-2822

Never mind the Scollard Street address: look for the entrance to this uptown Buca at 60 Yorkville Avenue. It's a modern Italian restaurant, majoring in appetizers like octopus salami with lemon, smoked rainbow trout and cured Ahi tuna. Main courses—black cod, raw steelhead trout and pork belly—are broadly similar. Gorgonzola cheese is offered as a sweet, along with tiramisu and panna cotta. The list of Italian wines is huge. The interior is all cool glass and steel, which makes it look impersonal, but the service, as it happens, is very friendly. This is a sister restaurant to the original Buca at 604 King Street W. If you like glass and steel, come here. If you like being underground, go to King Street (telephone (416) 865-1600). Rob Gentile is in charge of both restaurants.

Open Monday to Wednesday 11 am to 3 pm, 5 pm to 10 pm, Thursday and Friday 11 am to 3 pm, 5 pm to 11 pm, Saturday

245

5 pm to 11 pm. Closed on Sunday. Licensed. Amex, Master Card, Visa. Book ahead.

TORONTO   MAP 204
BYBLOS   ☆
11 Duncan Street   **$175**
(647) 660-0909

Byblos is Mediterranean in style, offering wines from Lebanon, Spain and Portugal, with a few bottles from France and Italy and a few from Napa, Sonoma and the Columbia Valley in Oregon. All the food is carefully pre-pared and presented. There's steak tartar, tuna ceviche, slow-braised lamb and deep-fried eggplant, all meant for sharing. The small dishes are the best and the best of them (it's a marvel) is the crispy eggplant with tahini aioli and bayildi sauce. The best of the large dishes is probably the whole sea-bass, though the fish is not well boned, so be careful. Byblos isn't cheap—-Nova 7 from Benjamin Bridge, for example, costs 70.00 a bottle.

Open Monday to Saturday 5.30 pm to 9.30 pm, Sunday 4 pm to 9.30 pm. Licensed. Amex, Master Card, Visa. Book ahead. &

TORONTO   MAP 204
CAFE BOULUD   ☆
60 Yorkville Avenue   **$225**
(416) 963-6000

There's something self-important about Café Boulud. The dining-room says "Look at me" to everyone sitting there. The menu is notable chiefly for the importance of every dish on it. (It features shrimp with garlic, raw oys-ters, tuna tartar, Pacific halibut, truffled boudin, veal stew, fresh sea-bass and New York steak.) The kitchen has a new rotisserie for its fish, and it's always competent, but seldom novel or exciting. The food prices are high and the wine prices are beyond belief. (The best buy on the wine-list is probably the Poplar Grove from the Okanagan, which at 70.00 costs only a little more than

it's worth.) Needless to say, the service is impeccable.
Open daily 5.30 pm to 10 pm (later on weekends). Licensed.
Amex, Master Card, Visa. Book ahead if you can. &

TORONTO   **MAP 204**
CAMPAGNOLO
832 Dundas Street W   **$150**
(416) 364-4785

We've said it before. Campagnolo is Italian and, like most
Italian restaurants, it's warm and friendly. They have, as
a matter of course, house-made spaghetti and house-
made tagliatelle, but the fact is that their best dishes aren't
Italian at all. For instance, they like to start with roasted
bone marrow, served with oxtail marmalade, and go on
to bone-in veal chops (expensive as veal always is) or Irish
organic salmon with zucchini flowers and chanterelles,
ending with salted caramel budino. The wines aren't
cheap, and the best buy is probably the sauvignon blanc
from Organized Crime at just over 50.00.
Open Wednesday to Sunday 6 pm to 9 pm. Closed on Monday
and Tuesday. Licensed. Master Card, Visa. Book ahead.

TORONTO   **MAP 204**
CANOE   ☆☆☆
Toronto-Dominion Centre   **$245**
66 Wellington Street W
(416) 364-0054

If you book a table by the window, you'll find that the
whole of Toronto Island is spread out before you. Meanwhile, the kitchen has developed an exciting menu that
starts with a lovely wood-mushroom soup with camelina
seeds and a fluke ceviche with fried seaweed, clay-pepper
dust, cranberries and sea-buckthorn. The Alberta lamb
that comes next is mixed with squash, kale and brown
butter. Better still is the Atlantic salmon with mustard
and sweet potatoes and the East-Coast halibut, which is
daringly prepared with wasabi and turnip purée. The

sweets are less important, but there's a good chocolate torte and a charming passion-fruit sorbet. There's some very good drinking on the wine-list, where the best buy is probably the Tawse pinot noir. (Tawse is one of the best Niagara vintages and it deserves to be better known than it is.) If you want a dessert wine, you'll find that the Pillitteri vidal ice wine is actually just as good as the Benjamin Bridge from Gaspereau.

Open Monday to Friday 11.45 am to 2.30 pm, 5 pm to 9 pm. Closed on Saturday and Sunday. Licensed. All cards. Book ahead. &

TORONTO   **MAP 204**
CARMEN   ☆
922 Queen Street W   **$130**
(416) 535-0404

Carmen was one of the ten best new restaurants in Toronto in 2013. The chef is Spanish and his menu features tapas and four or five paellas. Our favourite tapas are the fried artichokes with aioli, the pork tenderloin with piquillo jam and the fried green tomatoes with red peppers and feta cheese. The paellas, which are expensive, come to the table in a hot pan and are big enough for four. The wines are Spanish, some of them quite rare in this country.

Open daily 5 pm to 11 pm. Licensed. All cards. Book ahead. &

TORONTO   **MAP 204**
CAVA   ☆
1560 Yonge Street   **$200**
(416) 979-9918

Cava has a tapas-style menu with all kinds of Spanish food and drink. There's serrano ham and the much better Iberico ham, both sliced off the bone right in front of you. There's blue cheese with sherry-roasted figs—a delightful dish. There's ceviche of Spanish mackerel, roasted Brussels sprouts with black garlic and a mousse of foie gras. Large plates run to grilled octopus, grilled sardines

and roasted sablefish with black rice and collard greens. There are no fewer than 24 riojas by the bottle and two by the glass. The meal ends well with a valhrona-chocolate soufflé with (not enough) coffee sauce.
Open daily 5 pm to 10 pm. Licensed. Amex, Master Card, Visa. &

TORONTO   MAP 204
THE CHASE
10 Temperance Street   **$250**
(647) 348-7000

The cooking here is direct and straightforward. The dining-room, in the penthouse on the fifth floor, is spacious and elegant and there's valet parking. The menu starts with avocado and curried shrimps, scallops in a purée of cauliflower and octopus salsa verde. There's lamb and beef to follow, but it's best to stick to the seafood (black cod, tuna and Arctic char). The sturgeon comes with Brussels sprouts, the char and tuna with artichokes, the black cod with fresh pasta. These are all expensive dishes, and in fact the Chase *is* expensive. The cheapest champagne costs 150.00 a bottle.
Open Monday to Friday 11.30 am to 5 pm (lunch), 5 pm to 11 pm (dinner), Saturday 5 pm to 11 pm. Closed on Sunday. Licensed. Amex, Master Card, Visa. Valet parking. Book ahead. &

TORONTO   MAP 204
DANDYLION
1198 Queen Street W   **$150**
(647) 464-9100

Dandylion is a warm and friendly restaurant, next to a pawnbroker's shop on Queen Street. They have a tightly edited menu of three appetizers, three main courses and three sweets. The presentation is unusual. Chicken is hidden under cabbage leaves, lamb under mustard greens, ice cream under shreds of phyllo and saskatoons. There are no shared plates; Dandylion dares to be different. The chef is Jay Carter, who worked for Susur Lee for ten years and moved to Centro before opening his own place. A typical menu starts with carrot soup with ginger and shrimps and goes on to monkfish with sunchokes and ends with olive-oil cake with peaches and pistachios. There aren't many wines, but there are four ciders and six beers, among them Orval, a Trappist 6-percent beer from Belgium.

Open Tuesday to Saturday 5.30 pm to 10.30 pm. Closed on Sunday and Monday. Licensed. Master Card, Visa.

TORONTO　　　　　　　　　　　　　　**MAP 204**
EDULIS　　　　　　　　　　　　　　　　☆☆
169 Niagara Street　　　　　　　　　　　**$240**
(416) 703-4222

Edulis is an intimate restaurant on a quiet downtown street. You don't need to shout to make yourself heard here, though you may be annoyed to find that the so-called set menus are actually blind tasting menus chosen by the chef. This, however, is one case where you'll be happy to be surprised. The cooking is all about seasonal cuisine, which doesn't mean just root vegetables in winter. Instead, your meal is likely to start with thin slices of raw fish, lightly dressed and served with radish and sesame seeds or perhaps with bonito served with house-made chorizo and butter beans. The roasted John Dory is beautifully cooked and comes in its own broth with onion petals; duck is cooked two ways, with pistachio, sausage and wild mushrooms. Dinner ends with a blood-orange sorbet, lemon mousse or a citrus salad. Five courses like this cost 65.00, seven cost 85.00. The wine-list is extensive but reasonably priced. The top wine costs 225.00, 100.00 more for champagne.

Open Wednesday to Saturday 6 pm to 10.30 pm, Sunday noon to 1.30 pm. Closed on Monday and Tuesday. Licensed. Amex, Master Card, Visa. Book ahead. ♿

If you use an out-of-date edition and find it inaccurate, don't blame us. Buy a new edition.

TORONTO   **MAP 204**
ENOTECA SOCIALE
1288 Dundas Street W   **$135**
(416) 534-1200

Before you book a table at Enoteca, you need to know
that there's only one fish dish on the menu and very little
meat. Basically, this is a pasta house and the big seller is
spaghetti. True, there are a number of useful appetizers—
arancini, chicken-liver mousse, tuna, mushroom bruschetta and raw oysters. For the main course there's
bucatini, gnocchi, rigatoni and sea-bass. The sea-bass is
very good indeed and the pasta is all made in house.
There are several wines by the glass, the best of which is
a barolo for only 12.00.
Open daily 5 pm to 11 pm. Licensed. Amex, Master Card,
Visa. Book ahead.

TORONTO   **MAP 204**
THE FAT PASHA
414 Dupont Street   **$95**
(647) 340-6142

The Fat Pasha is fun if you take things slowly, one at a
time. Start with the roasted cauliflower, and when you're
finished that ask for some cabbage with caraway or, if
you're hungry, some za'taar chicken. Next comes
tabouleh or falafel. Don't bother with the hummus,
which is oily and heavy. Instead, finish your meal with
some bread pudding with maple syrup, which is a lot
lighter than the sticky-date pudding. White wine goes
better with this style of cooking (Jewish, Middle Eastern)
and they have a couple of useful white wines from Prince
Edward County. Ask for the Norman Hardie. The Fat
Pasha is usually crowded and always noisy. Just point to
what you want on the menu, and with luck you'll get it.
Open Monday and Tuesday 5 pm to 11 pm, Wednesday to Sun-
day 11 am to 3 pm, 5 pm to 11 pm. Licensed. Master Card,
Visa. Book ahead if you can. &

TORONTO   **MAP 204**
FRANK
Art Gallery of Ontario   **$145**
317 Dundas Street W
(416) 979-6688

Frank is a good place to know about if you want to visit
the Art Gallery of Ontario, and that's about it. The menu
and surroundings are unpretentious, not to say perfectly
ordinary. Lunch costs 35.00 for three courses, and it starts
with a single scallop, attended by mushy peas and a pea-
shoot salad, neither of which has much flavour. Then
comes pan-seared trout (or, much better, fillet of salmon
on the à la carte). Finally, there's Eton Mess, which
sounds a lot better than it is. But don't miss either the
sculpture or the paintings, much of both quite superb.
Open Monday to Friday 11.30 am to 2.30 pm, 5.30 pm to 10
pm, Sunday 11 am to 2 pm (brunch). Closed on Saturday. Li-
censed. Amex, Master Card, Visa. &

TORONTO   **MAP 204**
FRANK'S KITCHEN
588 College Street   **$180**
(416) 516-5861

You don't go to Frank's Kitchen for red-checked table-
cloths or classic Italian cuisine. You go for a novel menu
and imaginative cooking. They start with an unusual and
charming *amuse bouche* of beet soup. After that they build
their meal around truffles—black and white and shaved
at your table. If you're lucky, a purée of cauliflower with
shaved truffles will be offered as an appetizer; if not, ask
for grilled octopus with squid ink in a blood-orange
vinaigrette or a plate of raw oysters. Follow that with
pork four ways or rack of local lamb. The lamb is certainly excellent. And they have a sauternes that doesn't
cost much—in fact, it's a great buy.
Open Tuesday to Sunday 6 pm to 10 pm. Closed on Monday.
Licensed. Amex, Master Card, Visa.

TORONTO   **MAP 204**

THE GALLERY GRILL

Hart House   **$140**
7 Hart House Circle
(416) 978-2445

The Gallery Grill may seem like a refuge for professors looking for dishes that were fashionable in the nineteen-seventies. Actually, it's not like that at all. The cooking is bright and lively and very much to the point. Suzanne Baby, the long-time chef, starts most of her meals with tomato soup laced with red peppers and goes on to such things as seared big-eye tuna with a superb tonnato of beets and hazelnut pesto. This is a striking dish and the best thing on a menu that also offers grilled octopus, turnip cake with shiitake mushrooms and quail with roasted sunchokes. The panna cotta that ends the meal, with its hibiscus crumble and wild blueberries, seems fresh and new. All the wines are sold by the glass, the half-litre and the bottle, and you won't do better than the viognier from Organized Crime or the pinot noir from Quail's Gate. The Gallery Grill is full of surprises, among them an array of cocktails, served every weekday from 4 to 7.30 pm.

Open Monday to Friday 11.30 am to 2.30 pm, Sunday 11 am to 2 pm (brunch). Closed on Saturday. Licensed. Amex, Master Card, Visa. ♿

TORONTO   **MAP 204**

GEORGE   ☆☆
111C Queen Street E   **$200**
(416) 863-6006

You need to know that George is not the chef. He did the design and did it for nothing. The owner was grateful and gave the restaurant the designer's name. The place isn't easy to find. Look for it upstairs at No. 111C. The menu runs strongly to seafood, offering yellowfin tuna, lobster, scallops, black cod and Arctic char, as well as breast of duck, Cornish game hen and rib-eye of beef.

253

The Arctic char comes with black rice and yogurt foam, but is apt to be overcooked. The lobster is first class and the scallops are well served by their excellent cauliflower velouté and their purée of miso. The chefs are never content to do the usual thing. They marry their tuna with curried yogurt, their breast of duck with pomegranates, their lobster with lemon-grass mayonnaise, their Cornish game hen with goat-cheese, their pork belly with cardamom mustard, their black cod with hemp seeds. The tasting menus are a good idea, if you can afford 110.00 for five courses, 135.00 for seven courses or 155.00 for ten.

Open Monday noon to 1.30 pm, Tuesday to Friday noon to 1.30 pm, 5.30 pm to 9.30 pm, Saturday 5.30 pm to 9.30 pm. Closed on Sunday. Licensed. Amex, Master Card, Visa. Book ahead.

TORONTO   MAP 204
THE GLOBE
124 Danforth Avenue   **$180**
(416) 466-2000

The glory of this restaurant is that wines by the bottle are sold at half price every Sunday; wines by the glass are sold at half-price between 4 and 6 pm every day of the week. Not content with that, they also sell raw oysters at half price every day from 4 to 6 pm. They have an excellent smoked rillette of pickerel and a fine croquette of pig's tails. Strigoli mushrooms come with homemade pasta, and if you have 39.00 to spare they also have loin of elk. The wine-list is short, but the wine-list is not. There are fifteen chardonnays, eight pinot noirs, five rieslings, six sauvignon blancs and six gewurztraminers—all at half price on Sunday. The interior of the restaurant—all weathered boards, old bricks and stainless-steel lighting fixtures—is well designed and very attractive. Peninsula Ridge is not, however, the best of the open wines. Choose another.

Open Tuesday to Thursday 6 pm to 10 pm, Friday to Sunday 11.30 am to 2 pm (brunch on weekends), 6 pm to 10 pm. Closed on Monday. Licensed. All cards. &

TORONTO   **MAP 204**
HONEST WEIGHT   ☆
2766 Dundas Street W   **$75**
(416) 604-9992

John Bil's little restaurant (it has about eight tables) is in
the so-called Junction, a depressing area of the city. But
it's open all day (except Monday) and though it takes no
reservations you can call ahead and they'll tell you when
you're likely to get a table. The fish is as good as you'll
get anywhere. The preparation is simple, but the service
is exemplary, the prices low. If you like you can buy fish
from the display case to take home. The rest of the daily
menu is chalked up on blackboards. Keep an eye out for
the okonomiyaki, a Japanese pancake stuffed with
seafood. It's good. There's usually also some nagaimo
yam topped with smoked fish. Otherwise they'll have
clams and saltspring mussels, several varieties of oyster
and spot prawns cooked in butter. John Bil is as nimble
with the sweet course as with fish. Ask for his rhubarb
crumble or something with chocolate. There's also a
short list of wines and craft beers, all fairly priced.
Open Tuesday and Wednesday 11 am to 8 pm, Thursday to Sat-
urday 11 am to 10 pm, Sunday 11 am to 8 pm. Closed on Mon-
day. Licensed for beer and wine only. Master Card, Visa.

TORONTO   **MAP 204**
HOPGOOD'S FOODLINER   ☆
325 Roncesvalles Avenue   **$120**
(416) 533-2723

Hopgood's is the brightest star in Roncesvalles Village—
more hip than hipster, more substance than show. The
two small rooms—one at the front and one at the back,
linked by a corridor past the central kitchen—are noisy
and vibrant. The heating ducts are exposed, the walls are
painted brick and the floors are reclaimed wood—some
of the planks are fourteen inches wide. They don't grow
trees that wide any more. Geoff Hopgood's grandparents

owned a chain of three IGA stores in Nova Scotia, and they were each called Hopgood's Foodliner. A huge colour picture of one of them, complete with a parking-lot full of cars from the fifties and sixties, is projected onto a screen over the bar. As you might expect, given his Maritime roots, Hopgood's menu concentrates on fish and seafood: salt-fish croquettes, scallop tartare with truffles and apple, and a snow-crab sammy that you will want to come back for. Most of the added touches are Japanese, from the daikon braised in dashi that comes with the albacore tuna to the spicy ndjua under the soft, buttery sablefish. The oyster bar has oysters from the East Coast, littleneck clams and on Thursday, Friday and Saturday Gaspé live scallops. Or you can come for Buck-a-Shuck Mondays—all the oysters you can eat for a dollar apiece, all night long.

Open Monday and Wednesday to Sunday 5.30 pm to 11 pm. Closed on Tuesday. Licensed. Master Card, Visa.

TORONTO   **MAP 204**
JACQUES   🖘
126A Cumberland Street   **$100**
(416) 961-1893

Jacques is still doing all the cooking at his eponymous restaurant upstairs on Cumberland Street, and he's filling every table. No wonder. He chooses his ingredients—his salmon and his fillet of beef—with care and skill, and cooks them correctly. The people who fill the tables are all cheerful and happy. The food is good—just try the tarte tatin—and the prices are low. The dining-room is quiet and conversation comes readily, which is a rare luxury. The vegetables are likeable if plain and the wines are all easy to drink, even the beaujolais nouveau. Everything is in fact exactly as it should be. Take Jacques out of the guide? Never.

Open Monday to Saturday noon to 3 pm, 6 pm to 11 pm, Sunday 5 pm to 10 pm. Licensed. Amex, Master Card, Visa. Book ahead if you can.

TORONTO   **MAP 204**
KAJI   ★★★
860 Queensway   **$325**
Etobicoke
(416) 252-2166

Mitsuhiro Kaji has been in a kitchen since he was thirteen
years old. First he apprenticed in Japan for ten years, then
he came to Canada in 1980. He's still in the kitchen
today, working five nights a week, offering two seasonal
omakase dinners, one featuring Wagyu beef, the other
lobster tempura. Course after course appears at your table
and everything is beautiful. The sushi is all flown to
Canada the day the fish is caught and it's served in the
restaurant the next day. It's all achingly tender. Kaji
thinks the commercial soy sauce is too salty, so he makes
his own. The vinegar is all imported from Japan. Before
he goes home for the night he throws away all the left-
overs. The toro tuna has been on his menu for years, as
have the lobster, the abalone, the sea bream and the udon
noodles. Spanish mackerel is a new delicacy. The menu
keeps changing, so you never know just what's coming
next. A taxi from downtown Toronto costs 60.00, but
you can avoid that by simply driving west on the Gar-
diner to Islington, turning north on Islington and east on
the Queensway. Kaji is on the left.
*Open Wednesday to Sunday 6 pm to 9 pm. Closed on Monday
and Tuesday. Licensed. All cards. Free parking. Book ahead.*

TORONTO   **MAP 204**
NORTH 44°   ★★
2537 Yonge Street   **$250**
(416) 487-4897

Sash Simpson is now the chef de cuisine at North 44° and
he's the best yet. The prices are still out of this world, but
so is the cooking. The Ahi tuna, the seared foie gras, the
beef carpaccio and even the raw oysters are all well and
carefully prepared. You've seen all of them before, but
the same isn't true of the hand-rolled gnocchi—we've

seldom had gnocchi as light as this before. The beef is all aged for eight weeks, which gives it a unique taste and texture. We admire the prime rib of beef, of course, but we love the duck three ways—crisp confit, pink breast and seared foie gras. To make duck like this, a chef needs imagination, skill and experience. To build a wine-list like this also requires experience. They have a whole page of champagnes, and cabernet sauvignons that start at 45.00 and rise to more than 700.00 for a Groth or a Caymus special select. They list sixteen single malts, including three Macallans. This was always a memorable restaurant; today it's even better than that.

Open Monday to Saturday 5 pm to 10 pm. Closed on Sunday. Licensed. Amex, Master Card, Visa. Valet parking. Book ahead. ♿

TORONTO   **MAP 204**
NOTA BENE   ☆☆
180 Queen Street W   **$210**
(416) 977-6400

Nota Bene is a thoroughly convincing restaurant. Their chilled sweet-corn soup is a masterpiece and so are their tuna sashimi and their ceviche of hamachi. The salmon is more expensive, and their pulled-pork tenderloin costs almost 40.00. But they make an exceptionally light sticky-toffee pudding and give you three cheeses for 16.00 (or five for 24.00). The wines are all priced to sell and a bottle of Hidden Bush can be had for less than 50.00. It's true that the best wines on the list cost more—Cakebread and Stratus are both priced at 120.00—but if you're looking for a Pauillac or a Nuit St.-Georges chances are you won't find either. If Hidden Bench isn't good enough for you, ask for a bottle of Tawse at 80.00.

Open Monday to Friday noon to 2.30 pm, 5.30 pm to 11 pm, Saturday 5.30 pm to 11 pm. Closed on Sunday. Licensed. Amex, Master Card, Visa. Book ahead. ♿

Nobody can buy his way into this guide and nobody can buy his way out.

TORONTO   **MAP 204**
ONE   ☆
Hazelton Hotel   **$200**
116 Yorkville Avenue
(416) 961-9600

Like all Mark McEwan's restaurants, One is lavish and expensive. Dinners start, rather grandly, with steak tartar,
oysters on the half-shell or yellowfin-tuna sashimi with
yuzu and jalapeno. Then there's wild salmon, black cod
and loin of lamb. The wine-list is expansive, offering
wines, as it does, from both the Old World and the New,
several of them from Canada. There's a fine Stoneleigh
sauvignon blanc from Marlborough and a chardonnay
from Thomas George in Russian River for 40.00 a glass.
Thomas George is not the best buy in the house. The
sauvignon blanc from Marlborough is a pleasant wine.
Try it and save a lot of money.
Open daily 11.30 am to 4.30 pm (lunch), 4.30 pm to 11 pm
(dinner). Licensed. Amex, Master Card, Visa. Book ahead. &

TORONTO   **MAP 204**
ORIGIN
109 King Street E   **$150**
(416) 603-8009

Origin is directly across King Street from St. James
Cathedral. It's essentially a tapas bar, though they also
have a raw bar and a regular à la carte. The meal starts
with an heirloom-tomato salad with basil and preserved
lemon and goes on to cinnamon-glazed apples with cranberries, honeyed yogurt and candied walnuts, smoked
salmon with cucumber and beef burgers with mayonnaise, avocado and arugula. The most interesting drinking is from Tawse, which is a new addition to the list and
better than either the Angel's Gate riesling or the sauvignon blanc from the Maule Valley in Chile. There's another Origin in Bayview, but this one is probably the
better of the two.
Open Monday to Friday 11.30 am to 3 pm, 5 pm to 11 pm,

259

TORONTO   MAP 204
PAI
18 Duncan Street   **$80**
(416) 901-4724

It all started with Wandee Young. Back in 1980 she opened Young Thailand on Eglinton Avenue—the first Thai restaurant in Canada. Now there's one on every streetcorner. But for the past few years, all the Thai talk in Toronto has been about the Regulars. Nuit Regular met her husband Jeff while he was backpacking in Thailand. They came back to Canada in 2008 to open Sukhothai, which is still run by Jeff's parents. Jeff and Nuit moved on to Khao San Road, to Sabai Sabai and now, most recently, to Pai, a crowded basement in the theatre district festively dressed in teak, brick and strings of bright pennant flags. The menu runs through a selection of the usual Thai favourites—spring rolls, satays, pad Thai, green curry (served inside a whole coconut) and a tasty treatment of massaman beef carpeted in deep-fried shallots. But it's the northern Thai specialties you come for (Nuit Regular grew up in north Thailand, at the opposite end of the country from Wandee Young)—things like the khao soi, made with egg noodles in golden curry, or the gaeng hunglay, a sweet-and-sour ginger curry of oxtail, or the grabong, a mountain of Thai tempura made from kabocha squash. As with all of Nuit Regular's restaurants, everything is made for sharing, and it's okay to eat with your hands.

Open Monday to Thursday 11.30 am to 10 pm, Friday and Saturday 11.30 am to 10.30 pm, Sunday 5 pm to 10 pm. Licensed. Master Card, Visa.

Where an entry is printed in italics this indicates that the restaurant has been listed only because it serves the best food in its area or because it hasn't yet been adequately tested.

TORONTO   **MAP 204**
PATRIA   ✩✩
478 King Street W   **$240**
(416) 367-0505

Charles Khabouth has built a spectacular restaurant just
off King Street and seen it full of diners every night.
They go there for Stuart Cameron's splendid Spanish
cooking and to enjoy the beautiful space he works in. The
thing to have here is the Iberico ham, if you can afford
it. The Spanish cheeses are wonderful too. After that
there are several paellas, each as good as the last. The
wine-list offers one or two wines from each of the prin-
cipal Spanish wine-growing regions. Drink red if convenient, because there are some fine riojas on this list. If
not, there are a few serviceable whites. The place is
packed, but in spite of that the service is always good,
solid and friendly. The prices are high, of course.
Open Monday to Saturday 5 pm to midnight, Sunday 10.30
am to 2.30 pm (brunch), 5 pm to midnight. Licensed. Amex,
Master Card, Visa. Book ahead.

TORONTO   **MAP 204**
RICHMOND STATION   ✩
1 Richmond Street W   **$160**
(647) 748-1444

Carl Heinrich is an outstanding chef. His slow-cooked
rainbow trout, for instance, is a brilliant dish, and he has
several other good things on his menu as well, things like
pulled-pork ravioli, caramelized perogies and even the
traditional coq au vin. His squash soup is delightful and
so is his roasted beet salad. His lemon posset is probably
the best of the sweets. In the evening he adds poached
halibut and Berkshire pork chops. As for his charcuterie,
it's on the menu all day. He has an excellent sangiovese
for 115.00, but his Daniel Chotard sauvignon blanc is
good enough for anybody at just 15.00 a glass. Everything his kitchen touches is perfect in its way.
Open Monday to Friday 11 am to 10 pm, Saturday 5 pm to 10

pm. Closed on Sunday. Licensed. Amex, Master Card, Visa.

TORONTO   **MAP 204**
SCARAMOUCHE   ☆☆
1 Benvenuto Place   **$240**
(416) 961-8011

Scaramouche, as everyone knows by now, has a stunning
view of the city by night. But there's a lot more to Scaramouche than the view. Keith Froggett is still in charge
of the kitchen and he has a very handsome menu and
does some beautiful things with it. His steak tartar, for
instance, tastes exactly as it should, which is rare in Canadian restaurants. His grilled-octopus salad is a delight.
And his yellowfin-tuna sashimi is wonderful. At his best,
Keith Froggett is brilliant. But of course he's not always
at his best. His warm lobster with ginger and sesame is a
good example. Lobster is, of course, an important luxury, but it's hard to deal with, hard for a kitchen that
wants to handle its dishes with real delicacy. Froggett's
lobster is just like the lobster you'll get in any Maritime
road house. But one has to admit that his pasta is all
house-made, his sea-bass fresh and lightly cooked. As for
his wine-list, it's long and very splendid. If money is a
problem—and Scaramouche is certainly expensive—ask
for a couple of half-glasses of the Proprietary bordeaux.
It costs 23.00 for two half-glasses, which is cheap for a
wine of this quality. If you insist on a whole bottle, we
can't help you.
*Open Monday to Saturday 5.30 pm to 9.30 pm. Closed on Sun-
day. Licensed. All cards. Free valet parking. Book ahead.*

TORONTO   **MAP 204**
LA SOCIETE
131 Bloor Street W: Floor 2   **$185**
(416) 551-9929

This place has a great location, a step or two from
Yorkville Avenue. They overlook Bloor Street and behind the restaurant there's an ample bar. The menu is

lively, starting with yellowfin-tuna tartar with avocado and going on to escargots de bourgogne, charcuterie, steak frites, tartar of beef and fried mussels. There's a biggish list of wines from the New World and the Old, featuring Stanners from Niagara, Groth from Napa and Laurent Perrier by the glass. The cooking is better than you might expect—try the tuna tartar and see for yourself.

Open Monday to Friday 11.30 am to 3 pm, 5 pm to 9.30 pm, Saturday and Sunday 11 am to 3 pm (brunch), 5 pm to 9.30 pm. Licensed. Amex, Master Card, Visa. &

TORONTO   MAP 204
YASU   ★★
81 Harbord Street   **$250**
(416) 477-2361

Yasu is small and simple. There's nothing inside but a plain white sushi bar with twelve seats facing two sushi chefs, each serving six diners. There's a small wine-list but no menu. The wine-list offers a few bottles of Louis Jadot chablis premier cru and Moet & Chandon, plus Asahi and Kirin beer from Japan. The sakes are listed on the facing page. There are seven of them by the glass and the bottle with a top price of 750.00. After you've chosen your wine or sake, you get to sit back and watch the chefs at work, and work they do for exactly two hours, creating identical sushis for each of the twelve diners. Most of these sushis few Canadians have seen before. There's striped jack, amberjack, sea-bass, ocean trout, monkfish, scallops, big-eye and blue-fin tuna, flounder, sea-urchin, salmon roe, grouper, cod, sea-bream, bonito and eel—fifteen varieties altogether. If you can't tell the difference between striped jack and amberjack, neither can most of the others at the bar. But you've had an experience the memory of which will stay with you for the rest of your life. The meal ends with a chilled dish of black-sesame ice cream. You pay the bill and leave. What more could anyone ask for?

Open Monday to Thursday at 6 pm (two sittings), Friday to

Sunday at 6 pm (three sittings). Licensed. Master Card, Visa. You must book ahead.

TORONTO   MAP 204
ZUCCA
2150 Yonge Street   **$160**
(416) 488-5774

Zucca is a small, noisy trattoria that specializes in home-made pasta and fresh fish. The fish of the day might be porgy, grilled whole with fresh herbs, lemon and olive-oil and always beautifully prepared. The pastas come as both an appetizer and a main dish. The capunti con melanzane is as good as any you're likely to find in Italy, and if you're feeling adventurous there's agnolotti di coniglio e porri or perhaps a dish of ravioli stuffed with whatever takes the chef's fancy. (The chef is still, after all these years, Andrew Milne-Allan.) The steaks come from Cumbrae and there's usually also some roasted Berkshire pork if you aren't in the mood for fish. Zucca has been around since 1997, and it's always been, as it still is, de-pendable and relaxing.
Open daily 5.30 pm to 10 pm. Licensed. Amex, Master Card, Visa.

TORONTO
See also CREEMORE, MARKHAM, PORT CREDIT.

TRINITY, Newfoundland   MAP 205
THE TWINE LOFT   ☆
Artisan Inn   **$150**
57 High Street
(709) 464-3377

Trinity is the oldest settlement in Newfoundland. Sir Richmond Whitbourne held the first Admiralty Court here in 1616, just two years after Champlain founded Port Royal. The parish church of St. Paul dates from 1734 and the rest of the town looks much as it did two centuries ago. The Twine Loft has a lovely setting overlooking Fisher Cove from a restored fishing loft next to the Artisan Inn. They have a licensed deck where after 3 o'clock you can sample one of the best selections of wine and spirits in the province. Marieke Gow is a trained sommelier and in the off season she travels the world in search of the right wines at the right price. She and her mother, Tineke, who is responsible for the Twine Loft's fine antiques, charm every visitor. Unfortunately, this has brought them so may travellers that they've had to shorten their hours and cut back on the music that used to be such an important part of the place. The menu changes from day to day. There are always a number of vegetarian dishes, for which there's an increasing demand. Two chefs work in an open kitchen, using garden greens and rhubarb from the kitchen garden for their famous rhubarb-custard tarts. Cod comes straight from the sea and wild blueberries come from the surrounding fields. Diners still speak of the beer-braised lamb, the salmon with hazelnuts and the partridge-berry pudding with hot butter. The Twine Loft is only a few minutes from the summer theatre, and they guarantee that you'll get there before the curtain rises.

Open daily at 5.30 pm and 7.45 pm (two sittings). Licensed. Master Card, Visa. Book ahead if you can. &

TRURO, N.S.   **MAP 206**
BISTRO 22
16 Inglis Place   **$100**
(902) 843-4123

There haven't been any good restaurants in Truro for many years, but all that has now changed. Dennis Pierce is a local boy and this is his first restaurant. He does all the cooking himself and has been known to prepare the sweets between the lunch and dinner shifts. There's nothing to drink except Nova Scotian wines, but all the food is fresh and locally sourced. Pierce is at his best with his salads, especially the mixed green, which is full of goat-cheese, avocado and walnuts. You won't go wrong with any of his soups either. He does very good things with both meat and fish, and his beef bourguignon is as good as any to be had in France. Be sure to ask for the mashed potatoes—they're wonderful. So are the sweets, which are all made in-house.

Open Tuesday and Wednesday 11 am to 2 pm, Thursday to Saturday 11 am to 2 pm, 5 pm to 8.30 pm. Closed on Sunday and Monday. Licensed. All cards. &

TWILLINGATE, Newfoundland   MAP 207
DOYLE SANSOME & SONS
25 Sansome's Place   **$60**
Hillgrade
New World Island
(709) 628-7421

This place is about ten miles south of Twillingate on Highway 340. It's right on the town dock, a fishery first and foremost and a restaurant second. You can catch your own lobster (in season) and they'll cook it for you and serve it on the dock or in their enclosed patio. It's a small and unpretentious restaurant, but you won't find better seafood anywhere. If you come here after August, when the lobster season ends, they'll give you fresh scallops, snow crab or the familiar deep-fried cod with chips and tartare sauce. They even have hamburgers and cheeseburgers if you want them. They also have fresh blueberry and partridge-berry pies. They don't take cards, but there's a cash machine nearby.

Open daily 10 am to 9 pm from early May until mid–September. Licensed. No cards. Book ahead if you can.

UCLUELET, B.C.   (MAP 203)
NORWOODS   ☆☆
1714 Peninsula Road   **$175**
(250) 726-7001

Working with local farmers, ranchers, fishermen and cheese-makers, Richard Norwood has created a changing menu that reflects his years of travel in Europe, Asia and the Americas. Everything is perfectly fresh. The captain of a fishing vessel may call a few hours before reaching port to let the chef know what he has, which they can be serving in the restaurant that same evening. You start with an amazing seafood sampler that comes with some of the tenderest octopus we have ever had. Next there's a green salad with goat-cheese from a farm in the Fraser Valley or, if you prefer, a bowl of carrot soup with red pepper, seasoned with fennel and coriander. The beef and lamb have both been highly praised, but we generally order the seared albacore tuna with a Korean sweet-and-sour sauce. We also really admire the chocolate torte, which comes with Grand Marnier and chocolate mousse. *Open daily 5 pm to 9 pm. Licensed. All cards. Book ahead.* &

VANCOUVER, B.C.   MAP 209
ABSINTHE
1260 Commercial Drive   **$80**
(604) 566-9053

Absinthe is a charming, 22-seat French-style bistro with a small, choice menu that changes every day. They have only three appetizers, three main courses and three sweets. These are all sold *prix fixe* for 28.00 to 35.00. It's a good idea to start with the tuna tartar, after which you can't do better than the pan-seared scallops with silky whipped potatoes. The rabbit in red wine is good too, in fact one of the best we've ever had. Finish up with the molten-lava cake or the rice pudding with salted caramel. *Open Wednesday and Thursday 5.30 pm to 8.30 pm, Friday and Saturday 5.30 pm to 9 pm, Sunday 5.30 pm to 8.30 pm. Closed on Monday and Tuesday. Licensed. Master Card, Visa. Book ahead.*

VANCOUVER   MAP 209
ACORN   ☆
3995 Main Street   **$120**
(604) 566-9001

Acorn has made vegetarian food fashionable. The credit for this must go to the chef, Brian Luptak; the flavours he's created are like nothing we've ever been offered. One of these is the cauliflower with pine mushrooms, apple jelly and spruce salt; another is the chestnut gnudi with ricotta cheese. Both of these come with parsnip purée, bitter greens, sunchoke chips and brown butter. For mains, they do brassica with rosemary roasted cabbage, capellini tossed with tomatoes, olives, arugula and olive-oil and king-oyster mushrooms with braised shallots, sherry gel and carrot meringue. For sweet, we recommend the quince compôte served with stilton, walnuts and clover honey. The wine-list is small but carefully chosen.

Open Monday to Friday 5.30 pm to 10 pm, Saturday 10 am to 2.30 pm (brunch), 5.30 pm to 11 pm, Sunday 10 am to 2.30 pm (brunch), 5.30 pm to 10 pm. Licensed. Master Card, Visa. No reservations.

VANCOUVER   MAP 209

ASK FOR LUIGI
305 Alexander Street   **$130**
(604) 428-2544

It's hard to believe that this place was once the restaurant of the year in Vancouver. There's no Luigi in the kitchen—Luigi is the grandfather of one of the owners. But the place has a lot of charm. It's a pasta house and it always has fresh homemade rigatoni, risotto spaghetti and gnocchi on hand, as well as panna cotta and bunido (bunido is a flowerless chocolate cake and it's much better than the panna cotta.) Start with the fried cauliflower—it's very good indeed. The evening menu is much like the menu at noon, except that they add ravioli, octopus and sea-urchin. There aren't many wines, but there's Fontanafredda barbera by the bottle and the half-litre.

Open Tuesday to Friday 11.30 am to 2 pm, 5.30 pm to 10 pm, Saturday and Sunday 5.30 pm to 10 pm. Closed on Monday. Licensed, Master Card, Visa. Book ahead if you can. &

Nobody can buy his way into this guide and nobody can buy his way out.

BANANA LEAF   ✎
1779 Robson Street   **$75**
(604) 569-3363

Of the five Banana Leaf restaurants, this one has the best
food and service. For one thing, their roti canai (curried
flatbread), is the best in town. You should also try their
crisp green beans tossed with shrimps and tomatoes. We
ourselves usually order the chilli crab Singapore style. It's
phenomenal and we keep coming back for more. When
it comes to atmosphere, however, we prefer the Banana
Leaf on Denman. They're at 1096 Denman Street (tele
phone (604) 683-3333). Their menu is limited, but what
they do they do well. Ask for either the black cod
caramelized with ginger or the Gulai seafood simmered
in a spicy sauce of turmeric, tamarind, galangal, coconut
and lemon grass. Some people prefer their noodle dishes,
the best of which is probably the fried-egg with tomatoes
and bean-sprouts. There's a good selection of Asian beers,
which go well with the food. All five Banana Leaf restaurants keep similar hours.
Open Sunday to Thursday 11.30 am to 10 pm, Friday and Sat-
urday 11.30 am to 10.30 pm. Licensed. Amex, Master Card,
Visa. ♿

VANCOUVER   **MAP 209**
BAO BEI   ✎
163 Keefer Street   **$75**
(604) 688-0876

This is a trendy place that deals exclusively in Asian fusion food. It's always full and they take reservations only
for parties of six or more. Start with one of their
schnacks—steamed scallop-and-nettle dumplings or
marinated eggplant with soy, garlic and ginger. After that
we suggest their steamed buns with pork belly, bean-
sprouts and sugared peanuts or their great take on beef
tartar with preserved mustard root, crisp shallots, water-
cress and burned scallion oil. For sweet they have an ex-

citing trio of house-made ice creams with distinctive Asian flavours (green tea, Vietnamese coffee and mandarin orange).

Open Tuesday to Saturday 5.30 pm to midnight, Sunday 5.30 pm to 11 pm. Closed on Monday. Licensed. Master Card, Visa. No reservations.

VANCOUVER   **MAP 209**
BAUHAUS   ☆☆
1 W Cordova Street   **$250**
(604) 974-1147

Opened in 2015, the Bauhaus already has a one-star rating in Michelin. It's the brainchild of the German film director, Uwe Boll, who has lived in Vancouver for some time. It was named the Best New Restaurant in 2015, but it's shockingly expensive. They serve traditional German dishes, but you don't need to order a schnitzel or rouladen. Instead, ask for lobster in lobster foam or roast duck, and for lunch ask for artichoke soup, trout or halibut. Everything is perfectly cooked and the service is impeccable. Our favourite is the trout, though the asparagus soup and the halibut are both about the best we've ever eaten. They offer a six-course tasting menu for 110.00 and there's a 100.00 discount on Travelzoo.

Open Monday to Thursday 11.30 am to 2.30 pm, 5 pm to 10.30 pm, Friday 11.30 am to 2.30 pm, 5 pm to midnight, Saturday 5 pm to midnight, Sunday 5 pm to 10.30 pm. Licensed. Amex, Master Card, Visa. ♿

VANCOUVER   **MAP 209**
BLUE WATER   ☆☆☆
1095 Hamilton Street   **$210**
(604) 688-8078

Blue Water is expensive, but it's a spectacular restaurant. It has about twenty West Coast oysters (seventeen of them from B.C.) They have a great sushi bar, offering nigiri sushi of all sorts—Maguro, Toro and Hamachi—as well as a surprising list of sashimi. The regular à la carte

270

starts with smoked sockeye salmon, dungeness crab and albacore-tuna carpaccio and goes on to an astonishing version of Alaska black cod, sturgeon and Arctic char. If you don't like fish, there's fine beef tenderloin for 43.50. They have several Mouton Rothschilds, Lafites and Latours, but, more to the point, there are choice wines from Burrowing Owl, Blue Mountain and Joie Farm, as well as excellent drinking from Gehringer. Blue Water has just about everything.

Open daily 5 pm to midnight. Licensed. All cards. Valet parking.
&

VANCOUVER   **MAP 209**
LA BUCA   ☆
4025 Macdonald Street   **$110**
(604) 730-6988

La Buca has the smallest kitchen we've ever seen, but the chefs work wonders in their cramped quarters. The menu is as small as the kitchen, but there are always some daily specials. This is an Italian kitchen and meals start with handmade ravioli stuffed with mascarpone cheese bathed in sage butter, followed by milkfed saltimbocca al limone or lamb chops with spiced anchovy butter. Or you can simply order the five-course tasting menu. Recently, La Buca has opened a sister restaurant called La Sorella. It offers a wide range of Italian comfort food and is located at 3369 Cambie Street (telephone (604) 873-3131.

Open Sunday to Thursday 5 pm to 9.30 pm, Friday and Saturday 5 pm to 10 pm. Licensed, Master Card, Visa. Book ahead.
&

VANCOUVER   **MAP 209**
BUFALA
5395 West Boulevard   **$100**
(604) 267-7499

Bufala is in Kerrisdale, where it's become a useful addition to Vancouver's fast-growing artisanal pizza scene. Unlike traditional Neapolitan pizza, which is meant to be eaten libretto-style (folded in half and eaten out of the hand), Bufala's pizza crust is crisp at the edges and soft in the centre. It gets its taste from its nine-year-old starter dough, mixed with bread flour and wholewheat flour from the family farm. They also offer burrata with pickled vegetables, carpaccio of albacore tuna and Italian meatballs with tomatoes and ricotta. The best of the bianchi (white pizzas) are the carpaccio, the pesto and the clam; the best of the rosse (red pizzas) are the Calabrian sausage, the quattro formaggi and the margherita (fresh tomatoes and basil). There's plenty of Italian wine and it's not expensive.

Open daily 11.30 am to 10 pm. Licensed. Amex, Master Card, Visa. &

VANCOUVER   MAP 209
CAFE KATHMANDU   🖐️
2779 Commercial Drive   **$85**
(604) 879-9909

The menu here will be unfamiliar to many readers. For an appetizer, just ask either for the bhatmaas, which are toasted soybeans with minced ginger, garlic and chilli, or for the choilaa, which are shredded chicken or pork simmered with lemon, garlic and coriander. Then go on to a goat curry with yellow dal and sweet-and-sour chutney. Café Kathmandu has a big vegan menu. Vegans won't do better than the raaio or mustard greens slow-cooked with gently-spiced potatoes. Nothing here costs more than 15.00 and beer is always on hand.

Open Monday to Saturday 5 pm to 10 pm. Closed on Sunday. Licensed for beer and wine only. Master Card, Visa. &

VANCOUVER   MAP 209
CAMPAGNOLO   ☆
1020 Main Street   **$135**
(604) 484-6018

Campagnolo has recently been redecorated in high style and it now stands out head and shoulders from the rough-

and-tumble of Main Street. If you come with a companion, order the salumi platter, followed by a helping of
Sloping Hills pork. Upstairs they have a more extensive
menu, and there's now a sister restaurant at 2297 E Hastings Street called Campagnolo Roma (telephone (604)
569-0456). It's open only in the evening from 6 to 11
from Wednesday to Sunday. The original restaurant has
a long, impressive list of red wines from Italy as well as
three grappas from Jacopo Poli, all at favourable prices.
*Open Monday to Friday 11.30 am to 2.30 pm, 5 pm to 11 pm,
Saturday 11.30 am to 2.30 pm (brunch), 5 pm to midnight,
Sunday 11.30 am to 2.30 pm (brunch), 5 pm to 11 pm. Licensed. Master Card, Visa. No reservations.*

VANCOUVER   **MAP 209**
CHAMBAR   ☆
568 Beatty Street   **$130**
(604) 879-7119

Chambar is now open for breakfast, lunch and dinner.
They have an entirely new menu, featuring such dishes
as curried chicken with anise and orange, deep fried frogs'
legs, grilled venison in a wine ragoût and an amazing
poutine with blue cheese and pink peppercorns. For all
that, mussels and fries with Belgian beer are still the heart
of the business. The new quarters are spacious and chic,
but noise remains a problem.
*Open daily 8 am to midnight. Licensed. Amex, Master Card,
Visa. Book ahead.* &

VANCOUVER   **MAP 209**
CHEF TONY   ☆☆
4600 No. 3 Road: Unit 101D   **$175**
Richmond
(604) 279-0083

The dim sum at Chef Tony is amazing. Every day the
kitchen staff prepare delicate doughs, batters and crusts,
using finely-milled imported flour. The resulting egg-
white buns, mushroom tarts and steamed Malay cakes are

heavenly. Innovative dishes like hand-chopped black-truffle siu mai and puffy pork buns keep this place full all the time. Chef Tony is known for his ambition and his swagger. He's also known for his creativity and self-confidence. Apart from the dim sum, the kitchen pre-pares roast squab, chilled poached free-range chicken with shaved truffles and sea-cucumber dressed in olive-oil and black pepper. The sweets are a knockout. Look for the feather-light steamed sponge-cake and the warm steamed-milk-and-egg-white dumplings. In the evening, ask for the chilled osmanthus jelly-cake. The service is attentive and altogether professional.

Open daily 10.30 am to 3 pm, 5 pm to 10 pm. Licensed. Master Card, Visa. Book ahead.

VANCOUVER   **MAP 209**
CIOPPINO'S   ★★★
1133 Hamilton Street   **$290**
(604) 688-7466

At Cioppino's they cook in the northern-Italian style, and every table has been full six days a week for as long as anyone can remember. Perhaps that's because Pino Posteraro is on the floor, and often in the kitchen, every night. Cooking is what the place is all about, cooking and fresh local produce. For instance, the prosciutto di Parma is made with prosciutto that's been aged 24 months. (If you prefer, you can ask for Iberico ham, cut from the black Iberian pig, for 88.00.) If you can't afford that, and who can, ask for the calamari, made with tender young squid, spinach and lemon. It's a beautiful dish. Then there's Pacific octopus, served with Tuscan white beans, and saltspring mussels, served in a spicy tomato broth. After that there's sablefish, rack of lamb, wild boar, osso buco and even Dover sole—an unexpected pleasure. The wine-list is magnificent. The top price on the list is some 4000.00 for a bottle of sassicaia—there are several to choose from, as well as a number of solaias and ornellaias. (If you turn the page, you'll find that they have countless grappas as well.) These are the exceptions; there's good

drinking at all prices.
Open Monday to Saturday 5.30 pm to 10.30 pm. Closed on
Sunday. Licensed. All cards. Valet parking. Book ahead if you
can. ♿

VANCOUVER   MAP 209
DIVA AT THE MET   ☆☆
645 Howe Street   **$175**
(604) 602-7788

At Diva they take the competition of the food trucks
very seriously indeed. That's why they offer a cheap
lunch of lasagne and kobe meatballs every day of the
week. The regular à la carte is more expensive, of course,
featuring tuna tartar, jerk chicken, beef short ribs, pan-
seared spring salmon and smoked black cod. (In the
evening they add bouillabaisse and breast of duck in a
purée of celery-root.) The cooking is apt and to the
point, the service friendly and efficient. The wine-list is
as good as ever, if not better. There's Edna Valley
chardonnay from California and several of the best wines
from the Okanagan—Wild Goose, Road 13, Blasted
Church, Blue Mountain, Black Hills and Joie Farm, most
of them priced at about 50.00 a bottle. The meal ends
well with a classic lemon tart.
Open Monday to Friday 11.30 am to 2.30 pm, 5.30 pm to 9.45
pm, Saturday and Sunday 5.30 pm to 9.45 pm. Licensed.
Amex, Master Card, Visa. Free valet parking.

VANCOUVER   MAP 209
THE FARMER'S APPRENTICE   ☆
1535 W 6 Avenue   **$150**
(604) 620-2070

The Farmer's Apprentice gets its name from the fact that
the menu was (and still is) determined by what local farmers were able to deliver each week. David Gunawan and
his partner, Dara Young, devise imaginative dishes from
the produce they're sent. Everything is organic, including
the whole wine-list. They offer meat, fish and cheese—

spelt, smoked sablefish, pork—as well as vegetarian fare—cauliflower, sea buckthorn and beeswax ice cream. Recently they've switched to a *prix-fixe* menu at 50.00 or 55.00 a head, depending on your choice of main course. Most people also take the optional wine pairing at 35.00 a head.

Open Monday to Friday 5.30 pm to 10 pm, Saturday and Sunday 11 am to 2 pm (brunch), 5.30 pm to 10 pm. Licensed. Amex, Master Card, Visa. No reservations.

VANCOUVER   **MAP 209**
FRANCESCO'S   ☆☆
860 Burrard Street   **$200**
(604) 685-7770

This place got a new name last year, because that's when Don Francesco Alonso died. Eating at Francesco's is more than just enjoying well-prepared Italian food. It's an opulent restaurant, where formally-dressed waiters cater to your every desire at a price that's as high as any in the city. They start with a rich and creamy lobster bisque and go on to venison with port wine and roasted potatoes, ending with an excellent tiramisu. Francesco's has a fine cellar of local and imported wines, many sold by the glass as well as the bottle. Unless price is no object, order by the glass.

Open Monday to Friday 11.30 am to 5 pm (lunch), 5 pm to 11 pm (dinner), Saturday and Sunday 5 pm to 11 pm. Licensed. All cards. Book ahead. ♿

VANCOUVER   **MAP 209**
GO FISH   🥢
1505 W 1 Avenue   **$45**
(604) 730-5040

Go Fish is a little shack on Fisherman's Wharf within easy walking distance of Granville Island. It has outdoor seating on a heated patio and a fine view of the harbour. Their halibut is lightly battered and served with crisps and coleslaw. The best of their soups is the red curry. The best of their fish is the spicy Pacific combo. They have no licence and no washroom. In summer you'll have to stand in line and you'll probably have to take your food elsewhere on the wharf if you want to eat in comfort. But the fish is well worth the wait; the helpings are big and the prices are reasonable. If you like you can call ahead and get your food to take away.

Open Tuesday to Friday 11.30 am to 6.30 pm, Saturday and Sunday noon to 6.30 pm. Closed on Monday. No liquor. Master Card, Visa. No reservations. &

VANCOUVER　　　　　　　　　　　**MAP 209**
HAWKSWORTH　　　　　　　　　　☆☆☆
Hotel Georgia　　　　　　　　　　　**$240**
801 W Georgia Street
(604) 673-7000

At this sumptuous restaurant in the Hotel Georgia, David Hawksworth has developed a fresh, exciting menu full of such novelties as hamachi sashimi with passion fruit, foie gras with charred figs, ancho-glazed pork belly with crisp pig's ear. There's nothing simple or plain about all this; instead, ingredients are piled on ingredients in a wild assembly of flavours. Discipline is seldom part of the game, except perhaps with the butter-poached lobster with hollandaise sauce, and it has to be said that David Hawksworth's cooking is often right over the top. In time, he'll no doubt settle down. Meanwhile, have fun with the amazing things on your plate. The wine-list is unbelievable. Take refuge in a glass of the Burrowing Owl or the Simulkameen. If you want to spend money, there's a Lafite for 4668.00 and a Mouton-Rothschild for 3150.00. Wines by the glass cost about 15.00.

Open Monday to Friday 11.30 am to 2 pm, 5.30 pm to 11 pm, Saturday and Sunday 10.30 am to 2.30 pm (brunch), 5.30 pm to 11 pm. Licensed. All cards. Valet parking. Book ahead.

We accept no advertisements. We accept no payment for listings. We depend entirely on you. Recommend the book to your friends.

VANCOUVER   MAP 209
JAPADOG   ☞
530 Robson Street   **$25**
(604) 569-1158

There are now six street stands selling Japadog products
all over the city, but the Japadog on Robson Street actually has an address. Their signature dog is the terimayo,
which is flavoured with mayonnaise, seaweed and teriyaki
sauce. They also sell a lot of their kurobuta dog, which
is made with a juicy pork sausage and is even tastier. If
you want something more distinctively Japanese, ask for
an ebi tempura dog. And if you like the spicy Asian street
fare, go for the kurogoma kimuchi (turkey sausage with
black sesame) or the shrimpy chili (spicy shrimp sausage).
They even have a sweet dog, which is made with a deep-
fried bun filled with any one of five different ice creams.
They also have plain Canadian dogs if you don't want to
experiment.
Open Monday to Thursday 10 am to 10 pm, Friday and Sat-
urday 10 am to midnight, Sunday 10 am to 9 pm. No liquor, no
cards. No reservations.

VANCOUVER   MAP 209
KINGYO IZAKAYA
871 Denman Street   **$90**
(604) 608-1677

Izakaya means *stay* and *sake shop*, which indicates that Izakaya was started as a sake shop that allowed customers to
sit on the premises to drink their sake. This is a funky
place that now serves much more than traditional sashimi
and sushi. Their savoury bowls are very popular at
lunchtime. Our favourites are the pork bowl and the avocado bowl, though we like all their carpaccio bowls too,
the scallop bowl and the sockeye-salmon bowl. For something different, try the stone-grilled beef tongue with
red yuzu pepper and green onions or the takowasabi, featuring raw, cooked or half-and-half-cooked octopus.
Many people admire their fried boneless chicken karaage

with special sansho salt or their slow-braised pork belly with dijon mustard and Japanese mayonnaise. If you get there early, ask for one of the ten bento boxes. The evening menu features kobe beef or grilled pork cheeks marinated with miso. There are some interesting sweets—almond tofu with dried goji berries and frozen green-tea crème brûlée with red beans. They also have sushi and sashimi, but why bother?

Open Monday to Thursday 11.30 am to 2.45 pm, 5.30 pm to 11.30 pm, Friday and Saturday 11.30 am to 3 pm, 5.30 pm to 1 am, Sunday 11.30 am to 2.45 pm, 5.30 pm to 11.30 pm. Licensed. Master Card, Visa.

VANCOUVER   **MAP 209**
LONGTAIL KITCHEN
810 Quayside Drive: Unit 116   **$85**
New Westminster
(604) 553-3855

Make your way to New Westminster for Angus An's mai-style chicken-curry noodles if for nothing else. (Though we suspect that you'll find yourself trying more than one item from Longtail's small but diverse menu.) Located in the River Market complex, Longtail offers a casual dining area in a small storefront setting, with a lot of raw wood and paper lanterns. Almost everything on the menu is either chicken or seafood and most cost less than 10.00. As well as the chicken-curry noodles, they have, among other things, curried lingcod, crisp-fried oysters and pad Thai. A number of local craft beers go well with the spicy food.

Open Sunday to Thursday 10 am to 7 pm, Friday and Saturday 10 am to 8 pm. Licensed. Master Card, Visa.

VANCOUVER   **MAP 209**
MAENAM   ☆
1938 W 4 Avenue   **$125**
(604) 730-5579

If you like Thai food well prepared, well served and fairly

priced, this is the place for you. There are no Buddhist shrines to be seen and no servers in Thai costume. The menu is varied and imaginative and there are some very impressive dishes, like the steamed mussels with Thai basil and lemon grass, the hot-and-sour soup with prawns, galangal, lemon grass and chilli jam, the eight-spiced fish and the red curry of duck. If you've never had banana-blossom salad have one now; it comes with sesame, tamarind and palm sugar. There's a good selection of Asian beers and some of the pairings they offer are quite remarkable. Just try Angus An's mussels with a dry riesling and judge for yourself. Our feeling is that Angus An is now doing for Thai food what Vikram Vij did years ago for Indian food.

Open Monday 5 pm to 10 pm, Tuesday to Thursday noon to 2.30 pm, 5 pm to 10 pm, Friday and Saturday noon to 2.30 pm, 5 pm to 11 pm, Sunday 5 pm to 10 pm. Licensed. Amex, Master Card, Visa. &

VANCOUVER   **MAP 209**
MARKET   ☆☆
Shangri-La Hotel   **$175**
1115 Alberni Street
(604) 695-1115

Since 2009, when it opened, Market has had its ups and downs. But right now it's in top form, with an inviting menu, first-class service and a stunning selection of wines. The wine-list has always been amazing, with its old Mouton-Rothschilds and its super-Tuscans at breath-taking prices. Recently they added a whole page of Château Margaux, where nothing costs less than 1900.00. You can drink quite cheaply and quite well, however, from the Okanagan, but it's the cooking of Montgomery Lau that makes Market what it is. His lamb is pretty rough, but albacore tuna has seldom been so good. It comes with avocado, ginger and (too many) radishes. The steamed shrimps come with avocado too, the seared scallops with caramelized cauliflower, which is a clever idea. The dungeness crab with sesame is usually less exciting than the sablefish with scallions and Thai basil. All the fish is also available simply grilled, but when the kitchen is at its best, as it is at the moment, it's probably wise to ask for the Thai basil or the caramelized cauliflower.

Open Monday to Friday 11.30 am to 2.30 pm, 5 pm to 11 pm, Saturday and Sunday 11 am to 3 pm (brunch), 5 pm to 11 pm. Licensed. Amex, Master Card, Visa. Book ahead. ♿

VANCOUVER   MAP 209
MASTER BARBECUE
4651 No. 3 Road: Suite 145   **$45**
Richmond
(604) 272-6568

For a long time we've lamented the loss of the orange and green doors in Chinatown, where you could get wonderful Hong Kong fare at very reasonable prices. Fortunately, this place does a good job of taking the place of the orange and green doors. Master Barbecue is a small hole-in-the-wall restaurant, but their barbecue dishes are all great. You come here for the roasted pork with its crunchy skin, the melt-in-your-mouth pork fat and the pork belly underneath. The fat isn't excessive and it does a good job of marrying the crackling to the juicy belly. The pork comes on a bed of white rice, which is how the restaurant serves it. Lineups are long and we prefer to order ahead and take our food away when we get there. *Open Monday, Tuesday and Thursday to Sunday 11 am to 3 pm, 5 pm to 8 pm. Closed on Wednesday. No liquor, no cards. No reservations.*

VANCOUVER   MAP 209
MEDINA CAFE   ☞
780 Richards Street   **$75**
(604) 879-3114

Café Medina offers rich sweets, hot chocolate and great espresso coffee. Despite the move from Beatty Street, they still have long lineups at the door. They also serve

Belgian waffles with lavender chocolate, sizzling fried eggs with braised short-ribs, applewood smoked cheddar and raspberry lattes. The waffles are topped with your choice of dark chocolate, salted caramel and orange marmalade. Gluten-free options are available on request. At noon try the albacore tuna with white beans and quinoa dressed in tahini. Unfortunately, they do not take reservations.

Open Monday to Friday 8 am to 3 pm, Saturday and Sunday 9 am to 3 pm. Licensed. Amex, Master Card, Visa. No reservations. ♿

VANCOUVER   MAP 209
MY SHANTI
15869 Croydon Drive   **$120**
Surrey
(604) 560-4416

My Shanti is Hindi for My Peace, and it's Vikram Vij's third restaurant. For years Vij has thought that dishes from Bengal (to name one of many such regions) are too rarely found in Indian restaurants. He'll tell you also that the mustard oil used here seldom gets the same respect as the olive oil used in Tuscany. There's no butter chicken at My Shanti, only the dishes native to the several regions of India. We've been surprised and delighted with many of the items on the menu, among them the wild-boar kebabs, the steamed fish and (our favourite) the goat curry. My Shanti is more expensive than most Indian restaurants, but it's cheaper than Vij's (see below).

Open daily 5 pm to 9 pm. Licensed. Amex, Master Card, Visa. No reservations. ♿

VANCOUVER   MAP 209
NICLI ANTICA
62 E Cordova Street   **$90**
(604) 669-6985

This is basically a pizzeria, but if you start with a salad, make it the salad di rucola featuring arugula, fennel, or-

anges, olives and shaved parmesan—a lovely combination
of flavours. Two can share your pizza, maybe three. Go
for the arugula and cavolo nero e funghi topped with
grana padano, fior di latte and prosciutto. It's always perfect, but if you like you can try the pesto with fior di
latte, fresh basil and tomatoes or the spicy diavolo, which
is made with sopressata and chilli oil.
Open daily 11.30 am to 11 pm. Licensed. Master Card, Visa.
No reservations.

VANCOUVER   **MAP 209**
OAKWOOD
2741 W 4 Avenue   **$140**
(604) 558-1965

The noon-hour menu at Oakwood is extremely small,
but it expands in the evening, when they offer bison tartar béarnaise and pulled-pork with miso. The best of the
mains are probably the pan-seared scallops or the braised
lamb with spiced lentils and apricots. This year we think
the best of the sweets is the coconut panna cotta with
fresh fruit and caramelized lemon grass. The wine-list is
short, but it features some of Joie Farm's best wines.
Open Tuesday to Friday 5 pm to 10.30 pm, Saturday and Sun-
day 10 am to 2.45 pm (brunch), 5 pm to 10.30 pm. Closed on
Monday. Licensed. Amex, Master Card, Visa. No reservations.
&

VANCOUVER   **MAP 209**
PEACEFUL RESTAURANT
532 W Broadway   **$85**
(604) 879-9878

Chinese restaurants used to be cheap. But the likes of the
Varsity Grill are no more. Their successors have mostly
gone upscale. The Peaceful Restaurant preserves something of the old style. How good is it? Well, over the
years it has headed more than one list of the best Chinese
restaurants in Vancouver. It's casual, but it's good. To start
with, they make a lot of dim sum: beef rolls, xiao long

bao, pork buns and potato rolls. The szechuan-style noodle dishes are all made in-house too and they're all great, especially the dan-dan noodles in a spicy pork-and-spinach sauce. Try also the szechuan braised fish, served on a bed of greens in a spicy sauce. The restaurant has three convenient locations, all with similar food and similar hours.

Open Sunday to Thursday 11 am to 9.30 pm, Friday and Saturday 11 am to 10 pm. Licensed for beer and wine only. No cards.

VANCOUVER   MAP 209
THE PEAR TREE   ☆☆
4120 E Hastings Street   **$125**
Burnaby
(604) 299-2772

The Pear Tree may have an inconvenient location, but it also has a lot of charm. Inside it's all pale grey, with sophisticated service and an arresting menu. Meals begin with lobster bisque or perhaps with gin-and-tomato soup, followed by beautiful lamb shanks with cauliflower fritters, which is a far better choice than the steelhead trout with butternut squash. Finish off with a fresh lemon tart with a sour-cream sorbet. The best thing to drink, in our opinion, is the Edna Valley chardonnay. Pay the 10.00 they ask for a glass and be thankful. The Pear Tree is not expensive.

Open Tuesday to Saturday 5 pm to 11 pm. Closed on Sunday and Monday. Licensed. All cards. &

VANCOUVER   MAP 209
LA PENTOLA DI QUERCIA
Opus Hotel   **$90**
350 Davie Street
(604) 642-0557

Following the closure of their celebrated Elixir dining-room, the Opus Hotel had no fine-dining facility. That all changed late in 2012 when La Quercia expanded into downtown Vancouver. For appetizers we suggest the carpaccio of Pacific octopus with sorrel and tomato or the poached asparagus with grated prosciutto and a quail egg. There's a good main treatment of loin of rabbit wrapped in prosciutto and served with grilled polenta and root vegetables. Of the sweets we recommend the tiramisu and the lemon cream. The wine-list is very good and it's won many awards.

Open daily 7 am to 11 pm. Licensed. All cards. ♿

VANCOUVER   **MAP 209**
PHNOM PENH
244 E Georgia Street   **$90**
(604) 682-5777

Phnom Penh is crowded even on a day that's too wet and cold to go outside. It's a family-run restaurant serving a mixture of Vietnamese and Cambodian food. There are said to be 200 dishes on the menu, all served with Asian spices and all very inexpensive. Our favourite dishes are the hot-and-sour soup, loaded with prawns and lemon grass, and the Cambodian butter beef, which is fanned out on your plate, barely steamed with shallots and flavoured with soy, lime and cilantro. You can drink wine or beer if you like, or you can just settle for one of their fruit moo milkshakes.

Open daily 10 am to 10 pm. Licensed. Amex, Master Card, Visa. No reservations.

VANCOUVER   **MAP 209**
LA QUERCIA   ☆☆
3689 W 4 Avenue   **$150**
(604) 676-1007

La Quercia was named the best new restaurant of 2009 and one still gets the feeling that nothing leaves the kitchen without the approval of the chef. The menu is essentially Milanese and it changes often. Some things, like vitello tonnato and branzino with fennel, reappear often. Their 50.00 *prix fixe* must be the best upscale buy in town, but the à la carte changes every day. Their pasta is heavenly; their gnocchi is as light as a cloud; and their agnolotti with ricotta and stinging nettles is stunning. Their roasted sablefish tends to sell out early. And if you don't want the hanger steak ask for the country-style pork chops instead. The flourless-chocolate cake is now probably the best of the sweets.

Open Tuesday to Sunday 5 pm to 10 pm. Closed on Monday. Licensed. Master Card, Visa. Book ahead. &

VANCOUVER   **MAP 209**
RANGOLI
1488 W 11 Avenue   **$80**
(604) 736-5711

Rangoli offers many of the same dishes as Vij's. The up-side is that you don't have to wait for a table. The down-side is that the flavours are not quite the same. Rangoli doubles as a restaurant and a market, selling ready-to-eat dishes and freshly-roasted Indian spices that are almost as good as at the parent restaurant and much cheaper. The menu changes often, but it always includes several meat dishes and several vegetables that are much better than the commercial products. Our eat-in favourites include the beef, lamb and lentil kebabs with dates and tamarind curry, the spicy pulled pork on sautéed greens and sour-cream chutney and the beef short-ribs in Kalonji curry with rice and pickled vegetables. They all come with naan. All the best sweets from Vij's are also sold next door at Rangoli.

Open daily 11 am to 10 pm. Licensed. All cards. No reservations. &

VANCOUVER   **MAP 209**
LA REGALADE
2232 Marine Drive   **$135**
(604) 921-2228

North Vancouver doesn't have a lot of good restaurants. La Régalade, on Marine Drive, may be crowded and noisy, but it's kept most of its old admirers. In fact Alain

Raye, the chef, has attracted a good many new customers. Start with his blue-cheese tart with pears or his confit of duck legs. At noon he has some very good salads and some first-class omelettes. In the evening we suggest the roast pork with apples or the braised lamb shank. The helpings are always generous.

Open Monday to Friday 11.30 am to 2 pm, 5 pm to 10 pm, Saturday 5 pm to 10 pm. Closed on Sunday. Licensed. Amex, Master Card, Visa. Book ahead if you can. &

VANCOUVER   MAP 209
SAI WOO   ☆
158 E Pender Street   **$180**
(604) 568-1117

The upstairs dining-room at Sai Woo is lovely; the cuisine is modern. The chef chooses your meal and you pay 100.00 for two. Recently we did this and had Peking duck in a Chinese pancake. Next came roast lamb with squash, shallots and kale and pan-seared sablefish with cassava cake and cauliflower. Panna cotta with lavender, vanilla crumble and licorice mint followed. Everything was exquisite.

Open Tuesday to Thursday 5 pm to midnight, Friday and Saturday 5 pm to 2 am, Sunday 5 pm to midnight. Closed on Monday. Licensed. Master Card, Visa.

VANCOUVER   MAP 209
SALADE DE FRUITS
1555 W 7 Avenue   **$80**
(604) 714-5987

Every evening Salade de Fruits serves several of the big French bistro dishes. They always have great steaks, but they're equally adept with the rack of lamb and the duck confit. In fact, we usually go for a dish of rabbit. The sweets are all great, especially the tarte tatin. There aren't many wines, but the prices are very reasonable. The service is competent and friendly.

Open Tuesday to Saturday 11.30 am to 2.30 pm, 5 pm to 8.30 pm. Closed on Sunday and Monday. Licensed. No cards. Book ahead.

VANCOUVER   MAP 209
SHANGHAI RIVER
7831 Westminster Highway   **$85**
Richmond
(604) 233-8885

When it comes to xiao long bao, the Shanghai River is always said to have some of the best in Vancouver. The xiao long bao is a kind of steamed bun traditionally made in Jiangnan. In Canada they're known as soup dumplings or just as plain dumplings. They're filled with steaming broth and minced crab or pork. The chef is good as well with smoked duck, eggplant with chilli garlic, marinated squid, honey-glazed beef and fried prawns with walnuts. He also likes to experiment with things like goose-liver shumai, black vinegar spare-ribs, sliced pork belly and spicy crab. The place is often full and you should always book ahead.

Open Monday to Friday 11 am to 3 pm, 5 pm to 10 pm, Saturday 10 am to 3 pm, 5 pm to 10 pm, Sunday 5 pm to 10 pm. Licensed. Master Card, Visa. Book ahead. &

VANCOUVER   MAP 209
TACOFINO COMMISSARY
2327 E Hastings Street   **$90**
(604) 253-8226

The newest Tacofino is a sit-down restaurant (not a truck) in east Vancouver. It offers everything the Tacofina Cantina in Tofino and the Orange and Blue Trucks in Vancouver offer and more. For one thing, they have a liquor licence. They have a pork-jowl taco stuffed with salsa fresca, a yam-tempura taco with cabbage and avocado in soy sauce and a Japanese-style taco with tuna, sesame, wakame, ginger and wasabi. They do other things as well, notably Brussels sprouts tossed in a jalapeno vinaigrette and an octopus salad with jalapeno

and spicy chilli oil.
Open daily 11.30 am to 3 pm, 5 pm to 10 pm. Licensed. Master Card, Visa.

VANCOUVER   MAP 209
THE TRUFFLE HOUSE
2452 Marine Drive   **$125**
West Vancouver
(604) 922-4222

The Truffle House is a popular boutique restaurant that serves mainly truffle-infused dishes. It's a tiny place with only a few tables and chairs. They serve brunch on Saturday and Sunday and dinner on Friday and Saturday. At noon they have a marvellous onion soup, quite the best in the city. The place is packed early in the day for a breakfast of two-egg omelettes with wild mushrooms and black truffles. For dinner they start with truffle gnocchi, a warm scallop-and-spinach salad and dungeness and snow crab with a lemon-and-tarragon aioli, followed by a risotto of wild mushrooms and truffles and roasted sablefish marinated in maple and soy. Afterward there's a variety of crêpes and a really good tarte tatin.
Open Monday to Thursday 8 am to 11 am (breakfast), 11 am to 3 pm (lunch), Friday 8 am to 11 am, 11 am to 3 pm, 5 pm to 9 pm, Saturday 8 am to 3 pm (brunch), 5 pm to 9 pm, Sunday 8 am to 3 pm (brunch). Licensed. Master Card, Visa. No reservations.

VANCOUVER   MAP 209
L'UFFICIO
3687 W 4 Avenue
(604) 676-1007

Everyone was disappointed when La Ghianda, La Quercia's little brother, closed a few years ago. Fortunately, L'Ufficio offers everything from multi-course dinners to casual meals, most of them served on small plates. In this it's like an Italian enoteca. The menu changes often, but it's usually a good idea to order the chef's special for

36.00. This might bring you a pork rillette, followed by a primi of fusiuatta all'amatriciana and a secondi of sweet-bread pie. The sweets are all great, and the best of them is the bunet from Piedmont, which combines chocolate, eggs and amaretto.

Open Tuesday to Sunday 5 pm to 10 pm. Closed on Monday. Licensed. Master Card, Visa. No reservations. &

VANCOUVER   **MAP 209**
VIJ'S   ☆☆
1480 W 11 Avenue   **$175**
(604) 736-6664

For more than twenty years people have been willing to line up for Vij's remarkable food—with no exceptions made for the rich or famous. No wonder. Vij has amazing flavours and flawless service. He offers a nice range of vegetarian dishes and we can without hesitation recommend many of his creations: spiced shiitake mushrooms, curried portobello mushrooms with porcini, curried chickpeas on sweet-potato cookies and jack fruit with cardamom and cumin. Vikram Vij is more expensive than he used to be, but he's still worth every dollar.

Open daily 5.30 pm to 9.30 pm. Licensed for beer and wine only. All cards. No reservations. &

VANCOUVER   **MAP 209**
WILDEBEEST
120 W Hastings Street   **$110**
(604) 687-6880

Unless you want a glass of whisky with your dinner, it's a good idea to come to Wildebeest for breakfast, when you can drink any one of five draft beers. Our favourite is the Strange Fellows beer, which goes well with the free-range scrambled eggs flavoured with bone marrow. They come with triple-cooked potatoes, which are a feature of almost every dish except the merguez sausages. Wildebeest is well served and very cheap.

Open Monday to Friday 5 pm to midnight, Saturday and Sun-

day 10 am to 2 pm (brunch), 5 pm to midnight. Licensed. Amex, Master Card, Visa. Book ahead if you can.

VANCOUVER   MAP 209
YEW SEAFOOD
Four Seasons Hotel   **$175**
791 W Georgia Street
(604) 692-4939

YEW has very good food for a hotel restaurant and it shows all day long. Their breakfast is so good that people often come from the Hotel Georgia next door, which doesn't have one. Later in the day, YEW has some of the freshest and best raw oysters in town and their tuna tataki is aptly served with grapes and walnuts, which give the raw tuna some welcome texture. For mains they have a fine paella of salmon, sablefish, spot prawns, mussels, clams and chorizo. YEW is nothing if not expensive, but you can have a tower of seafood for only 99.00 for four, which is a pretty good buy. The sweets are all wonderful, especially the tarte tatin and the butterscotch pudding with figs.
Open daily 7 am to 10.30 am, 11.30 am to 2.30 pm, 5 pm to 10 pm. Licensed. All cards. &

VANCOUVER   MAP 209
ZEST   ☆
2775 W 16 Avenue   **$295**
(604) 731-9378

Zest has won numerous awards for its exquisite Japanese cuisine. Actually, what they do is a fusion of the Japanese and Italian cuisines. They have created an intimate space of warm colours, textures and intoxicating scents. When we were last there we began with cream-of-cauliflower soup topped with flakes of prosciutto, and went on to a seafood sunomono filled with dungeness crab, tiger prawns, octopus, surf clams and wakame seaweed—an amazing blend of flavours and ingredients. They also offer sushi and sashimi rolls stuffed with albacore tuna, sockeye salmon, organic greens, cucumber and flying-fish roe. Their wild sablefish is marinated for twenty hours with yuzu juice, sautéed kale, beets and togarashi chick peas; their roasted breast of duck is served with organic quinoa, fried leeks, smoked tomatoes and mustard-greens and their deep-fried panko-crusted pork tenderloin comes with a pea-shoot salad dressed in sweet miso. Omakase (placing your trust in the chef) plays an essential part at Zest. You can safely place your trust in the chef's sashimi, his five-piece sushi or his vegetable tempura. An omakase dinner costs all of 90.00. This is more than most sushi bars, but it's worth it. Look for Zest behind a Starbucks at the corner of W 16 Avenue and Macdonald Street.

Open Tuesday to Sunday 5 pm to 10 pm. Closed on Monday. Licensed. Amex, Master Card, Visa. Book ahead.

VANCOUVER
See also GIBSONS.

VIBANK, Saskatchewan	**(MAP 160)**
THE GROTTO	☆
101 2 Avenue	**$140**
(306) 762-2010	

Located about 30 miles east of Regina, the Grotto occupies the premises of an old convent. Here they offer fresh Mexican dishes as well as several southern barbecues. On Wednesday and Friday they serve a variety of tacos, tamales, smoked ribs and street-style corn. On Saturday it's southern-style barbecues like Carolina ribs, pecan-smoked breast of duck, smoked prime-rib steak and their special show-stopper, which is the Texas Platter. The Texas Platter is a huge tray piled high with brisket, ribs, chicken, baked beans and corn-bread. Dinners end with a chocolate flan, mango-and-pineapple pie or a piece of *tres-leches* cake. You have to book ahead because often all the tables are booked for several weeks (maybe months) at a time.

Open Tuesday 9 am to 2 pm, Wednesday and Friday 9 am to 9

pm, Saturday 5 pm to 9 pm. Closed on Sunday, Monday and Thursday. Licensed. Master Card, Visa. You must book ahead.

VICTORIA, B.C. MAP 211
THE BLUE FOX 🐾
919 Fort Street **$60**
(250) 380-1683

The Blue Fox has huge plate-glass windows and old brick walls. Like the Village Café, they serve breakfast every day at 8 o'clock or earlier. This means ten different varieties of eggs benedict, along with big beef burgers, Moroccan chicken, and pork quesadillas. People write to us about the Bubble and Squeak and the Eggs el Jimador (pulled pork with sweet bell peppers and jalapeno aioli). The helpings are enormous, the prices low.
Open Monday to Friday 7.30 am to 4 pm. Licensed. Master Card, Visa.

VICTORIA MAP 211
BRASSERIE L'ECOLE ☆☆
1715 Government Street **$135**
(250) 475-6260

This place is supposed to be a Parisian-style bistro, but actually it's more elegant than most Parisian bistros and the cooking is, if anything, better. The menu reflects Sean Brennan's desire to use local products cooked in the French country style. It's chalked up on a blackboard and changes regularly, but it always features steak with fries and usually offers oysters and mussels as well. The oysters on the half-shell are about the best in town, but they also offer an endive salad and lentil fritters with parsnips and sunchokes. For sweet, if you're tired of crème brûlée, ask for the tarte tatin. It's a good one. There's a great little wine-list.
Open Tuesday to Saturday 5.30 pm to 11 pm. Closed on Sunday and Monday. Licensed. Master Card, Visa. No reservations. ♿

Nobody but nobody can buy his way into this guide.

293

VICTORIA   **MAP 211**
CAFE BRIO
944 Fort Street   **$140**
(866) 270-5461

Café Brio is good, but not as good as it used to be. They
still have a nice parsnip soup. They still have house-made
charcuterie. And they still have buffalo brie and goat-
cheese from Salt Spring Island. But their rockfish is very
disappointing and their roast chuck was never a good
idea. The wines from Road 13 are hardly enough to carry
the restaurant. The interior, however, is mellow and
warm and the service is attentive and well informed.
Open daily 5.30 pm to 10 pm. Licensed. Master Card, Visa.
&

VICTORIA   **MAP 211**
CHOUX CHOUX CHARCUTERIE
830 Fort Street   **$45**
(250) 382-7572

Choux Choux is expensive, but it's worth every dollar.
Everything on the menu is delicious and everything can
be eaten there or taken away. Sometimes the plat du jour
will feature a baguette and a splendid house-made soup.
We've tried the truffled eggs, the steak tartar, the organic
chicken on a bed of Tuscan beans, the grilled bratwurst
sausages with green beans and the cassoulet. Their soups
are always good, but you have to arrive early if you want
to order the plat du jour before it sells out, as it often does
by noon.
*Open Tuesday to Friday 10 am to 5.30 pm, Saturday 10 am to
5 pm. Closed on Sunday and Monday. No liquor, no cards. No
reservations.*

This is a guide to Canadian restaurants from coast to
coast—the first ever published and the only one of its
kind on the market today. We accept no advertisements.
Nobody can buy his way into this guide and nobody can
buy his way out.

VICTORIA   **MAP 211**
FOO   🖎
769 Yates Street   **$60**
(250) 383-3111

Foo faces a small parking-lot off Yates Street, where
everyone, even customers, has to pay to park their car.
Inside, bare tables encircle the room; outside, there are
tables on the sidewalk. The menu is written up on blackboards. It never changes, but there are specials every day.
What Foo is all about is Asian street food sold at rock-
bottom prices. There's red-coconut curry, tuna tataki
with soba noodles, caramel chicken with fresh ginger and
Chinese greens, chilli-glazed octopus and sweet-and-sour
pork belly. There are a few local beers, including White
Bark wheat beer and Lone Tree cider. Everything is cheap
and everything tastes real.
Open Monday to Saturday 11.30 am to 10 pm, Sunday 11.30
am to 9 pm. Licensed for beer and wine only. Master Card, Visa.
No reservations. &

VICTORIA   **MAP 211**
JAM
542 Herald Street   **$60**
(778) 440-4489

Jam is located at the edge of Chinatown, where it serves
modern comfort food. It's big seller is scrambled eggs
with spinach, goat cheese and pesto. You should also try
the so-called Charlie Bowl, which means two fried eggs
with ham, green onions and cheddar. Or the Herald
Street omelette, which comes with hash-brown potatoes
and Monterey Jack cheese, spinach, green onions,
chopped tomatoes, mushrooms and onion or tomato jam.
If you aren't weight-watching, go for the Three Pigs
(sausages dipped in pancake butter and served with maple
syrup and fruit). They also have deep-fried avocado,
pineapple-and-coconut pancakes, French toast with apples and soft tacos with chorizo and tortillas. At
lunchtime they offer a nice selection of soups, salads and

sandwiches. Expect lineups on weekends.
Open daily 8 am to 3 pm. Licensed. Master Card, Visa. Book ahead.

VICTORIA   MAP 211
LITTLE JUMBO
506 Fort Street: Unit 102   **$90**
(778) 433-5535

Finding your way to Little Jumbo isn't easy. Just go to
No. 506 and push through the door. Go down a blank
hallway until you come to the place, which has recently
become a full-service restaurant. They still have small
plates and extremely good wine pairings, but more and
more people are coming here for a complete meal. Their
charcuterie is excellent and their wine-list recently won
a silver medal. They have a reliable torchon of foie gras
and first-class smoked sablefish with romesco sauce. The
main dishes lean to important meats like lamb shanks and
triple-A striploin steak. If you go for a sweet, make it the
flourless-chocolate torte with bourbon and fresh berries.
*Open Tuesday and Wednesday 5.30 pm to midnight, Thursday
to Saturday 5.30 pm to 1 am, Sunday 5.30 pm to midnight.
Closed on Monday. Licensed. No reservations.*

VICTORIA   MAP 211
MATISSE   ☆☆
512 Yates Street   **$170**
(250) 480-0883

Matisse has a comfortable dining-room, quiet music and
an eloquent menu. The kitchen is at its best with foie
gras, but the à la carte offers halibut and sablefish with a
cheese soufflé for only 30.00. There's always some rabbit—they're good with rabbit—as well as guinea hen
with truffles and bison flat-iron steak. Their lamb comes
from Australia, which is a long way from Alberta, where
some of the best lamb in the world is to be had. They
have at least two remarkable wines, one red (Mission Hill
reserve merlot) and one white (Poplar Grove pinot gris).

Both cost just 40.00 a bottle or 10.00 a glass. The service is very attentive.
Open Wednesday to Sunday 5.30 pm to 10 pm. Closed on Monday and Tuesday. Licensed. Amex, Master Card, Visa. ♿

VICTORIA   MAP 211
OLO   ☆
509 Fisgard Street   **$160**
(250) 590-8795

Ullah has changed its name to Olo, but little else has changed. It's always been known for its inventive menu, which features Holliewood Zen oysters, sweetbreads with hot sauce and dry-aged cheddar cheese. They've always cooked well, and this year their clams in dashi broth, their lingcod with pickled squash, their spelt chitarra breast of duck and their mashed potatoes with buttermilk—especially the mashed potatoes with buttermilk—are all great. The service is attentive and concerned. And their wine-list is fascinating, offering excellent drinking from Joie Farms, Venturi-Schulze, Tantalus, Black Swift and Wild Goose, among others, most of them at very modest prices.
Open daily 5 pm to 11 pm (later on Friday and Saturday). Licensed. Master Card, Visa. Book ahead.

VICTORIA   MAP 211
PADELLA
2524 Estevan Avenue   **$95**
(250) 592-7424

Padella is open on Sunday when many other restaurants are closed. It's in Oak Bay, which is only a short drive from downtown Victoria. The décor will remind you of a traditional Italian trattoria. The food here in Oak Bay is delicious and the wine-list is sensible. It's best to let Kyle Gignac and Zoe O'Doherty, the husband and wife team who own the place, choose your meal. They'll start you with an antipasto plate of fried eggplant with dried salted cod and go on to a kale salad with twice-fried bacon. The house-made gnocchi with Italian sausage and red pepper, the smoked sockeye salmon with lemon and dill and the lamb with eggplant are, they think, the best of the main courses. The chocolate truffles and the chocolate panna cotta are certainly both irresistible.

Open Wednesday to Sunday 5 pm to 9 pm. Closed on Monday and Tuesday. Licensed. Master Card, Visa. Book ahead.

VICTORIA   **MAP 211**
PRIMA STRADA
230 Cook Street   **$90**
(250) 590-8595

Prima Strada has two locations, one on Cook Street, which is sleek and modern, the other on Bridge Street, which is in an old garage. They both supply authentic Neapolitan thin-crust pizzas baked in their wood-fired brick ovens. Both make first-class rucola e crudo, which combines tomato, parmesan and mozzarella, served on arugula with prosciutto. But there's more to Prima Strada than pizza. They also have excellent polpi, or juicy Italian meatballs in a hot tomato sauce, and their salads, especially the roasted-beet salad with mascarpone, hazelnuts and fresh mint, are great.

Open Sunday to Thursday 11.30 am to 9 pm, Friday and Saturday 11.30 am to 10 pm. Licensed. Master Card, Visa. &

VICTORIA   **MAP 211**
RED FISH BLUE FISH
1006 Wharf Street   **$80**
(250) 298-6877

Red Fish Blue Fish is on the pier below Wharf Street in the heart of downtown Victoria. Are you looking for the best fish and chips in Victoria, or perhaps for a sophisticated taco? Red Fish Blue Fish has them both. Their tacones are a light-hearted spin on the traditional seafood taco. Our favourite is the scallop tacone, but others prefer the tuna, which comes with a nice mayonnaise. If you want something really hot, ask for the tempura cod. All the tacones can also be had tostada-style in a crisp corn tortilla. All the fish is fresh and out of this world, but it has to be said that the average wait time is 30 minutes or more.

Open daily 11.30 am to 6.30 pm. Licensed. Master Card, Visa. No reservations.

VICTORIA   MAP 211
SHINE CAFE   ☞
1548 Fort Street   **$60**
(250) 595-2133

Shine is a family operation, and it's open only for break-fast and lunch. It majors in omelettes, the best of which, we think, is the so-called Forager, served on a bed of mushrooms, spinach and avocado. The pancakes with maple syrup is a better dish for lunch, though at noon they also have soup, salads and sandwiches. There isn't much to drink aside from the Bad Apple, which is apple cider spiked with Sailor Jerry's rum. The original location is here on Fort Street, but they now have a branch that's more convenient for visitors to the city. It's at 1320 Blan-shard Street (telephone (250) 595-2134). The menus are the same.

Open daily 8 am to 3 pm. Licensed. Master Card, Visa. No reservations.

VICTORIA   MAP 211
STAGE
1307 Gladstone Avenue   **$110**
(250) 388-4222

Stage is very dark and very noisy, but they have first-class tapas and a number of fine wines, and both are very cheap. The Yalumba viognier costs only 38.00 a bottle; Joie's Noble Blend is more expensive at 49.00, Black Hills sauvignon more again, the Wild Goose pinot blanc less at 37.00. Their shrimps, served with cucumber and cilantro, are beautifully fresh and tender; the tuna, sadly, comes on a bed of cold raw beans, but the Sooke trout is nicely served with spring onions, radishes, lemon and crème fraîche. Their charcuterie is lively and exciting—just try the smoked elk or the salt-cured foie gras. They don't take sweets seriously, and unfortunately there isn't much to eat after the savouries but crème brûlée.

Open daily 5 pm to midnight (earlier on Sunday and Monday). Licensed. Master Card, Visa. No reservations. ♿

VICTORIA   MAP 211
TACOFINA VICTORIA
787 Fort Street   **$90**
(778) 406-1787

This is a new sitdown location in downtown Victoria. They offer the same tacos and burritos that are on offer at any of the Tacofina trucks. They also have an excellent tortilla soup. And remember: you can have a beer with your meal here, and that makes a difference.

Open daily 11 am to 11 pm. Licensed. Master Card, Visa.

VICTORIA   MAP 211
IL TERRAZZO
555 Johnson Street   **$150**
(250) 361-0028

Look for Il Terrazzo in Waddington Alley, behind Willie's Bakery. It's crowded and the noise is overwhelming. They cook in the northern Italian style, which means brodetto di pescatore to begin with or fried squid with cucumbers and cilantro, or perhaps seared scallops with smoked tuna. After that you may be tempted by the osso buco or the rack of lamb. The lamb, however, is tough and tasteless; better the roasted salmon with mango or the baked local halibut. The wine-list is large and comfortable, offering, among other good things, a Liberty School and a Joie Farm from Peter Lehmann. Take your pick.

Open Monday to Friday 11.30 am to 2 pm, 5.30 pm to 10 pm, Saturday and Sunday 5.30 pm to 10 pm. Licensed. Amex, Master Card, Visa. ♿

VICTORIA   **MAP 211**
VILLAGE CAFE   🖐️
2518 Estevan Avenue   **$60**
(250) 592-8311

This is a great place for breakfast. It's located in Estevan
village, which is a longish way from the centre of the city.
But if you're on your way to Vancouver it's convenient
to the Swartz Bay terminal. Its cuisine is Jewish and they
do a lot of Montreal smoked meat and a lot of Reuben
and Estevan sandwiches. Everyone likes the free-run
poached eggs with cumin and garlic and the French toast
with maple syrup and fresh fruit. There's a second Village
Café at 4517 W Saanich Road in Royal Oak (telephone
(778) 265-8898. It's open from Wednesday to Sunday 8
am to 3 pm, 5 pm to 9 pm.
Open daily 8 am to 3 pm. Licensed. Master Card, Visa.

VICTORIA   **MAP 211**
ZAMBRI'S   ☆
820 Yates Street   **$160**
(250) 360-1171

Zambri's has changed a lot in the last couple of years.
There's a new emphasis on fresh, young vegetables;
there's a new interest in the produce of local farms; and
there's a fresh approach to wines. For instance, look twice
at the tiny new potatoes, which often take the place of
chanterelles. Alberta lamb is as good as any in the world,
but local farm-raised lamb makes the Okanagan product
look as good as any from Alberta. The tiramisu that follows is a good one, but don't miss the flight of grappas,
which makes Alexander the equal of Jacopo Poli—something that isn't easy to do. There are all the usual antipas-
tos and primis—spaghetti, penne, orechiette, tagliatelle,
but you can always ignore them in favour of the local
wild salmon, the local albacore tuna or the local lamb
chops—or even the filetto of beef tenderloin with polenta and truffle oil. The wine-list is all Italian, which is
sensible enough unless you're looking for something

from Poplar Grove or Mission Mill.
Open Monday to Thursday 11 am to 3 pm, 5 pm to 9 pm, Friday and Saturday 11 am to 3 pm, 5 pm to 10 pm, Sunday 10.30 am to 2.30 pm (brunch), 5 pm to 9 pm. Licensed. Amex, Master Card, Visa. &

VICTORIA
See also GALIANO ISLAND, SALT SPRING ISLAND, SIDNEY, SOOKE.

VICTORIA–BY–THE–SEA, P.E.I. (MAP 37)
LANDMARK CAFE ☆
12 Main Street **$85**
(902) 658-2286

Eugene Sauvé has been in charge of the kitchen at the Landmark for 26 years, and his whole family (including his former wife) now works in the restaurant. Eugene is a great cook and his grilled haddock is as good as anything on the Island, maybe better. The same is true of his meat pies, his lobster rolls and his lasagne. He also makes scallops in garlic butter and a fine Cajun-chicken stir-fry. He has only a couple of wines, Peller and a little-known local wine. (The Peller is the better of the two.) He's a big, friendly man, and he makes sure that everybody has a good time at the Landmark.
Open daily 11.30 am to 2.45 pm, 5 pm to 8 pm from 1 June until 30 September. Licensed. Master Card, Visa. Book ahead. &

WAINWRIGHT, Alberta MAP 213
THE HONEY-POT
823 2 Avenue **$100**
(780) 842-4094

The Honey-Pot has been owned by the same family for three generations. Alex Heath is running the place now, with the help of his daughter, Michele. Fifty years ago it began offering meals to the soldiers of Western Command. The soldiers were lucky to find such a place in

Wainwright, and there's still nothing else like it. That's because the family have never taken anything for granted. You'll still get top-quality Alberta beef in your steak sandwich. Your fish and chips will still be made with hand-battered haddock. The salmon on your dinner plate will still be fresh from Sooke and it'll still be topped with lemon and dill. There are still six beers on tap, including the local Ribstone Creek, which is sold in twenty-ounce British pints. The vegetables are always fresh and there's a different homemade soup every day, though most people seem to prefer the boneless chicken wings. They have a nutella mousse, but if you don't feel like nutella there's the so-called Foggy Bottom, which features bananas, strawberries and chocolate ganache.

Open Monday to Saturday 11 am to 9.30 pm. Closed on Sunday. Licensed. Amex, Master Card, Visa. &

WATERLOO, Ontario   **MAP 214**
MASALA BAY   ☆
3B Regina Street N   **$85**
(519) 747-2763

Waterloo is the high-tech capital of Canada, home of the University of Waterloo, the Perimeter Institute of Theoretical Physics and the Stephen Hawking Institute. Masala Bay is a small Indian restaurant where Hawking has been photographed with the proprietors. Their food is traditional and very cheap. The best things come from the tandoor oven and the naan is superb. People write to us about the tikka and the aloo gobi, which is the best in town. Actually, our favourite is the bhoona gosht or beef curry. There's a good buffet at noon, but the evening helpings are too large for comfort. There are very few wines, but they do have two or three draft beers on tap.

Open Monday to Thursday noon to 2 pm, 5 pm to 9.30 pm, Friday 11 am to 2 pm, 5 pm to 10 pm. Closed on Saturday and Sunday. Licensed. All cards. &

Our website is at www.oberonpress.ca. Readers wishing to use e-mail should address us at oberon@sympatico.ca.

WATERLOO   **MAP 214**
NICK & NAT'S UPTOWN 21   ☆☆
21 King Street N   **$150**
(519) 883-1100

Nick & Nat's is small and seats only about 40 people, but
it's rapidly becoming a local institution. Its emphasis is
on local produce and craft beers. They also have a useful
Canadian wine-list. The menu changes frequently, depending on the season, but there's always a four-course
prix fixe for 50.00. If you order the *prix fixe* they'll probably start you off with mushrooms on toast, seared tuna
or grilled octopus. Next there might be an ethereal
pumpkin soup. The main courses will all be seasonal—
beef brisket, perhaps, or mussels with fries or duck confit.
The mussels are always fresh, the fries perfect (crisp on
the outside, creamy and rich on the inside). The brisket
is served on a bed of whipped potatoes and grilled rapini,
and it's salty and completely satisfying. The homemade
sorbets that end the meal are exquisite and the crème
brûlée is about the best in town.
Open Tuesday to Saturday 5 pm to 9 pm. Closed on Sunday and
Monday. Licensed. All cards.

WATERLOO   **MAP 214**
SOLE   ☆
83 Erb Street W   **$140**
(519) 747-5622

Sole is housed in what was once the Seagram cooperage
building. The menu was shortened last year, but they've
kept their salads and most of their appetizers, as well as a
variety of fish. In the evening the most exciting dishes,
we think, are the pork belly with (amazingly fresh) scallops on a bed of puréed parsnip, the poached salmon seasoned with lime and the roasted-chicken ballotine stuffed
with sausage and sage. The steaks are good too and come
with delicate garlic mash. Our longtime favourite sweet
is the carrot cake with pecans. There's an extensive list of
beer and wine, and the carafes are all excellent buys.

*Open Monday to Thursday 11.30 am to 11 pm, Friday 11.30
am to midnight, Saturday 11 am to midnight, Sunday 11 am to
9 pm. Licensed. All cards.* &

WATERLOO   **MAP 214**
TWH SOCIAL
Walper Hotel   **$120**
1 King Street W
(519) 745-8478

The old Walper Hotel is being renovated and the ground-
floor pub replaced by the TWH restaurant and bar. Jeff
Ward, formerly of Oliver & Bonacini and Marisol, is in
charge of the kitchen. He has eight appetizers, one of
which is gorgeous. The beef carpaccio comes with slivers
of cremini mushrooms and is richly marbled and full of
flavour. The mains include chicken, pork and steak, and
there are some good specials, the best of which is the osso
buco on a bed of polenta with braised spinach. The cooking and presentation are both reliable.
*Open Monday to Thursday 11 am to 11 pm, Friday 11 am to
midnight, Saturday 4 pm to midnight. Closed on Sunday. Licensed. Amex, Master Card, Visa.* &

WELLINGTON, Ontario   **(MAP 145)**
DRAKE DEVONSHIRE
24 Wharf Street   **$150**
(613) 399-3111

The *Globe* named this place one of its ten best restaurants
of the year, which is surprising because its sister restaurant, the Drake in Toronto, is certainly not. The dining
area faces the lake and is open all week. Dinners start with
a charcuterie plate or salt cod, followed by pan-seared
trout with ginger and parsnip or a schnitzel of lamb with
roasted beets and hummus. They have two or three
sweets, one of which is usually apple pie with blackberry
custard. There are also a couple of *prix-fixe* menus at a
top price of 65.00. The noon-hour menu is similar but
shorter. They stock eighteen open wines, all of which are

305

quite expensive. We don't think as highly of the restaurant as others do, and it's certainly no place to go if you're looking for a quiet, intimate meal.

Open Monday to Friday 11.30 am to 2 pm, 5 pm to 9 pm, Saturday and Sunday 8 am to 2 pm (brunch). Licensed. All cards. Book ahead if you can.

WELLINGTON (MAP 144)
EAST & MAIN
270 Main Street   **$150**
(613) 399-5420

East & Main is a relative newcomer to this area, but already it's packed at all hours, and you should book ahead. There are good reasons for its success. The cooking is good, the portions ample, the service attentive. The wine-list offers twenty local whites and twenty local reds. You can start dinner with gravlax cured in vodka and go on to braised lamb shanks with zinfandel or cider-brined pork tenderloin with red cabbage The best of the sweets is either the chocolate torte or the blueberry streusel cake.
Open Monday and Thursday to Sunday noon to 2.30 pm, 5.30 pm to 9.30 pm. Closed on Tuesday and Wednesday. Licensed. Master Card, Visa. Book ahead.

WHISTLER, B.C. MAP 216
ALTA   ☆☆
4319 Main Street   **$185**
(604) 932-2582

Alta is offering good cooking at a reasonable cost in a town known everywhere for its astronomical prices. Nicholas Cassettari is a strong believer in locally-sourced ingredients. His beers come from a brewery down the street and many of his wines are local and organic. He starts with elk tartar and foie-gras parfait, and continues with Wagyu beef and (better still) coriander-cured Arctic char. The sweets, at least one of them made with lavender, are as perfect as everything else. The service is casual but prompt, the atmosphere lively.

Open daily 5.30 pm to 10 pm (shorter hours in summer). Licensed. Amex, Master Card, Visa. Book ahead. &

WHISTLER   **MAP 216**
ARAXI   ★★
4222 Village Square   **$200**
(604) 932-4540

Araxi is probably Whistler's best-known restaurant, though it's certainly not, as Gordon Ramsay once said, the best in Canada. It was the creation of Jack Evrensol and was named for Jack's wife. Evrensol went on to form a group called Top Tables that included Blue Water and West. At the moment they're planning a second restaurant in Whistler, with a menu designed by Araxi's chef, James Wait. It was Wait who brought the fashion of local ingredients and seasonal menus to Whistler, long before they became clichés in the trade. His *sous-vide* venison is fork-tender and his breast of duck from Yarrow Farm is beyond criticism. As for his steaks, they're as good as any in the province. He has 9000 bottles of wine in his cellar, many of them offered at affordable prices. From Monday to Thursday in the spring and fall there's a five-course menu at a price of 32.50. The oyster bar, open daily from 3 o'clock to 5, shucks up to a thousand oysters of twelve different varieties every day.

Open daily 11 am to 2 pm, 5 pm to 11 pm from 1 June until 30 September, daily 5 pm to 10.30 pm from 1 October until 31 May. Licensed. All cards. Book ahead. &

WHISTLER   **MAP 216**
BEARFOOT BISTRO   ★★
4121 Village Green   **$350**
(604) 932-3433

The Bearfoot Bistro is primarily for people with plenty of money in their pocket. Such people love to cut off their champagne cork with a sabre. They love to sip their vodka in the ice-room, which is kept at minus-32 degrees celsius—they lend each guest in the room a Canada

Goose parka while they're there. They even love a menu that offers shaved white Alba truffles and beluga caviar. But André St.-Jacques makes few mistakes, and his three-course *prix fixe* is not unreasonable at 99.00, especially when his chef is Melissa Craig, who's one of the best in the business. You start with scallop sashimi or oysters on the half-shell and go on to Alaska black cod smoked in tea or local breast of duck with fig juice and finish with yuzu. (If you want the nitro ice cream you'll have to pay a *supplément* of 20.00 for it.) They have over 1100 labels in their cellar and the waiters are familiar with them all. *Open daily 5.30 pm to 1 am from 1 May until 15 December (shorter hours in winter). Licensed. All cards. Book ahead.* &

WHISTLER   MAP 216
RIMROCK CAFE   ☆☆
Highland Lodge   **$200**
2117 Whistler Road
(877) 932-5589

We've always been fond of the Rimrock, partly because it was the first restaurant we were able to recommend in Whistler. That was in 1989. Now, almost 30 years later, most people agree that it's still the best restaurant in town. Rolf Gunther was in charge of the kitchen when it opened and he's still in the kitchen today. Gunther has always been interested in seafood and trucks still come here all the way from Vancouver to bring him what he needs. It used to be oysters; now it's game—bison, venison, elk and caribou. Prices are pretty high, and wild salmon with lobster-mashed potatoes costs 37.00, venison tenderloin with porcini gnocchi 45.00, mixed grill (a fine dish) 55.00. But this is an upscale dining-room and high prices are to be expected. Dinners always start well with lobster bisque with armagnac and end well with sticky-toffee pudding.
Open daily 5 pm to 9.30 pm (shorter hours in winter). Licensed. All cards. Book ahead if you can.

Every restaurant in this guide has been personally tested.

WHISTLER   MAP 216
SPLITZ GRILL
4369 Main Street: Unit 104   **$60**
(604) 938-9300

If you have a family to feed, this is the place for you.
They never lower their standards or raise their prices.
They play loud music, but if you don't like that, you can
always sit in the car. They have beef burgers, chicken
burgers, bison burgers and even salmon burgers, all
finished with either barbecue or teriyaki sauce. You then
get to add any one of at least twenty different toppings.
The burgers are huge, but if your children want more to
eat, the fries and the onion rings are both first-rate. Then
there's a huge choice of ice creams and a chocolate milkshake, which has few equals that we know of. A jumbo
hot-dog costs just 4.95, less than that for children. Look
for the Splitz Grill in the Alpenglow Hotel, close to the
centre of town.
Open daily 11 am to 9 pm. Licensed for beer and wine only.
Master Card, Visa.

WHITEHORSE, Yukon   *MAP 218*

If you come to Whitehorse in the daytime, you'll be glad to know
about the Baked Café and Bakery at 100 Main Street (telephone
(867) 633 6291). Their coffee is so good that people line up for
a cup. They have a full range of baked goods and a couple of fine
homemade soups. The scones are great and so are the quiches. You
go up to the counter for your food, which you then take to a table.
They're open on weekdays from 7 am to 7 pm, on Saturday from
8 am to 6 pm, on Sunday from 8 am to 5 pm. They have a licence
and take most cards. The Sanchez Cantina at 211 Hanson Street
(telephone (867) 668-5858) claims to have the only authentic
Mexican food in the Yukon. The owners go home every winter,
but regulars think the kitchen is always pretty good, especially
with its bean soup and chicken enchiladas. Orlina Sanchez makes
nearly everything from scratch. This is a family business and Or-
lina seems never to stop smiling. They're open for both lunch and
dinner every day but Sunday, have a licence and take most cards.

309

WHITEHORSE   **MAP 218**
THE WHEELHOUSE
Waterfront Station
2237 2 Avenue   **$135**
(867) 456-2982

Visually, the Wheelhouse is stunning. It's a replica of the
old stern-wheelers that plied the Yukon River before the
highways were built. The Waterfront Station is purpose-
built, and the interior could be mistaken for a museum
of local artifacts. The menu is short, but features local
produce. Look for elk bolognese, bison shepherd's pie
and grilled Arctic char. They all come with three fresh
vegetables. Regulars consider the place expensive (around
30.00 a plate), but tourists will be thrilled to find it. The
service, once rough and ready, has now become thoroughly professional.
Open Wednesday to Sunday 5 pm to 11 pm. Closed on Monday
and Tuesday. Licensed. Master Card, Visa.

WINDERMERE, Ontario   **(MAP 149)**
WINDERMERE HOUSE
2508 Windermere Road   **$175**
(705) 769-3611

Windermere House, as everyone knows, burned to the
ground several years ago and was rebuilt to look the same
as before. The dining-room, run by Oliver & Bonacini,
is now back at the top of its form. It has an expansive if
rather commercial menu and an ambitious wine-list.
Meals start with truffled-mushroom soup or, more ex-
pensively, with shrimp tempura, mussels or citrus-cured
albacore tuna. The mussels and the tuna are both offered
as main courses as well for about twice the money.
There's also beef tenderloin (seven ounces for 42.00) and
rib-eye (twelve ounces for 40.00). The sweets are, with
one exception, rather commonplace. (The exception is
the chocolate marquise with hazelnut praline, seasonal
berries and chantilly cream.) They have only a handful
of white wines (ten to be exact), but the list of red wines

is long and interesting. The best of these is the Stag's Leap cabernet sauvignon from Napa, the cheapest the merlot from Henry of Pelham, which is a real buy at 39.00.

Open Tuesday to Sunday 6 pm to 9 pm from 15 May until 30 June, Tuesday to Sunday 6 pm to 10 pm from 1 July until 31 August, Thursday noon to 9 pm, Friday and Saturday noon to 10 pm, Sunday noon to 9 pm (brunch) from 1 September until 15 October. Closed on Monday from 15 May until 31 August, from Monday to Wednesday from 1 September until 15 October. Licensed. Amex, Master Card, Visa. &

WINDSOR, Ontario   MAP 220
TOSCANA   ☆
3891 Dougall Avenue   **$125**
(519) 972-5699

Jonathan Reaume has no patience with regional cuisine, claiming that he has the best suppliers everywhere in the world. His lamb, for instance, comes from Colorado. His chicken is free range and organic. He has a new menu this year, but he's kept most of our favourites—lightly-cooked calf's liver, grilled Atlantic salmon with fennel and orange, smoked Lake Erie trout with naan. The menu is supposed to be Italian, and it does include such Italian staples as veal and pasta. The most interesting pasta is the fettuccine with beef tenderloin and Iberico ham, for only 18.00. There are also several interesting salads, among them the farro (asparagus, tomato, and dried cranberries). His liver is carefully cleaned and lightly cooked; his beef is always tender. But the most remarkable thing about Toscana is the abundance of sushi and sashimi. There's also an ambitious lunch menu, which offers a lot more than soup and sandwiches. There's a big list of wines from the Old World and the New, a good many of which are offered by the glass as well as the bottle.

Open Monday to Friday 11.30 am to 2.30 pm, 5 pm to 10 pm, Saturday 5 pm to 10 pm. Closed on Sunday. Licensed. Amex, Master Card, Visa. &

Nobody but nobody can buy his way into this guide.

WINDSOR

See also KINGSVILLE.

WINNIPEG, Manitoba   **MAP 221**
BISTRO DANSK
63 Sherbrook Street   **$100**
(204) 775-5662

Some things never change, among them the menu at
Bistro Dansk. For almost three decades they've offered
the same pork schnitzel, fried trout and Danish meatballs.
But their herring, with its sauce of sour cream and
tomato, is a marvellous creation. The same is true of their
cream puff with chocolate sauce, and even their hazelnut
tart. The wines are well chosen and not too expensive,
and there are some good European beers on the list as
well. Lunch is much the same, though at noon there's also
an excellent chicken soup that many people swear by, as
well as a variety of open-face sandwiches—the shrimp
and beef is the best. If you want a sweet, Paul Vocadlo
will make you a palacinka at almost any hour of the day.
Bistro Dansk has good food, modest prices, excellent
service and lots of nearby parking.
Open Tuesday to Saturday 11 am to 2.30 pm, 5 pm to 9 pm.
Closed on Sunday and Monday. Licensed. Amex, Master Card,
Visa. Book ahead. &

WINNIPEG   **MAP 221**
CAFE CE SOIR
937 Portage Avenue   **$75**
(204) 414-7647

This is a small, unassuming restaurant a few minutes from
downtown Winnipeg and it's about as close as Winnipeg
gets to genuine Parisian cuisine. They have a few tables
and a refrigerator between the kitchen and the customers.
But Edith Piaf is on the soundtrack. The baguettes are
warm from the oven and the menu features escargots de
bourgogne, coq au vin, onion soup with gruyère, mussels
with fries and liver pâté. For Sunday brunch they offer a

great chicken sandwich that may be the best thing on the menu. A new provincial law allows diners to bring their own bottle and pay a corkage fee of only 8.00, which is a remarkable bargain. The service is agreeable but slow. *Open Tuesday and Wednesday 11 am to 2 pm, 5 pm to 11 pm, Thursday and Friday 11 am to 11 pm, Saturday 10 am to 2 pm, 5 pm to 11 pm, Sunday 10 am to 2 pm (brunch). Licensed. All cards. Book ahead on weekends.* &

WINNIPEG

WINNIPEG   **MAP 221**
CHEW   ☆
532 Waterloo Street   **$170**
(204) 667-2439

Chew is small and you have to book ahead. The menu is small too and most people seem to start with roasted mushrooms, beef tartar or scallops and go on to line-caught albacore tuna with beets and edamame or braised lamb shank with heirloom carrots in a purée of white beans. Bargains like pork belly have now pretty well disappeared from the menu, but the prices aren't out of line. The wine-list is strong, especially on the red side. *Open Tuesday to Sunday 11 am to 11 pm. Closed on Monday. Licensed. Master Card, Visa. You must book ahead.* &

WINNIPEG   **MAP 221**
EAST INDIA COMPANY   ☆
319 York Avenue   **$65**
(204) 947-3097

The East India Company is, in our opinion, the best Indian restaurant in Winnipeg. It's a well-dressed place, with good service and sitar music playing softly on the soundtrack. The daily buffet has all the usual samosas, panirs, curries and vindaloos. Sometimes they also have shrimps or mussels, often lamb with lentils and usually some hot naan. There are always a number of vegetarian dishes, as well as delicately-scented sorbets and Indian beers. At 23.00 per person the buffet has to be one of the best deals in town. Parking is free at night and for an

hour at noon.
Open Monday to Friday 11 am to 2 pm, 5 pm to 10 pm, Saturday 5 pm to 10 pm, Sunday noon to 8 pm. Licensed. Amex, Master Card, Visa. Book ahead. &

WINNIPEG   MAP 221
IGI BARBECUE AND SUSHI BISTRO
1875 Pembina Highway: Unit 10   **$75**
(204) 477-9909

This is a huge place near the University of Manitoba campus, where students in their hundreds (if not thousands) come to buy dragon rolls, maki, donburi and make-your-own barbecues—everything Chinese, Japanese and Korean—for 30.00 or so, depending on what you order. Nigiri and maki sushi are made at one counter, barbecues at another. The waiters are very friendly and are glad to tell you how to prepare barbecued beef, lamb, chicken, pork and shrimp. Lovely whole lobsters come to your table in hand-woven baskets. Everyone is welcome—you don't have to be a student to enjoy the fun.
Open Monday 11.30 am to 3 pm, Tuesday 4.30 pm to 10.30 pm, Wednesday to Friday 11.30 am to 3 pm, 4.30 pm to 10.30 pm, Saturday and Sunday 11.30 am to 3 pm (brunch), 4.30 pm to 10.30 pm. Licensed. Master Card, Visa. &

WINNIPEG   MAP 221
NORTH GARDEN
33 University Crescent: Unit 6   **$50**
(204) 275-2591

North Garden is a bundle of contradictions. First of all, it's actually in south Winnipeg, not north. It has no garden. But the menu has all the varieties of fried noodles and many Chinese vegetables, like bok choy and gai lan. It has grand platters of fresh fish (even lobster in season) and great dim sum. Everything is beautifully displayed on platters or served in hot pots. It has excellent service, adequate parking and prices even students can afford to pay. Suits are almost never to be seen and running-shoes are everywhere. In other words, North Garden is casual, cheap and sometimes amazingly good.

Open Monday to Thursday 10 am to midnight, Friday and Saturday 9 am to 1 am, Sunday 10 am to midnight. Licensed. All cards. Book ahead if you can. &

WINNIPEG
THE PALM ROOM
Fort Garry Hotel
222 Broadway Avenue
(204) 942-8251

MAP 221
☆
$125

The Fort Garry was restored to its original Edwardian grandeur several years ago by Richard Bel and Ida Albo. Nowadays doormen park your car and chefs carve the roasts. On weekdays they serve hamburgers and roast chicken. Helpings are big enough for a truck driver, though everything is served with conscious formality. There's always an abundance of roast beef and fresh seafood. Prices are surprising. The antipasto plate costs only 18.00, the pot roast 25.00. Every night there's live music.

Open Monday to Thursday 11 am to midnight, Friday and Saturday 11 am to 1 am, Sunday 10 am to midnight. Licensed. Amex, Master Card, Visa. &

WINNIPEG
PEASANT COOKERY
283 Bannatyne Avenue: Unit 100
(204) 989-7700

MAP 221

$100

At Peasant Cookery they cook French—or maybe we should say French Canadian, given their baked chicken with maple syrup, their poutine and their tourtière. The menu is long, running from salads to onion soup, from pasta with bacon and clams to mussels with chorizo. But it offers a plate of cold cuts for just 19.00 or beef brisket for a few dollars more. There's a lovely bar next door and a terrace in summer. The service is good, though parking is not. You come here for the atmosphere as much as the food and you pay for what you get. But in Toronto you'd pay twice as much and be thankful.

Open Monday to Thursday 11.30 am to 11 pm, Friday 11.30 am to midnight, Saturday 5 pm to midnight, Sunday 5 pm to 10 pm. Licensed. All cards. &

WINNIPEG

MAP 221

RAE & JERRY'S
1405 Portage Avenue   **$125**
(204) 783-6155

Rae & Jerry's is still the best steak house in Winnipeg. You go in the door and you're back in 1957, the year the restaurant opened. People are all eating shrimp cocktails, twenty-ounce T-bone steaks or prime ribs of beef and slices of pecan pie, just as they used to do fifty years ago. The beef is as good as ever and the pecan pie is still a must-have dish. Helpings are large, and if you haven't got room for the pecan pie ask instead for the bread pudding. People complain that nothing ever changes at Rae & Jerry's, but after all, that's the whole point of the place. Prices are quite high now, but if you eat at the bar everything is much cheaper. The wines are plentiful and reasonably priced and the service is friendly and prompt.

Open Monday to Saturday 11 am to 11 pm, Sunday 11 am to 8.30 pm. Licensed. Amex, Master Card, Visa. Free parking. Book ahead. &

WINNIPEG

MAP 221

RIPE
842 Corydon Avenue   **$85**
(204) 284-7916

Ripe is a bistro, a rare thing in Winnipeg. The front room could pass for a brasserie in Paris, with its grand bar and its outside terrace. Tom Pitt, the owner and chef, started the place with the idea that rich food is good and leaving hungry bad. For instance, his mussels come in a cream sauce spiked with pernod—all for 12.00. At noon, however, he has plain shepherd's pie and plain steak-and-mushroom pie, and they're probably the two best things in the house. He serves rack of pork and sausages with sauerkraut at a price most other restaurants charge for soup. For the sweet course there's usually an apple-pie tart with melted cheddar and a chocolate brownie with ice cream. On Wednesday you can have two appetizers for the price of one. The bar is always well stocked and the well-chosen wine-list is reasonably priced.

Open Tuesday to Friday 11 am to 2 pm, 5 pm to 10 pm, Saturday 10 am to 2 pm, 5 pm to 10 pm, Sunday 10 am to 2 pm, 5 pm to 9 pm. Closed on Monday. Licensed. All cards. Book ahead if you can. ♿

WINNIPEG   **MAP 221**
LA SCALA
725 Corydon Avenue   **$125**
(204) 452-2750

Perry Scaletta began his career as a bicycle racer, but for the last twenty years he's been the owner and chef at La Scala. Here he improvises lively, Italian-style dishes, working from an Asian-Italian fusion menu. His trademark dishes are Chinese dumplings, linguine with prawns, penne arrabiata with chorizo, rib steak, Thai chicken with cashew nuts, fish stew and osso buco. There's a big, reasonably-priced wine-list that offers an unusual number of Italian cabernets. In summer the sidewalk terrace is filled to capacity; in winter you move inside, where the dining-room is always snug and warm. La Scala is a friendly place with an interesting menu, good cooking and a charming host.

Open Monday to Friday 11.30 am to 1.30 pm, 5 pm to 11 pm, Saturday and Sunday 5 pm to 11 pm from 1 May until 31 August, Monday to Thursday 5 pm to 8.30 pm, Friday and Saturday 5 pm to 10 pm from 1 September until 30 April. Closed on Sunday in winter. Licensed. Amex, Master Card, Visa.

This is a guide to Canadian restaurants from coast to coast—the first ever published and the only one of its kind on the market today.

WINNIPEG   **MAP 221**
SYDNEY'S AT THE FORKS   ✩✩
1 Forks Market Road: Unit 215   **$190**
(204) 942-6075

Sydney's is probably the best restaurant in Winnipeg and also the most inconvenient. It's hard to find and if you don't have a car there are no taxis to be had anywhere. If you can put up with that, you'll find that the menu is novel and interesting, the cooking (at its best) wonderful. They start with such unusual things as heart of veal, curried carrots, pike en papillote (a beautiful dish) and buttermilk-fried quail. The main dishes are rather less remarkable: half-rack of lamb, loin of pork (brined with ginger beer), confit of duck leg and New York steak. The lavender-and-ginger crème brûlée that ends the meal is merely ordinary. All this costs 55.00. There are only four Canadian wines on the list, but one of them is Burrowing Owl, which says a lot.
Open Monday 5 pm to 9 pm, Tuesday to Friday 11.30 am to 2 pm, 5 pm to 9 pm, Saturday 5 pm to 9 pm. Closed on Sunday. Licensed. All cards. Book ahead. ♿

WINNIPEG   **MAP 221**
TRE VISI
926 Grosvenor Avenue   **$195**
(204) 475-4447

Tre Visi on Grosvenor Avenue is a new restaurant. It has a small menu, starting with lovely squid marinara and continuing with vitello piccata, gnocchi with pesto and fettuccine alla diva, which means shrimps with asparagus, mushrooms and tomatoes. There are all the usual sweets—tiramisu, tartufo al cioccolato and crème brûlée. Then there's a very cheap sauvignon blanc from Marlborough and a useful list of chiantis and valpolicellas, as well as an unusual zinfandel from 7 Deadly Zins in California. The atmosphere is bright and cheerful, the service friendly and efficient. The prices are modest.
Open Tuesday to Friday 11.30 am to 2.30 pm, 5 pm to 9 pm,

Saturday and Sunday 5 pm to 9 pm. Closed on Monday. Licensed. Amex, Master Card, Visa. Book ahead if you can. ⅃

WOLFVILLE, N.S.   **MAP 222**
BLOMIDON INN   ☆☆
195 Main Street   **$150 ($325)**
(877) 542-2291

The bad news is that Sean Laceby has left the kitchen that has been his for so many years. He's been replaced by Donna Jackson, who is turning out meals that look and taste a lot like the work of Sean Laceby. Is her salmon overcooked? One has to admit that it is not. Does the lobster bisque taste of tomato? It does not. Such is the power of history. All the established dishes are still in place: the lobster, the beef tenderloin, the free-range chicken, the pork, even the tuna. All are tenderly and deftly cooked. The service is still all it should be. And the wine-list, always remarkable, still has most of the great French and Italian labels, to say nothing of local bottlings from Grand Pré, Benjamin Bridge, Gaspereau and Luckett's.
Open Monday to Friday 11.30 am to 2 pm, 5 pm to 9.30 pm, Saturday and Sunday 10 am to 3 pm (brunch), 5 pm to 9.30 pm. Licensed. Master Card, Visa.

WOLFVILLE   **MAP 222**
CELLAR DOOR   ☞
Luckett Vineyards   **$50**
1293 Grand Pré Road
(902) 542-2600

Pete Luckett made an instant success of his grocery stores, which he calls Pete's Frootiques. He then opened a vineyard called Luckett's. That was in 2010 and the Luckett Vineyards were rated the top tourist attraction in Wolfville just two years later. The wines are still young, of course, but the restaurant offers spectacular views of Minas Basin and Cape Blomidon. The Cellar Door itself is reserved for private parties, but the outside patio has seating for ordinary travellers. Here you can have a soup, a sandwich (Italian ham with figs, say) and a salad (patty-pan squash with chanterelles, perhaps). They also have cheese-and-charcuterie platters, as well as one or two excellent sweets. The German tasting varietal, Ortega, is the best of the wines on offer, though it's often sold out. Good news—they have a red telephone booth from which you can call anyone in North America free of charge.

Open daily 10 am to 5 pm from 1 June until 31 October. Licensed. Amex, Master Card, Visa. Book ahead if you can.

WOLFVILLE   **MAP 222**
TROY   ☆
12 Elm Avenue   **$145**
(902) 542-4425

Erkut Surmeli learned his trade in Turkey before he moved to Cambridge, where he opened his first restaurant. He met his future wife there and with her moved on, this time to Nova Scotia, where he opened a second restaurant. Ten years later he was joined by Michael Erdall Toker, a long-time friend. Together he and Toker opened Troy in the spring of 2013. Troy is basically Turkish in style, though most of their ingredients come from just down the road. Their scallops come from Digby, however, their beef from Prince Edward Island. Their cheese is made in a small fromagerie in nearby Aylesport, their beers in a local boutique brewery. The set menu, priced at 32.00, begins with warm pita bread, served with cold red peppers, grape leaves stuffed with rice, pine-nuts and black currants, yogurt with cucumber, garlic and mint, hummus and smoked eggplant, tagine, olive-oil and garlic. Hot appetizers—squid, lamb sausage and pan-fried lamb's liver, sumac and parsley—follow. A Turkish salad comes next, then a variety of kebabs and, finally, baklava. Helpings are big and you'll be full long before you get to the baklava.

Open Tuesday to Saturday 11 am to 9 pm, Sunday noon to 8 pm. Closed on Monday. Licensed. All cards. ♿

WOLFVILLE
See also GRAND PRE.

WOODY POINT, Newfoundland   **(MAP 164)**
THE OLD LOFT
Water Street   **$85**
(709) 453-2294

The Old Loft has never been a gourmet restaurant, but
people keep coming back for a meal here, so they see no
reason to change. They give you a big helping of traditional Newfoundland food at a very low price. That
might mean an open-face turkey sandwich piled high
with turkey and stuffing and coated with gravy. Or it
might mean a complete turkey dinner with all the trim-
mings. The vegetables aren't unusual, but they come
straight from the ground. The fries are hand-cut and perfectly cooked. The cod and the halibut are both caught
locally and pan-fried in the kitchen. The salmon and the
mussels are both farmed, but they're correctly cooked.
The highlight of the place is the moose pie, with its remarkable pastry. Pastry is what the Old Loft is really all
about. Clarice Bursey is a keen baker, but it's her mother,
Rose, who makes the wonderful pastry for the moose pie
and the partridge-berry pie. She also makes the bread,
which you can buy to take out. You'll find the Old Loft
on the second floor of a former fish-house on the south
arm of Bonne Bay in Gros Morne National Park. It was
settled over a hundred years ago, and the big old house
has been lovingly cared for ever since. To get there, turn
off Highway 431 on the road to Trout River; the restaurant is right on the highway.
*Open daily 11.30 am to 9 pm from Victoria Day until Thanks-
giving. Licensed for beer and wine only. Amex; Master Card,
Visa.*

If you wish to improve the guide send us information
about restaurants we have missed. Our mailing address is
Oberon Press, 145 Spruce Street: Suite 205, Ottawa, Ontario K1R 6P1.

WYEBRIDGE, Ontario   **(MAP 139)**
MAD MICHAEL'S   🖐
8215 Highway 93   **$90**
(705) 527-1666

For years we recommended Explorers in Midland. Explorers still has some fine cooking and a great wine-list, but after a couple of readers sent us critical letters we started going down the road to Mad Michael's in Wyebridge. It's a barbecue joint, but (you won't believe this) all the ingredients are fresh and local. They even make their own tomato ketchup. They have Texas-style pork ribs with lots of meat and little bone, sliced beef brisket, jerk chicken and smoked lamb with jalapeno jelly, as well as some irresistible things for vegetarians. They have pies for 6.00 and butter tarts for 2.00, and you'll never find a better piece of pie, or a better butter tart for that matter. They have a licence, but you shouldn't leave without trying the homemade lemonade or ginger beer. One diner describes Mad Michael's as beyond excellent—his words. *Open Thursday to Sunday noon to 8 pm from mid–May to mid–October. Closed Monday to Wednesday. Licensed. Amex, Master Card, Visa.*

YARMOUTH. N.S.   **MAP 225**
OLD WORLD BAKERY   🖐
232 Main Street   **$45**
(902) 742-2181

Nobody seems to know what the future holds for the Yarmouth-to-Bar-Harbour ferry service. But the Old World Bakery expects to survive, whatever happens. The new owner is Nathan Bain and he has kept nearly everything the same, including the baklava and other Greek family recipes. The bread—rye, whole-grain, sourdough and sweet-potato—is fantastic, and every morning at 7 o'clock six kinds of freshly-baked muffins get put out on the counter. There's a different homemade soup every day as well as big, filling sandwiches. (Our favourite is the smoked lamb.) The lamb, like the turkey and the sausage, is smoked on the premises. The coffee is fairly traded and it's always a treat.

Open Tuesday to Saturday 7 am to 6 pm. Closed on Sunday and Monday. No liquor, no cards. &

YARMOUTH
See also MIDDLE WEST PUBNICO.

YELLOWKNIFE, N.W.T.   MAP 226
BULLOCK'S BISTRO   ☆
3534 Weaver Drive   **$150**
(867) 873-3474

Everybody loves Bullock's. (If you don't love it, you hate it.) Inside, everybody is jammed together and the noise is deafening. It used to be a working fish shack—a small log structure with rickety chairs, bumper stickers on the walls and graffiti everywhere. But the fish is about as good as it gets. Most of it—all the whitefish, cod, pickerel and trout—comes from Great Slave Lake. The fish is grilled, pan-fried, poached, blackened Cajun-style or deep-fried in a beer batter. The fish chowder has more fish than broth, but it's usually sold out before noon, no matter how much they make. In that case, keep an eye out for the kingfisher skewer plate, which is cooked with a pound of butter and seasoned with spices. One diner writes that his pickerel was the best of a lifetime, another that his cod was the best he'd ever had; for a third it was the bison steak. If you want something to drink, help yourself from the cooler, where's there's always plenty of beer.

Open Sunday to Tuesday 11 am to 10 pm, Wednesday to Saturday 5 pm to 10 pm. Licensed. Master Card, Visa. Book ahead if you can.

This is a guide to Canadian restaurants from coast to coast—the first ever published and the only one of its kind on the market today. Every restaurant in the guide has been personally tested. Our reporters are not allowed to identify themselves or to accept free meals.

YELLOWKNIFE   **MAP 226**
THE LODGE AT THE VILLAGE   ★★★
Aurora Village   **$150**
5114 52 Street
(867) 669-0006

After travelling the world and studying the food and
wine of more than thirty countries, Pierre LePage settled
in Yellowknife. In 2011 he sold all his businesses to cook
and manage Aurora Lodge. The Aurora Village is said to
be the best place to see the aurora borealis, and thousands
of tourists fly in for the purpose, many from Japan. The
Lodge has a big dining hall with a bar at one end. Dinners
are served by reservation only, since there are only three
employees, one of them Pierre himself. But the cooking
is always fabulous. The old washboard road has been
resurfaced and now they're really only twenty minutes
from town, as they always said. Prices are high but no
higher than at Bullock's or the Wildcat. The best thing
on the menu is the pan-seared reindeer striploin with
saskatoons and birch syrup. Start with the breast of duck
with parmesan cheese and sea-salt and end with the cranberry bannock with Yukon jack.
Open daily 1 pm to 1 am by reservation only from the middle of
August to early October and from the middle of November to early
April. Licensed. All cards.

YELLOWKNIFE   *MAP 226*
WILDCAT CAFE
3904 Wiley Road   **$95**
(867) 873-4004

Nobody goes to Yellowknife and comes away without stopping at
the Wildcat. This old log shanty near the Pilot Monument dates
from the nineteen-thirties. Since then it's been extensively re-
stored, but it still looks like something left over from pioneer days.
The kitchen has always been at its best with breakfast. Last year
the chef was good too with lunch and dinner, but there'll be a new
chef this summer and of course we can't say how good he'll be.
Come and see for yourself. It's open Monday to Friday from

11.30 am to 10 pm, Saturday and Sunday from 10.30 am to 9 pm, has a licence and takes most cards. Further reports needed.

We will soon be preparing the next edition of this guide. To do that, we need the help of our readers, many of whom routinely send us information and comments on restaurants that interest them, whether or not they are already in the guide. Please address us by mail at 145 Spruce Street: Suite 205, Ottawa, Ontario K1R 6P1, by fax at (613) 238-3275 or by e-mail at oberon@sympatico.ca

First published July 1971. Reprinted September 1971, November 1971, January 1972. Second edition published June 1972. Reprinted July 1972. Third edition published June 1973. Reprinted July 1973. Fourth edition published June 1974. Fifth edition published June 1975. Book-of-the-Month Club edition published July 1975. Sixth edition published June 1976. Seventh edition published June 1977. Eighth edition published June 1978. Ninth edition published June 1979. Tenth edition published June 1980. Eleventh edition published June 1981. Twelfth edition published June 1982. Thirteenth edition published June 1983. Fourteenth edition published June 1984. Fifteenth edition published June 1985. Sixteenth edition published June 1986. Seventeenth edition published June 1987. Eighteenth edition published June 1988. Nineteenth edition published June 1989. Twentieth edition published June 1990. Twenty-first edition published June 1991. Twenty-second edition published June 1992. Twenty-third edition published June 1993. Twenty-fourth edition published June 1994. Twenty-fifth edition published June 1995. Twenty-sixth edition published June 1996. Twenty-seventh edition published June 1997. Twenty-eighth edition published June 1998. Twenty-ninth edition published June 1999. Thirtieth edition published June 2000. Thirty-first edition published June 2001. Thirty-second edition published June 2002. Thirty-third edition published June 2003. Thirty-fourth edition published June 2004. Thirty-fifth edition published June 2005. Thirty-sixth edition published June 2006. Thirty-seventh edition published June 2007. Thirty-eighth edition published June 2008. Thirty-ninth edition published June 2009. Fortieth edition published June 2010. Forty-first edition published June 2011. Forty-second edition published June 2012. Forty-third edition published June 2013. Forty-fourth edition published June 2014. Forty-fifth edition published June 2015. Forty-sixth edition published June 2016.